D1252497

An Approach to Congreve

AN APPROACH

TO CONGREVE

Aubrey L. Williams

New Haven and London Yale University Press 1979

PR
3368
.R4
W5

Copyright © 1979 by Yale University. All rights reserved. This book may not be reproduced, in whole or in part, in any form (beyond that copying permitted by Sections 107 and 108 of the U.S. Copyright Law and except by reviewers for the public press), without written permission from the publishers.

Set in Press Roman type.
Printed in the United States of America by
Vail-Ballou Press, Binghamton, N.Y.

Published in Great Britain, Europe, Africa, and Asia (except Japan) by Yale University Press, Ltd., London. Distributed in Australia and New Zealand by Book & Film Services, Artarmon, N.S.W., Australia; and in Japan by Harper & Row, Publishers, Tokyo Office.

Library of Congress Cataloging in Publication Data

Williams, Aubrey L
    An approach to Congreve.
    Includes index.
    1. Congreve, William, 1670–1729–Religion and ethics. I. Title.
PR3368.R4W5   822'.4   78–10381
ISBN 0–300–02304–9

To Carmen

minuentur atrae
carmine curae

Contents

Preface

A pervasive trend in recent discussions of William Congreve is evident in the number of critics who maintain that his plays reflect a post-Christian universe, a secularized or despiritualized world, one "abandoned," indeed, "by the deity." The "world of Congreve's plays is Epicurean and Hobbist," says one critic, and "being Epicurean, the plays lack the religious dimension." Congreve's dramatic vision, another alleges, "is consistent with the epicurean contempt for supernatural forces, and guilt rarely crosses his mind nor does it cross the minds of any of his characters." Congreve's "vision is secular," declares another, and we are informed by yet another that his plays offer a morality that is "secular and requires no reinforcement from any supernatural frame of reference, or from any cluster of religious allusions." Those "who examine the heroes" of Congreve's plays, concludes another, will find the plays themselves to be "pagan."

Against such views, as well as against the views of those who see almost all of late seventeenth-century drama as lacking "any sense of cosmic orderliness,"* this study attempts to provide the evidence and a context for an approach that takes into account the essential compatibility of Congreve's one novella and five plays with traditional Christian "explanations" and "configurations" of human life. By no means, of course, do I wish to suggest that his works are

---

*Quotations are taken from the following critics: W. H. Van Voris, *The Cultivated Stance* (Dublin: The Dolmen Press, 1965); Malcolm Kelsall, "Those Dying Generations," and John Barnard, "Passion, 'Poetical Justice,' and Dramatic Law in *The Double-Dealer* and *The Way of the World*," in *William Congreve,* ed. Brian Morris (London: Ernest Benn, 1972); Harriet Hawkins, *Likenesses of Truth in Elizabethan and Restoration Drama* (Oxford: The Clarendon Press, 1972); Irvin Ehrenpreis, *Literary Meaning and Augustan Values* (Charlottesville: University Press of Virginia, 1974); Virginia Ogden Birdsall, *Wild Civility: The English Comic Spirit on the Restoration Stage* (Bloomington: Indiana University Press, 1970).

merely fictionalized or dramatized arguments for morality or religion. I rather wish to broaden and complicate our awareness of
what may be going on in all his works by offering a challenge, and
possibly a check, to those past and current views which tend to
narrow and simplify his artistic range by their almost total neglect of
what I take to have been the still dominant fact of late seventeenth-
century English life: a still commonly shared, and fundamentally
Christian, vision of human existence.

The introductory first chapter thus seeks to demonstrate how
strongly this vision still was held in common by playwrights and
playgoers alike. Chapters 2 and 3 aim at showing how mutually
reciprocative were certain images and explanations of life set forth
not only by the preachers but also by the poets and critics of the
period. Chapter 4 attempts to engage the issues raised by Jeremy
Collier's attack on Congreve and the stage in general. The last six
chapters, in their examinations of Congreve's six major works, are
an attempt to provide the reader with an opportunity to decide
for himself whether the playwright's imaginative vision is consistent
with a Christian normative order—or with some putative Epicurean
or Hobbesian or "despiritualized" order—or with no order whatever.

Portions of this study have been given in lectures or printed as
essays. A kind of prolegomenon to the whole, entitled "Poetical
Justice, the Contrivances of Providence, and the Works of William
Congreve," was given as the annual Tudor and Stuart Lecture at
The Johns Hopkins University on April 25, 1968, and subsequently
appeared in *ELH* 35 (1968): 540-65. Whatever fragments of that
bygone effort, on a most memorable occasion, appear in the present
study are reprinted with the kind permission of the editor of *ELH*.
A somewhat different version of Chapter 5 appeared in *Imagined
Worlds: Essays on some English Novels and Novelists in Honour of
John Butt*, ed. Maynard Mack and Ian Gregor (London: Methuen &
Co., 1968), pp. 3-18, and is reprinted with permission from the
publisher. A much shorter version of Chapter 8 was given as a John
Hodges Memorial Lecture at the University of Tennessee on April
16, 1971, and was subsequently printed as such in *TSL* (1972),
pp. 1-18. I wish to express my gratitude to my hosts, particularly
Percy G. Adams, on that happy visit, and to the University of

Tennessee Press for permission to reprint portions of the lecture. Parts of Chapter 9 were given as a paper at a Clark Library Seminar on December 5, 1970, and printed as such in 1971. My memories of the hospitality accorded me then are yet green, and I gratefully acknowledge the permission to reprint granted me by the William Andrews Clark Memorial Library, University of California, Los Angeles. A modified version of Chapter 4 appeared in *PMLA* (1975), pp. 234–46, and is reprinted by permission of the Modern Language Association of America. A rather different version of Chapter 1 originally appeared as an article of the same title in *SLI* 10 (1977): 57–76, and I am grateful to the editors for permission to reprint.

In my protracted labors over this study it would be somewhat consolatory to think I had kept the advice of Horace in view, but I rather suspect the ten years spent on it were due more than anything else to the worrisome spirit in which I seem obliged to set down one word after another. A decade has certainly been sufficient time for me to accumulate more debts to libraries and librarians, students, colleagues, and friends, than I can adequately acknowledge here. Still, I must try to express, first of all, my gratitude to the several graduate assistants (most of them now professors) who somehow maintained, outwardly at least, a mien of good cheer during the terms of their servitude in this cause: Gail Compton, Michael Conlon, James L. Fortuna, Joan Metcalfe, James Thompson, Matthys Ouderland, Gisela Casines. I received much benefit from discussions, not to mention downright disputes, with these and other former students, particularly J. Paul Hunter, Richard Atnally, J. Douglas Canfield, M. Thomas Hester, Clifford Earl Ramsey, John Fischer, John David Walker, Robert Kalmey, Marianne Mayo, Joseph Popson, Larry P. Vonalt, John A. Jones, Jay Vonalt Booth.

I am much obliged also to several of my colleagues at the University of Florida who have read and commented on portions of the manuscript: Robert Bowers, Alistair Duckworth, John T. Fain, T. Walter Herbert, Jack Perlette, and Manning J. Dauer. Gareth Schmeling and Harold Gene Moss, of the Humanities Perspectives on the Professions, have eased my labors in ways they understand well, and Robert Thomson has provided more than once the clues I needed to discover some remote or arcane fact. Over the years

I have also been blessed with expert administrative help, especially from Patricia Bradford Rambo, Jimmy Perkins, Lee Hendrickson, Louise Brown, Beth Ramey, Sara Byers.

Two summer grants-in-aid, in 1971 and 1974, from the American Council of Learned Societies, mended considerably the pace of my labors. Two weeks of seclusion on Ossabaw Island, granted my wife and me by The Ossabaw Island Project, were especially helpful in writing the chapter on *Love for Love:* to Eleanor Torrey West, Calypso of that isle, much thanks. A summer appointment as director of a postdoctoral seminar on Pope at the William Andrews Clark Library, UCLA, enabled me to read through most of the interminable materials of the Collier controversy, and I am grateful indeed to the kindness shown me there by William Conway, Edna C. Davis, and Robert Vosper.

There are some special, not to say uncommon, debts: to Dorothy E. Maddocks, of Ripon, Yorkshire, for endowing me with a genuine "Black Box," that is, the kind of deed box which critics have seen, quite wrongly in my opinion, as a peculiarly talismanic object in *The Way of the World.* To David Mann, for his extraordinary courtesy in sending me the computer print-out (all four feet and 38 pounds of it, as I remember) of his *Concordance to the Plays of William Congreve* several years before its appearance in book form. To Irving Kallman, bookseller and bibliophile and bestower of firewood. To Ben Ross Schneider, Martin Battestin, Henry Knight Miller, and John M. Aden, whose words or works have been a sustaining force. To Phillip Harth, for telling comments set down in his reading of the manuscript. To the staff of the Beinecke Rare Book and Manuscript Library, Yale University, and especially to Marjorie Wynne, my tutelary spirit in Yale libraries for over three decades. To three members of the library staff at the University of Florida who have been indispensable to my work for many a year: Alice McNairy, of the acquisitions department, who has filled more of my requests than she would probably like to remember; Laura Monti, rare and gracious mistress of rare books and manuscripts; Jesse Ray Jones, reference department, my passe partout to the libraries of the world. Most uncommon perhaps of all, to three successive deans of the Graduate School at the University of

Florida: Linton E. Grinter (civil engineering), Harold Hanson (physics), Harry Sisler (chemistry), each of whom found ways to generate substantial sums whereby the University of Florida has acquired a collection of seventeenth- and eighteenth-century research materials that should serve scholars in the humanities and social sciences for centuries to come.

Finally, there are those old and cherished friends who have nourished, in ways no doubt unknown to them, all or most of my personal and professional life: my comrade-in-arms Jackson I. Cope, who nevertheless should be held innocent of what he instigated when he prompted the invitation for me to give a lecture before the Tudor and Stuart Club at the Johns Hopkins University; Frank A. Doggett; J. B. and Suzanne Pickard; the late and beloved Charles Archibald Robertson; and my late dear friend, William K. Wimsatt, whose strictures, and whose sweetness, abide with me still, and Margaret Wimsatt,

> The fairest garden in her looks,
> And in her mind the wisest books.

In the end, my deepest sense of obligation is to Maynard Mack, who presided over my beginnings and who, so far at least, has "indulg'd my labours past."

My wife, Carmen, I trust, will make the proper application, this particular month, of the lines from Horace which accompany my dedication of this book to her.

A. L. W.

Gainesville, Florida
Ides of April, 1978

1

Introduction

Of "One *Faith*": Authors and Auditors in the Restoration Theater

> *Dorax:* Religion bears him out; a thing taught young,
> In age ill practiced, yet his prop in death.
> Dryden, *Don Sebastian*, I.i.283–84.

One of the more curious facts about the criticism of Restoration drama, both past and present, has been its persistent neglect or only perfunctory notice of the one experience that contemporary playwrights and audiences had most in common: a shared upbringing and schooling in the basic doctrines and precepts of the Christian religion. Whatever the shadings and distinctions among Anglican, Roman, and dissenting congregations, and whatever the familiarity with Hobbes or Epicurus displayed in the age, there yet remains the simple and surpassing reality of each individual's generally similar indoctrination in the Christian view of man's present and future states and of his utter dependency on the will of God. It was an indoctrination that began with parental and tutorial guidance at home, where children as young as three or four years of age were likely to be given "two *Bibles,* one in Latin and one in English, together with a *Catechism* and a *Book of Common Prayer.*"[1] It was insistently enforced subsequently at grammar schools whose primary ends were "distinctly religious," both "in the curriculum and in the text-books employed," and which normally required not only attendance at prayers and church services but a continuing mastery of catechisms along with readings in both English and Latin (and sometimes Greek) versions of the Scriptures.[2] For those who went on to the universities, their tutor was

1

likely to be, as that of the earl of Rochester was, some "pious divine."[3] And before we conclude that the notorious earl is merely an example of how badly such an education may be wasted upon someone, let us rather suspend judgment for the moment and return to him a bit later.

We have recently had some good and cautionary advice from Robert Hume to the effect that Restoration playwrights "do not work to a tidy formula," that the "modern critic must expect to find a continuing state of confusion and change in both theory and plays," and that we "should not uncritically lump the pronouncements of the 1690's," most of them made in answer to Jeremy Collier, "with those of the 1660's."[4] Nevertheless, there is one particular critical "pronouncement," put forward by an unknown writer in 1698, which should never be forgotten in our approaches to the plays of any decade in the Restoration. The pronouncement in no sense implies a "tidy formula" by which plays were written, but it does suggest, I think, that behind the confusion and changes in dramatic theory and practice, as well as behind the continuing state of human confusion and discord represented so vividly on the stage itself, there existed for the majority of Restoration society a large body of shared theological and cosmological assumptions, an extensive and common vocabulary of special ethical or religious import, and an array of emblematic situations and predicaments, whose existential significance would have been consciously, or perhaps at times subconsciously, apprehended. The pronouncement, a sharp reminder of something most critics seldom seem to consider, is simply this: "Our Plays are no Heathen Compositions; our *Authors* and *Auditors* profess one *Faith.*"[5]

There are those who will regard such professions of faith as suspect, as representing perhaps, "only lip-service to inherited moral platitudes."[6] But depreciation of such professions seems most characteristic of those who attempt somehow to get at *the* meaning of Restoration plays without any notice at all of the religious modes of thought to which everyone in the age had been habituated since childhood. And while the tendency to make contexts and backgrounds supply the meaning of literary works is something I wish to

avoid, I also think that the failure to consider seriously the implications of a religious nurture common to authors and auditors alike
has had various kinds of unhappy consequences. One finds critics,
for example, resorting to Hobbes to account for the brutish and
"appetitive conflicts"[7] of human nature so often displayed on the
stage, and totally ignoring the traditional Christian view, instilled
in everyone, of a fallen and depraved humanity—and thus recorded
in Article 9 of the 39 Articles of Religion of the Church of England:
"man is very far gone from original righteousness, and is of his own
nature inclined to evil, so that the flesh lusteth always contrary to
the spirit, and therefore in every person born into this world, it
deserveth Gods wrath and damnation." The "appetitive conflicts"
in human nature were surely fully apprehended long before Hobbes,
and for many in such familiar terms as these: "For the good that I
would do I do not: but the evil which I would not, that I do," and
"But I see another law in my members, warring against the laws
of my mind, and bringing me into captivity to the law of sin which
is in my members."

One may attempt to account for the very imperfect human nature
imitated on the Restoration stage by a variety of recent theories—
Hobbesian, rationalistic, aesthetic—but that imitation seems to me
more likely a reflection of the general Christian *belief,* as Article 9
has it, in "the fault and corruption of the nature of every man,
that naturally is engendred of the off-spring of *Adam."* Dryden
needed no theory, Hobbesian or otherwise, to make him conclude
that the real "perfection" of "stage-characters consists chiefly in
their likeness to the deficient faulty nature, which is their original,"[8]
nor did John Sheffield, whose words in *An Essay upon Poetry*
(1682) are quoted with approval by Dryden:

> Reject that vulgar error which appears
> So fair, of making perfect characters;
> There's no such thing in Nature, and you'l draw
> A faultless Monster which the world ne'er saw.

Depraved though man might be, he nevertheless was still regarded
as living in a world whose Creator was concerned in his every deed
and who daily intervened on earth to chastise, to punish, to reward.

Those who find the plays of the Restoration to lack a sense of
"cosmic orderliness,"[9] or find that to Congreve "the natural world
appears chaotic,"[10] seem to ignore the very obvious order intrinsic
to a large body of plays which usually evince the defeat of vice
and folly and the reward of the good (however flawed the good may
be). They also seem oblivious to the fundamental Christian vision,
preached endlessly by Restoration clergymen to congregations
which included playgoers and playwrights alike, of a universe providentially designed, providentially sustained, providentially governed.
Nothing could have been more commonly heard from the pulpits
than these representative words of Archbishop John Tillotson
when he preached that the "providence of God many times preserves
good men from those ends which happen to others, and by a particular and remarkable interposition, rescues them out of those calamities which it suffers others to fall into; and God many times blesseth
good men with remarkable prosperity and success in their affairs."[11]
Or these of Bishop John Wilkins: "Both Virtue and Vice" are
"generally, and for the most part, sufficiently distinguished by
Rewards and Punishments in this Life."[12] We are concerned, after
all, with a period when, as Jacob Viner has pointed out,

> it was for many men psychologically impossible to believe that
> God did not constantly have man in his providential care, and
> that the physical order of the cosmos was not one of the tools
> he had designed to serve that purpose. The period [the seven-
> teenth and eighteenth centuries] in fact abounded, as never
> before, and perhaps never since, in attempts to demonstrate the
> manner in which the cosmos served man, much of it written by
> men with as good claims to be regarded as scientists as any men
> of their time.[13]

We shall be primarily concerned, indeeed, with a dramatist who
ended his *Mourning Bride* with these lines:

> Seest thou, how just the Hand of Heav'n has been?
> Let us that thro' our Innocence survive,
> Still in the Paths of Honour persevere;
> And not from past or present Ills Despair:

> For Blessings ever wait on vertuous Deeds;
> And tho' a late, a sure Reward succeeds.[14]

When Norman Holland remarks that the success of Nahum Tate's adaptation of *King Lear* "suggests, if nothing else, the remarkably bad taste in drama of Restoration and eighteenth-century audiences,"[15] he seems woefully to miss the point that Tate's *Lear* was so immensely popular precisely because it fulfilled so perfectly a pattern of order and justice in which both author and auditors believed—or *wanted* to believe. Tate's alterations may be offensive to modern critics, but nevertheless his version apparently fulfilled expectations or yearnings so deeply ingrained in the spectators that they went away satisfied and confirmed in their view of the way things did, or should, work out, the view expounded by Edgar in his closing address to the *living* Cordelia:

> Thy bright Example shall convince the World
> (Whatever Storms of Fortune are decreed)
> That Truth and Virtue shall at last succeed.

The vision of a world such as that depicted by Tillotson and Wilkins, or by Tate and Congreve, may strike many today as preposterous, but the credence given the vision at the time may be illustrated by reflections Dryden wrote down some twenty-five years after the first performance of his *Tyrannick Love*. Fretting over the possibility that the "misfortunes" of characters "wholly perfect (such as, for example, the character of a saint or martyr in a play)" would "produce impious thoughts in the beholders," making them "accuse the heavens of injustice, and think of leaving a religion where piety was so ill requited," Dryden remorsefully blamed himself for following so "dangerous" a practice in his dramatization of St. Catharine's martyrdom.[16] Even more fascinating, and no doubt suspect or incredible to some, is Colley Cibber's reported outburst when informed that Richardson planned for Clarissa to suffer the ultimate extremities of rape and death: "G-d d—n him, if she should; and that he should no longer believe Providence, or eternal Wisdom, or Goodness governed the world, if merit, innocence, and beauty were to be destroyed: nay (added he) my mind is so hurt with the thought of her being violated, that were I to see her in Heaven, sitting on the knees of the blessed Virgin, and crowned with glory, her suffering would still make me feel horror, horror distilled."[17]

The fact that Dryden wrote some plays of considerable prurience, or that Cibber's personal life was blatantly peccant, in no way proves to me that either man was insincere in his concern that a providential order be validated in literary terms. It does suggest to me that the humanity of Dryden and Cibber is as complicated and paradoxical, even perhaps as inconsistent, as anyone else's, a matter I would elaborate upon by a further look at that historical person who has been deemed not only the archetypal Restoration rake but also the actual model for Dorimant in *The Man of Mode*— John Wilmot, the earl of Rochester, whose early education seemed repudiated by a life of riot and debauchery well known to all. What by some may not be so well known, or usually even considered, is the manner of his dying: his progress over the year or so before his death, at thirty-three, from vague acknowledgment of a misspent life to the most passionate avowals of repentance, belief in God and His Providence, love of Christ, and his hopes, even his assurance, of eternal salvation.[18]

The outrageous sins committed by Rochester during one period of his life were in no way evaded or palliated by the clergy who attended him during his last year, nor were they glossed over at the funeral sermon preached by his chaplain, the Reverend Robert Parsons:

> His sins were like his parts, from which they sprang, all of them high and extraordinary. He seemed to affect something singular and paradoxical, in his impieties as well as his writings, above the reach and thought of other men; taking as much pains to draw others in, and to pervert the right ways of virtue, as the apostles and primitive saints did to save their own souls and them that heard them. For this was the heightening and amazing circumstance of his sins, that he was so diligent and industrious to recommend and propagate them; . . . framing arguments for sin, making proselytes to it, and writing panegyrics upon vice.[19]

Fully cognizant as they were of his past depravities, the clergy who

administered to Rochester during his terminal period included not
only his chaplain, but also "Dr. Marshall, the learned and worthy
rector of Lincoln College in Oxford," as well as "his diocesan, the
Lord Bishop of Oxford," and, of course, the Reverend Gilbert
Burnet, who took the time, amidst pressing affairs in London, to
comply with Rochester's appeals for his company—and whose later
narrative of Rochester's conversion was to go through five editions
between 1680 and 1700.

I stress such attendance on so profligate a son of the Church of
England to point up what should not need stressing: the fact that
contemporary clergymen of undoubted probity and learning in no
way considered Rochester, whatever his offenses, to be beyond their
care and cure—nor beyond the intervention of the "hand of God"
which then, Burnet reports, reached out and "touched him." Both
Burnet and Parsons, moreover, record Rochester's conversion as
occurring at the exact moment when Parsons "read him the fifty-
third chapter of the prophecy of Isaiah, and compared that with
the history of our saviour's passion": whereupon, as Rochester later
told Burnet, "he felt an inward force upon him, which did so enlighten his mind and convince him, that he could resist it no longer;
for the words had an authority which did shoot like rays or beams
in his mind; so that he was not only convinced by the reasonings
he had about it, which satisfied his understanding, but by a power
which did so effectually constrain him, that he did ever after as
firmly believe in his Saviour as if he had seen him in the clouds."[20]

Recollection of Rochester's conversion, or of the language he
is reported to have used ("I am assured of God's mercy to me
through Jesus Christ")[21] may seem an odd and even grotesque
intrusion in an approach to such drama as that of the Restoration
is so often reputed to be, a drama reported by some to be Epicurean
in its premises and nihilistic in its outlook, by others to be Hobbesian in its vision and values—a drama, in short, that is supposed
to reflect a society grown cynical and irreligious, sexually degener-
ate, emotionally bankrupt. But the society and drama reported on
by such critics is essentially a fabrication that is distractive from
the actual complexities of individual and communal life in the
period—and from the complexities of the art begotten in it. Cer-

tainly we should not fail to consider the gross immorality of King
Charles II or the viciousness of his influence. But then we also
should not fail to consider the fact that, as Gilbert Burnet told
Charles in his courageous, and celebrated, letter of remonstrance,
there was nothing that "so alienated the body of [his] people"
from him as the way he had given himself up "to so many sinful
pleasures."[22]

Rochester's statement that he became "convinced" in his faith
"by the reasonings he had about it" is very much at odds with the
school of thought which emphasizes, as Norman Holland does,
"the separation of faith from reason" or the growth of "a sense
of schism" in the late seventeenth century. It is Holland's view,
indeed, that "a whole pattern of separations" lies behind the comedies of the period, so that "spiritual reality was, in effect, separated
more and more from everyday life." There occurred, he argues, an
"infinite separation of God from man," a removal of God "from the
real world," and he agrees with those who have argued that at this
time "God drops out of the space and time of the real world" and
that the idea of Providence underwent a drastic revision, changing
from the conception of a "continuous participation of God in the
ordinary affairs of the world" to the conception of "a great over-all
clockwork system which functioned through natural laws."[23]

There can be no question that great changes were *incipient* in
the period and that indeed such changes ultimately were to lead to
the kinds of separations argued by Holland and others.[24] But it is
totally misleading to maintain that, for the vast majority of those
who met in the Restoration theater, any such drastic separations
had occurred. Holland's views would not have had much bearing
on the "everyday life" of those who heard, and I think believed,
these words of the Reverend Isaac Barrow, preached on November 5,
1673: "Divine and humane influences are so twisted and knit
together, that it is hard to sever them."[25] Neither would his views
have had much import for those who read, and I think believed, the
words of the Reverend Peter Browne when he wrote that it is by
the "use of Reason" that "the truths of all reveal'd Religion are
establish'd and remain unshaked and the same for ever, in spite of
all the opposition of their subtlest enemies."[26]

A good illustration of the way reason and faith were thought to be allied, rather than "separated," may be taken from a crucial scene in Dryden's *Tyrannick Love.* There, when Maximin tells St. Catharine that "Though Heav'n be clear, the way to it is dark," she replies:

> But where our Reason with our Faith does go,
> We're both above enlightened, and below.

A few minutes later Maximin commands his "Heathen Philosopher," Apollonius, to dispute St. Catharine's religion with her, only to witness his counselor's conquest by her reason and his conversion to her faith. "Where Truth prevails," Apollonius says, "all arguments are weak," and he adds:

> To that convincing power I must give place;
> And with that Truth, that Faith I will embrace.[27]

Later on in the play other conversions occur, notably those of Berenice, wife to Maximin, and of Porphyrius, her lover, and both declare their faith to have been prompted by their reason. To St. Catharine, Berenice says: "Your Arguments my reason first inclin'd,/ And then your bright example fix'd my mind" (IV, i, 434–35); and shortly thereafter Porphyrius asserts his independence from Maximin by declaring:

> Faith is a force from which there's no defence;
> Because the Reason it does first convince.
> And Reason Conscience into fetters brings;
> And Conscience is without the pow'r of Kings.

Such assertions by the obviously virtuous characters carry not only implicit authorial endorsement but also suggest an approving audience that would have been immensely surprised to hear that God had dropped "out of the space and time" of their world. I have taken them from so religious a play as *Tyrannick Love,* moreover, because I wish also to use its epilogue as evidence of the way the sacred and the profane could be so brilliantly, as well as unashamedly, accommodated to one another in the Restoration theater. The epilogue, of course, is that remarkable piece of bawdy spoken by

Nell Gwyn when, as the stage directions note, "she was to be carried off dead by the Bearers." Cast in the role of Valeria, Maximin's daughter, and having killed herself in the last act out of unrequited love for Porphyrius, Nell arises from her stretcher to address the audience:

> I come, kind Gentlemen, strange news to tell ye,
> I am the Ghost of poor departed *Nelly.*

Having promised to dance about their "Beds at nights," like some kind of sprightly succubus, Nell concludes:

> But farewell, Gentlemen, make haste to me,
> I'm sure e're long to have your company.
> As for my Epitaph when I am gone,
> I'll trust no Poet, but will write my own.
>
> *Here* Nelly *lies, who, though she liv'd a Slater'n,*
> *Yet dy'd a Princess, acting in S.* Cather'n.

Does the bawdy strain of the epilogue negate the drama of martyrdom and of heroic love and death which preceded it? I think not, no more than the so-called obscene figures in medieval churches may be said to violate or negate the cosmic "frame" of their existence. And while no one can possibly be sure of the actual audience response to Nell's words, I would guess that the obvious wit and salaciousness of the moment may have been complicated by their recognition of the memento mori in the invitation, however sexually suggestive, of a *"departed* Nelly"—"make haste to me,/I'm sure e're long to have your company"—as well as by their recognition in her epitaph of one of the commonest of theological and philosophical metaphors (the world of the stage as analogous to the stage of the world) and by that metaphor's insistence on human potentialities and possible transformations whereby even slatterns may "act well" the parts assigned them—even those of princesses.*

---

*The world-stage metaphor, of course, stressed not so much the part one was assigned by God, but *how well* one played the part. It may not be altogether beside the point here to recall Cibber's comment about the "many Actors" who "made it a Point to be seen in Parts," even those "flatly writ-

Editors of the California Dryden, along with a good many other critics, have argued that Restoration audiences "must have experienced a kind of perverse pleasure in seeing the roles of women of exemplary virtue played by actresses who were anything but that in everyday life," and they add that the "fascination of this contrast between role and reality is apparent in Pepys's report of the action backstage after Nell Gwyn had played an angel in Dekker and Massinger's *The Virgin Martyr*" a few years prior to her role in *Tyrannick Love*.[28] The possibility of a "perverse pleasure" being "experienced" on such occasions cannot be ruled out, of course, though such an emphasis seems to me superficial and highly reductive. I should like, therefore, to complicate the matter by quoting in full Pepys's account of his response to the scene in *The Virgin Martyr* when Nell Gwyn, playing a page-boy who is really an angel in disguise, descends to the stage to the accompaniment of a "windmusique" which he found "so sweet," he says, "that it ravished me, and indeed, in a word, did wrap up my soul so that it made me really sick, just as I have formerly been when in love with my wife; that neither then, nor all the evening going home, and at home, I was able to think of any thing, but remained all night transported, so as I could not believe that ever any musick hath that real command over the soul of a man as that did upon me: and makes me resolve to practice wind-musique, and to make my wife do the like."[29]

The California editors (whose bias seems to have fathered their thought) state that it was "the scene with the angel," rather than the "wind-musique" which accompanied it, that "ravished" Pepys's soul, and they also ascribe to him and others a "perverse pleasure" *during the performance* of the play on the basis of a scene *after*

---

ten," only "because they stood in the favourable Light of Honour and Virtue," and his humorous account of an actress who carried "this Theatrical Prudery to such a height, that she was, very near, keeping herself chaste by it: Her Fondness for Virtue on the Stage, she began to think, might persuade the World, that it had made an Impression on her private Life." One epilogue spoken by this actress contained the line, "Study to live the Character I play." See *An Apology for the Life of Colley Cibber,* ed. B. R. S. Fone (Ann Arbor: University of Michigan Press, 1968), p. 79.

the play, when he marvels at the impudence exhibited by both
Beck Marshall and Nell Gwyn amidst the men who hovered about
them—the "play being done" and they "off of the stage."[30] There is
nothing, in fact, in Pepys's words to indicate shock or fascination
or a "perverse pleasure" in seeing Nell act the part of an angel in
boy's attire; he simply says that going back stage he saw "Nell, in
her boy's clothes, mighty pretty." Scholars and critics apparently
have become both captives and abettors of a mythic Restoration
sexuality, one that when tested seems remote indeed from the
complicated personal realities as they are revealed in a Rochester
and a Pepys, or a Dryden and a Cibber.

In his preface to *Tyrannick Love,* Dryden states that he "considered that pleasure was not the only end of Poesie; and that even
the instructions of Morality were not so wholly the business of a
Poet, as that the Precepts and Examples of Piety were to be omit-
ted." He stated further that he would "maintain, against the Enemies of the Stage, that patterns of piety, decently represented,
and equally removed from the extremes of Superstition and Prophaneness, may be of excellent use to second the Precepts of our
Religion." And then, in words that are strikingly in accord with
those used by Pepys to describe the sensations aroused in him by
the "wind-musique" he so much admired, Dryden goes on: "By
the Harmony of words we elevate the mind to a sense of Devotion,
as our solemn Musick, which is inarticulate Poesie, does in Churches;
and by the lively [i.e. lifelike] images of piety, adorned by action,
through the senses allure the Soul: which while it is charmed in a
silent joy of what it sees and hears, is struck at the same time with
a secret veneration of things Celestial, and is wound up insensibly
into the practice of that which it admires."

There are doubtless those who will wish to confine Dryden's
"patterns of piety" and his "lively images of piety" rather strictly
to such patently religious plays as *Tyrannick Love, The Virgin
Martyr,* or *The Mourning Bride,* but it is my contention that such
patterns and images are to be found throughout the entire range of
Restoration drama. And while the work of William Congreve will
be used as the particular justification for my views, I would also
argue that such patterns and images are commonly adjusted and

reconciled to a large assortment of plays heroical, tragical, comical, and tragicomical. Such patterns and images, along with a variety of emblematic situations, often go unregarded, or they are dismissed as the conventional and nonreferential commonplaces and stock-in-trade of the Restoration theater—as if such commonplaces were insignificant formulae having only small rather than great importance in guiding audience response and in discovering authorial intent and dramatic meaning.[31] I have in mind, along with the illustrations that will be offered in the course of this study, all those episodes which take place in darkness or in prison cells or in a maze of corridors and paths, as well as all those scenes which seem dominated by interruptions, mistaken identities, fortuitous encounters, and other such seemingly random and adventitious happenings—as in Etherege's *She wou'd if she cou'd* (1668), where a whole series of both "lucky" and "unlucky" interruptions and discoveries culminate in Lady Cockwood's "pious resolution" to confine herself henceforth to the "humble Affairs" of her own family; or in Dryden's *Marriage-a-la-Mode* (1671), where there occur so many fortuitous interruptions of assignations and intended adulteries; or in Otway's *The Atheist* (1683), where Courtine says he will "go out into the middle of" a London street, "play at Blindmans-buff by myself, turn three times around"—and thereby "catches" the very despised wife he thought he had left back in the country; or in Vanbrugh's *The Provok'd Wife* (1697), where Lady Brute's surrender to Constant in the arbor at Spring Gardens is interrupted by the sudden rush upon them of Lady Fanciful and Mademoiselle, causing Lady Brute to dash off home in a fright, "as if the Devil," she says, "were in me."

One of the "liveliest," as well as one of the bawdiest, examples of a play structured according to such patterns of "providential" interruptions and mishaps is Dryden's *Mr. Limberham, or, The Kind Keeper,* often branded as his smuttiest achievement, but which he defended as "an honest satire against our crying sin of *keeping*" and as a play whose "crime" was that "it expressed too much of the vice it decried." For me at least, the bawdy of the play is too broad and buffoonish to represent a serious threat to anyone's morality. And at the very least we should note that for three acts all of Woodall's efforts to comply with the lechery of the wife, the kept mistress, and the landlady are totally frustrated by unexpected appearances of the husband or the kind keeper or his own father. And while all this is certainly the "conventional" stuff of comedy, the emblematic or metaphoric dimension it also carries was clearly signaled to a contemporary audience in the ludicrous episode at the end of act 3, where Woodall is attempting to mount Limberham's mistress on his bed while Brainsick's wife keeps jabbing at him with a pin from beneath the bed and where all such goings on are suspended by the sudden entrance of the hankering and sharp-set landlady, who exclaims, when all have been exposed: "So, so; if Providence had not sent me hither, what folly had been this day committed!"

Is Dryden here satirizing or deriding the whole concept of providential intervention in human affairs? I do not believe the author of *Tyrannick Love* and of *Religio Laici* had any such intention, and rather think his comic vision and his religious vision were so far from being "separated" that it never occurred to him that they could be or should be employed apart from one another. I would argue, moreover, that in all likelihood his audience would have viewed the scene not with shock and outrage but with an amused recognition of the way an awesome concept could be illustrated and enforced in the most comical, even farcical, terms. The action on stage is indeed bawdy, and no doubt designed to titilate an audience; at the same time the audience is also reminded of the theological "frame" within which, they had been taught since childhood, all human action, even the most bawdy, takes place. The scene displays a lapsed human nature in a most ludicrous way, but the audience of that time, at least, was also sent a message it would have grasped instantly.

To recognize the message today is not to turn the scene "solemn" or take all the "fun" out of it. Such recognition does lead to an expansion and complication of response to the scene, and so it becomes something more than a piece of mere ribaldry. If some today are offended or shocked at the idea of Providence intruding among the tumbled sheets of the scene, then it can only be because we have outlived that Christian vision within which no human conduct or transaction was considered too small or too ugly for providential regulation—the vision within which it was maintained that Providence "extends it self, not only to all created beings, and to all human affairs," but "even to the sins of Angels and men."[32]

The fact, moreover, that both the poltroonish kind keeper and the wife-despising husband are finally cuckolded, after more than a sufficiency of "fortunate" interruptions and "lucky" discoveries for any ordinary heads, scarcely affects the matter; for after their persistence in ignoring the evidence thus placed before their eyes, it is scarcely an impeachment of Providence when each is shown, in Woodall's words, to have taken "pains enough" for "his [own] cuckoldom." Even the most extravagant amount of providential interruption may not overcome what can only be considered the basest irresolution on the part of a Limberham or the most wilful impercipience on the part of a Brainsick. As the proverb had it, "If you leap into a well, Providence is not bound to fetch you out."

The cross-purposes and contraventions of sexual pursuit in *The Kind Keeper* approach the outlandish, but they are simply a variant on a basic pattern to be found in a host of Restoration plays, among them the works of Congreve. Over and over again the patterns illustrated, for most receptive audiences, the directive power of that Providence which, it was believed, did so often preserve man in spite of his errors and stumblings and which also somehow guided his uncertain steps through the earthly darkness wherein he wanders. Farcical and smutty as the action of *The Kind Keeper* may be, that action nonetheless may be accurately glossed by words from a much more sober play, Dryden's version of *The Tempest,* where Prospero says at one point that "man's life is all a mist, and in the dark, our fortunes meet us," and adds:

> Whether we drive, or whether we are driven,
> If ill 'tis ours, if good the act of Heaven.
>
> [III, v, 155 ff.]

And to drive the point home near the end of a play so obviously "providential"[33] in its action and outcome, Dryden has *"the good Gonzalo"* offer this explanation of the way the interests of justice have been so happily resolved and all parties reconciled:

Look down sweet Heav'n, and on this Couple drop
A blessed Crown, for it is you *chalk'd out the
Way* which brought us hither.
                                    [V, ii, 143-45; my italics]

Whether adjusted to high and tragic rant, or to low and comic
persiflage, such patterns illustrate the common ground and the
shared understanding with which authors and audiences alike faced
the ordinary as well as the extraordinary contingencies, exigencies,
quandaries, and predicaments of mortal life. In the graver plays
the patterns offer the dramatic exemplifications of that Providence
which both had been taught would be sure, "in all the Troubles and
Disturbances, all the cross, difficult, and Perplexing Passages that
can fall out," to "guide all to this happy issue; *That all Things shall
work together for Good to those that love God."** In the more
jocose and satirical plays the patterns also are present, offering their
own appropriate ratification of the commonly preached idea that
"nothing is so casual and uncertain, as to be exempted from the
disposal of Providence. For what seems accidental to us, is not
Chance, but Providence."[34]

No one author and no one auditor could be considered as fully
representative of those who met in the Restoration theater, but
even so I would suggest that Dryden, whose career and plays
spanned the years from 1660 to 1700, may be as representative as
any other playwright, and that Pepys, whose diary of the 1660s
reveals so nakedly his most private thoughts and feelings, may be
as representative as any other theater-goer. In considering such
men, moreover, it seems to me as important to remember Dryden's
oft-declared and lifelong abhorrence of atheism and impiety as it
is to dwell on the evident salaciousness of some of his plays, and that
our image of Pepys as prurient ogler be complicated by remem-
brance of his state of mind after his wife had confronted him with
her knowledge that he had renewed acquaintance with a former

---

*See Robert South, *Twelve Sermons Preached Upon Several Occasions,*
2 vols. (London, 1715), 1: 273. The biblical citation is Romans 8:28, often
invoked as authority for providential rewards in this life as well as in the
life to come.

mistress. He passed the afternoon, Pepys wrote, "in the greatest agony in the world," and then he tells of being

> most absolutely resolved, if ever I can master this bout, never to give her occasion while I live of more trouble of this or any other kind, there being no curse in the world so great as the differences between myself and her, and therefore I do, by the grace of God, promise never to offend her more, and did this night begin to pray to God upon my knees alone in my chamber, which God knows I cannot yet do heartily; but I hope God will give me the grace more and more every day to fear Him, and to be true to my poor wife.[35]

A few months after this, Pepys's growing blindness forced him to leave off his diary, which he closes with these words: "And so I betake myself to that course, which is almost as much as to see myself go into my grave: for which, and all the discomforts that will accompany my being blind, the good God prepare me!"

We do not know how many affairs Pepys actually had in the course of his life, or if he kept his resolve to be faithful to his wife (who died about a year after his promises to her and to God). We do know that, whatever his sexual frailties were, he was also "a loyal son of the Church of England," and that during the High Anglicanism of his later years he also "enjoyed a quiet and well-regulated domesticity, his household being presided over by Mary Skinner, with whom he had had a long and affectionate association, never consecrated by marriage but accepted as respectable by all his friends, since shortly after his wife's death." When he died at seventy, in 1703, his friend John Evelyn wrote in his diary that "Mr. Sam: Pepys" was "universally beloved, Hospitable, Generous, Learned in many things, skill'd in Musick, a very great Cherisher of Learned men." I do not think that the "Generous" Mr. Pepys, one of the kindest "keepers" of his age (and also one about whom there can be "no doubt of the sincerity of his religious feelings"),[36] would have been surprised, troubled, or offended by the quittance and the rewards accorded to Manly in *The Plain Dealer,* to Dorimant in *The Man of Mode,* to Mirabell in *The Way of the World.*

The world of the Restoration stage is a most fallen world, and human nature is there displayed in all the possible varieties of vice and folly—and also displayed in its capacity for self-denial, generosity of spirit, acts of trust and faith. The surface of this world is crisscrossed by haphazard encounters and by fortuitous mistakes and wanderings, as well as by the most devious indirection and opportunistic maneuvering. But behind the surface of so fallen a world, and working in and through all such human misadventure and misbehavior, there is usually implied, or explicitly affirmed, both an immanent and a transcendent order of Providence. The distributive justice enforced in the majority of Restoration plays, their punishment of vice and folly and their reward of the relatively good either in this life or the next, in no way bespeaks a world governed by chance or fortune or one suffering from Epicurean divine neglect.

To recognize the presence of such an order of justice is not, as some recent critics seem to think, to reduce the "dramatic realities" of Restoration plays, nor is it to read them "as if they were solemn theological treatises."[37] The "dramatic realities," indeed, cannot be fully appreciated until we have a better sense of the common ground of faith and the common explanations of life shared by those who met in the Restoration theater. Restoration audiences may have felt a "perverse pleasure" in seeing Nell Gwyn play a virtuous princess or appear as an angel in page-boy attire. But I suspect they had also been very well prepared, by lifelong habits of thought, to recognize under the robes and pantaloons a sister to us all, part angel and part whore, the potentialities for redemption in the most slatternly, the mysterious capacity to rise as well as to fall that should complicate our image of Pepys or Dryden or Rochester, or, for that matter, our image of Mellefont or Valentine or Mirabell.

2

Providential Justice in the Theater of the World

God *Almighty,* is that *Skilful Dramatist,* who always connecteth that of ours which went before, with what of his follows
after, into good *Coherent* Sense; and will at last make it appear,
that a *Thred* of exact Justice did run through all.

Ralph Cudworth,
True Intellectual System of the Universe (1678)

"Restoration man," an influential critic has said, "could no longer
seriously believe that society was divinely ordered," for "God
could no longer be said to take a direct interest in ordinary events."[1]
In spite of such words, the fact of the matter is that men of the
Restoration *were* saying that God took a "direct interest" in human
affairs, men as various, but as representative of the age, as Sprat
and Boyle and Newton, as Milton and Dryden and Pepys. Such
words, moreover, are grossly at odds with the convictions expressed
in the amazing amount of Providentialist apologetics which streamed
forth during the Restoration period and on into the eighteenth
century. Such apologetical literature, of course, often had Hobbes
and Epicurus in view, and most especially the Epicurean postulate of
a completely fortuitous creation whose "gods," such as they might
be, were utterly indifferent to earthly events. In contrast to such
Epicurean assumptions, late seventeenth-century Providentialists
stressed the traditional and still overwhelmingly accepted Christian
premise of a radically dependent universe, deliberately created by
God at a particular moment in time and yet also continuously
preserved in existence and supervised, to the smallest detail, by

his sustaining hand. In this traditional vision, the universe is seen, in Bishop Edward Stillingfleet's words, as a *"continued Creation,"* for "the *duration* or *continuance* of a *creature* in its *Being* doth immediately depend on *Divine providence* and *Conservation."* The "subsistence" of "all *Beings,* which come from an *Infinite* power," depends on "a continual *emanation* of the same *power* which gave them *Being;* and when once this is withdrawn, all those *Beings* which were produced by this *power* must needs *relapse* into nothing."* If the universe was compared to a watch or clock, as it often was and had been for centuries,[2] it was for most a clock that nevertheless still required a "continual emanation" from the God who gave it being:

> Thus God set up the world, as a fair and goodly Clock, to strike in tune, and to move in an orderly manner, not by its own weights . . . but by fresh influence from himself, by that inward, and intimate spring of immediate concourse, that should supply it in a most uniform, and proportionable manner.†

The utter and continuing dependency of all things upon the will of God was stressed in such a way, indeed, as to foster a sharp

---

Origines Sacrae, Or A Rational Account of the Grounds of Christian Faith, 3d ed. (London, 1666), p. 475. Cf. these words by the Reverend Richard Kingston, in *A Discourse on Divine Providence* (London, 1702), pp. 130–31: *"Preservation then,* is that benign Action of God, by which he continues the existence of things he created; so that (as a Learned Man [Stillingfleet?] has observed) *Preservation,* is but a continual Creation; for it is certain, (as the more celebrated *Philosophers* confess) *Preservation,* and Creation are not really two distinct Actions, but only different as to our Conceptions, because we conceive them in different respects, and our understandings consider them as two different things; the first, as it gives us Being and existence, the second, as it maintains, and continues what was given by the first."

†Nathaniel Culverwell, *An Elegant, and Learned Discourse on the Light of Nature: With several other Treatises* (London, 1661), p. 16. A foretaste of a view to prevail somewhat later is to be seen in this passage from Bernard Le Bovier de Fontenelle, where mention is made of those who "will have the World to be in great, what a Watch is in little, which is very regular, and depends only upon the just disposing of the several parts of the Movement." *Conversations With A Lady, On the Plurality of Worlds,* 4th ed. (London, 1719), p. 10.

sense of cosmic precariousness; man and the rest of the creation
were repeatedly imagined (as in Stillingfleet's words quoted above)
as poised on the brink of nothingness, as barely preserved, by God's
hand, from a relapse into chaos. It is not with God, wrote John
Arrowsmith in 1659, "as with carpenters and shipwrights,"

> who make houses for other men to dwell in, vessels for others
> to sail in, and therefore after they are made look after them no
> more; God who made all things for himself, looks to the preser-
> vation of all. It is accordingly said of Christ, *All things were
> created by him and for him, and by him all things consist.* The
> creatures are all as vessels, which if unhooped by withdrawing of
> Gods manutenency, all the liquor that is in them their several
> vertues, yea their several Beings would run out, and they return
> to their first nothing.[3]

That *"Almighty Wisdom* and *Goodness which first made all things,
doth also perpetually conserve and govern them,"* declared John
Smith in 1673, "lest stragling and falling off from the Deity, they
should become altogether disorderly, relapsing and sliding back into
their first *Chaos."*[4] Man, said John Norris in 1689, "so depends
upon God's continual Influence for the continuation of that Being
which he receiv'd from Him, that should God but never so little
withdraw it, he must necessarily fall back into his first Nothing."[5]
God, says Richard Kingston in 1702, has been represented by some
"as a great hand, which over an *Abyss,* bore up the vast Globe of
the World; or as a Secret Life hidden in every thing to preserve its
Being." But if God "should but withdraw his Hand, or take away
that support which he gives the World, it would immediately return
into its first *Chaos."*[6]

Such views, and such imagery, were an essential part of a traditional Christian vision still strong and vividly "real" for most men of
the Restoration (though not perhaps for some factitious "Restoration man"), and perhaps the best evidence of this is the way Pope,
at the close of his *Dunciad,* could take so awesome, and so appalling,
a possibility as the relapse of all things into chaos and old night and
give that possibility an imaginative immediacy. Pope's contemporaries, and his predecessors too, would have understood better than

we the theological premises which underlie the wondrous fantasy
of his poem.

Accepting the world as not merely the one-time creation, but as
also the "continued" creation, of God, it was highly improbable to
most men of the Restoration that He could be indifferent to what
He had wrought. To say that "God refuseth either to govern or care
for the World," says Sir Charles Wolseley, is "an affirmation highly
unreasonable" and a denial of "the necessary effects and emanations
of that goodness which we must needs ascribe to him."[7] There is
"not the least thing that falls within the Cognizance of Man,"
Robert South told a Westminster Abbey congregation in 1685, "but
is directed by the Counsel of God"; for *"Not an Hair can fall from
our Head, nor a Sparrow to the Ground, without the Will of our
heavenly Father,"* such a "universal Superintendency has the Eye
and Hand of Providence over all, even the most minute and inconsiderable Things."[8] In the words of William Sherlock, "To talk of
a General Providence, without God's Care and Government of
every particular Creature, is manifestly unreasonable and absurd."[9]

Throughout the Restoration period one of the most common, and
striking, ways of illustrating God's "universal Superintendency"
over all things was by means of the world-stage metaphor. Roy W.
Battenhouse has stressed the centrality of the metaphor in Calvin's
writings, as well as its importance to Marlowe and Elizabethans in
general, and Thomas B. Stroup has richly illustrated its widespread
use in English drama before the Restoration.[10] But it is just as important that we also recognize how common it was for spokesmen of
the later seventeenth century to employ, as their Elizabethan fore-
bears did, the image of God as a divine dramatist who has the world
for his theater. The Reverend George Hickes, for example, in a sermon devoted almost exclusively to the signs or marks by which
God's providential actions may be recognized, comments thus upon
the events leading to the Restoration of Charles II: "Certainly the
seasonable Contrivance of so many Scenes into every Act, and of so
many Acts into one Harmonious Play, must needs have been the
Study and Invention of a very Skilful Author, even of the All-wise,
and Almighty Dramatist, who hath the World for his Theatre, and
seldom less than a Kingdom for his Stage."[11] One of the ancient

users of the metaphor is thus recalled by Joseph Addison:

> *Epictetus* makes use of another kind of Allusion, which is very
> beautiful, and wonderfully proper to incline us to be satisfied
> with the Post in which Providence has placed us. We are here,
> says he, as in a Theater, where every one has a Part allotted to
> him. The great Duty which lies upon a Man is to act his Part in
> Perfection. We may, indeed, say that our Part does not suit us,
> and that we could act another better. But this (says the Philoso-
> pher) is not our Business. All that we are concerned in is to excel
> in the Part which is given us. If it be an improper one the Fault is
> not in us, but in him who has *cast* our several Parts, and is the
> great Disposer of the Drama.[12]

It was Plotinus, according to Battenhouse,[13] from whom the
Elizabethans derived their analogies between God and dramatist, and
Plotinus was still being credited with the analogy during the late
seventeenth century. Rebuking those who grumble against God's
governance of this world, Ralph Cudworth says that they who
"blame the Management of things as *Faulty,* and *Providence* as
Defective," because *"Judgment* is not presently Executed upon
the *Ungodly,"*

> are like such Spectators of a *Dramatick Poem,* as when wicked
> and injurious Persons are brought upon the Stage, for a while
> Swaggering and Triumphing; impatiently cry out against the
> Dramatist, and presently condemn the Plot; whereas if they
> would but expect the winding up of things, and stay till the
> last Close, they should then see them come off with shame and
> sufficient punishment. The Evolution of the World, as *Plotinus*
> calls it, is a truer Poem, and we men Histrionical Actors upon the
> Stage, who notwithstanding insert something of our *Own* into
> the *Poem* too; but God *Almighty* is that *Skilful Dramatist,* who
> always connecteth that of ours which went before, with what of
> his follows after, into good *Coherent* Sense; and will at last make
> it appear, that a *Thred* of exact Justice did run through all.[14]

Such assurances that God's providential justice would prevail on
his great stage, no matter the impercipience of man, are to be found

everywhere. Fallen men, said Henry More, like "Fools and Children," are "unfit Spectators of Things in Motion and Transition,"
and so "it is no wonder if the stupid World be much amuzd at
Providence, till that great *Dramatist,* God Almighty, draw on the
Period towards the last *Catastrophe* of things," when "certainly
Heaven and Earth will ring with the *Plaudite* or Acclamation, *Verily
there is a Reward for the Righteous; doubtless there is a God that
judges the Earth.*"[15] Every "Event that happens in the World," says
John Sharp, archbishop of York, "*is beautiful in its season;* as
Solomon expresses it," for "how unaccountable soever it may
appear to us, yet there is a good Reason to be given, both why it
happens at all, and likewise why it happens at that *time,* and with
those *circumstances* that it doth. It helps to adorn the Great *Drama*
and Contrivance of God's Providence, and Ministers to excellent
Ends, tho' we poor Creatures do little apprehend how it makes for
them."[16] We do "in this world (for the most part) see only the
dark side of Providence," said Bishop John Wilkins, but at "the last
and great day of *manifestation,* when the whole plot of Divine Love
shall be laid open, then we shall be able to discern the Beauty of
Providence in all the rugged passages of it."[17] And for those who
cared not to await a Last Judgment in another world but who
delighted in lurid instances of God's judgments against "murderers,
whoremongers, adulterers, ravishers, & tyrants" on the stage of the
world, there was Thomas Beard's *The Theatre of Gods Judgments,*
a compilation of literally thousands of examples of *"the admirable
justice of God against all notorious sinners, both great and small,"*
and which, though first published in 1597, was reprinted at least
twelve times right on up through 1704 and 1708 and 1770.

II

Although it was recognized that the "dispensations of God's
providence in this world, toward good and bad men, are many
times very promiscuous, and very cross, and contrary to what might
be expected from the wise and just sovereign of the world," and
that "virtuous and holy men are often ill treated in this world"
while "bad men many times flourish," nevertheless, most of the
Restoration clergy would apparently have been in accord with

Archbishop Tillotson when he went on to affirm that God also gives "particular and remarkable instances of his rewarding and punishing justice in this world, which may be to us an earnest of a future and general judgment." God "is pleased," he says, "sometimes in the dispensations of his providence, clearly to separate and distinguish the *precious from the vile,* remarkably to deliver good men, and *to snare the wicked in the works of their own hands.*"[18]

In another sermon the archbishop states that "natural reason" tells us "that God loves righteousness, and hates iniquity, and consequently that it must be agreeable to his nature to countenance and encourage the one, and to discountenance the other; that is, to give some publick testimony of his liking and affection to the one, and of his hatred and dislike of the other; which cannot be done, but by rewards and punishments" in this life.[19] Sherlock agrees, declaring that "though the Divine Providence does not always make a difference between Good and Bad men, as to their external Fortunes, yet sometimes God makes a very remarkable difference between them" and so gives "signal Demonstrations of his Anger against Bad men, and of his Care and Protection of the Good."[20]

God does not send his "Judgments upon this theatre of the world for his sport and pastime," says Tillotson, but rather uses such "acts of his providence" in order "to reclaim us."[21] The Reverend George Hickes, Dryden's friend and the nonjuring cleric whom the exiled James II quixotically appointed to the bishopric of Thetford, again made use of the stage metaphor to declare that "God is naturally the Protector of innocent Men, and righteous Causes, and tho' in Wisdom he cannot acquit, and condemn, reward, and punish here, as he means to do hereafter, when the great *Tragicomedy* is done; yet lest in the mean time the Spectators should have sinister Thoughts of his Providence, he is forced to come as it were, from behind the Curtain, and kill a bloody Tyrant, like *Herod,* with Blasphemy perhaps in his Mouth, and sitting in his Royal Apparel upon his Throne."[22]

If called upon to justify their conviction that the innocent and virtuous are watched over and rewarded in this life, the clergy them-

selves could call upon, as they frequently did, Romans 8:28: "And
we know that all things work together for good to them that love
God, to them who are called according to his purpose." It is the
text Tillotson cites when he says that "The providence of God is
more particularly concerned for good men, and he takes a more
particular and especial care of them."[23] And so with the Reverend
Thomas Pierce, when he says that "by the Wisdom of God's *Disposal,*" even "the evil of *sin,* in other men, is many times of great use
to *secure* our *Innocence.*"[24]

In the dispensation of his Providence, there was no need, it was
maintained, for God to suspend the laws of nature or to alter the
wills and hearts of individual men. In the first place, says Sherlock,
"God has bestowed different Vertues and Powers on Natural Causes,
and neither acts without them, nor against the Laws of Nature,"
and in addition he also exercises "an Absolute Government over
Mankind, who are Free Agents, without destroying the Liberty
and Freedom of their Choice, which would destroy the nature of
Vertue and Vice, of Rewards and Punishments."[25] In the words of
Bishop Wilkins, "That which is *most free,* the hearts and affections
of men, do follow the guidance of [God's] Decrees; Men may do
after their own counsel and inclinations, but they are still suitable
to his Providence; there is nothing more in our command than
our thoughts and words; and yet both *the preparation of the heart,
and the answer of the tongue, is from the Lord,* Prov. 16.1."[26]

When Maskwell, in his soliloquy in act 3 of *The Double-Dealer,*
asks whether the trap he has conceived for Mellefont and Lady
Touchwood is the product of his "Brain or Providence," his question, I believe, would have reminded his audience of the innumerable times they had read or heard it proclaimed that even those
"particular Interests of Gain, Honour, Pleasure, Revenge, which
sway men's desires and actions, are wisely contrived to the promoting of God's decrees and Glory."[27] And so, too, for those who
had heard so frequently, in one way or another, that nothing is
"more equal in Justice, and indeed more Natural in the direct
Consequences and Connexion of Effects and Causes, than for Men
wickedly Wise to out-wit themselves, and for such as wrestle with
Providence, to trip up their own Heels."[28] Whether as theater-goers

or as church-goers, most persons in the late seventeenth century, I believe, would have seen little reason to question the words of John Smith when he observed that a "wise man" who "looks from the Beginnings to the End of things" will behold all things "in their due place and method acting that part which the Supreme Mind and Wisdom that governs all things hath appointed them, and to carry on one and the same Eternal design, while they move according to their own proper inclination and measures, and aim at their particular Ends."[29]

While it is "very difficult, and ordinarily presumptuous, to determine precisely what things happen by God's special Providence, and Assistance, and what do not, because his secret Influences upon the Understandings, and Wills of Men, cannot be distinguished from their own Judgment and free Choice," nevertheless it is exceedingly common to find preachers delivering to their congregations "the Marks and Characters, which the Sence of Mankind, and the common Divinity of all Nations hath set down, as Rules whereby to know, when any Human Event is the Lord's special doing."[30] The kinds of "Human Event" with which the clergy and others deal, usually turn out to be inherently dramatic and also highly ironical in nature: last-minute rescues and escapes of the innocent or virtuous, the downfall of rich and powerful wickedness, the sudden disclosure of evil plotted in darkest secrecy, the frustration of craft and fraud, the ensnaring of bad men in their own snares. Individual instances of such events as witnessed God's interposing hand are the topics of a multitude of sermons in the period, but for the convenience of their particular congregations two of the more noted clergy of the day, Barrow and Hickes, delivered sermons in which the "Marks and Characters" of Providential interposition are collected and placed in seven categories.[31] Since the seven distinguishing marks offered by Hickes seem imitative of Barrow's, we may conflate their categories and include in them certain similar marks offered by others. It should be noted, however, that the "marks" are not really as "distinctive" as they are said to be in the two sermons, for the categories tend at times to blur into one another.

We may "perceive God's Hand," Barrow says of his first "character," when "effects are performed by no visible means, or by means disproportionate, unsuitable, repugnant to the effect." Examples of such "effects" are those occasions when "great feats are accomplished" by "weak forces" and when "impotency triumpheth over might"; when "great policy and craft do effect nothing, but are blasted of themselves, or baffled by simplicity"; when "plots, with extream caution and secrecy contrived in darkness, are by improbable means, by unaccountable accidents disclosed and brought to light"; when "ill men by their perverse wiliness do notably befool and ensnare themselves, laying trains to blow up their own designs, involving themselves in that ruine and mischief into which they studied to draw others."

A second "character of special Providence," Barrow says, is "the Seasonableness, and Suddenness of Events," when that which could not "well be expected, doth fall out happily, in the nick of an exigency, for the relief of innocence, the encouragement of goodness, the support of a good cause." Thus when "pestilent enterprizes (managed by close fraud, or impetuous violence) are brought to a head, and come near to the point of being executed," the "sudden detection, or seasonable obstruction of them, do argue the ever-vigilant Eye, and the all-powerful Hand to be engaged."

> God ever doth see those deceitful workers of iniquity, laying their mischief in the dark; he is always present at their cabals, and clandestine meetings, wherein they brood upon it. He often doth suffer it to grow on to a pitch of maturity, till it be thoroughly formed, till it be ready to be hatched, and break forth in its mischievous effects; then in a trice he snappeth and crusheth it to nothing.

It is scarcely surprising, in the light of these words, that Barrow's sermon on the marks of providential intervention, like so many other similar sermons, was delivered on an anniversary of the Gunpowder Plot, November 5, 1673.

Other characteristic marks of God's hand (again not always distinguishable from one another) as listed by Barrow are: 3. "the great Vtility and Beneficialness of Occurrences, especially in regard to the publick state of things, and to great personages, in whose welfare the publick is much concerned"; 4. the "Righteousness of

the case, or the Advantage springing from Events unto the main-
tenance of Right, the vindication of Innocence, the Defence of
Truth, the encouragement of Piety and Vertue"; 5. the "Correspondence of Events to the Prayers and desires of good men"; 6. the
"proceedings of God (especially in way of judgment, or of dispensing rewards and punishments) discover their original" and are "apt
to raise in them a sense of God's Hand" when "Craft incurreth
disappointment, and Simplicity findeth good success," or when
"bloudy Oppressours *have bloud given them to drink,* and come to
welter in their own gore (an accident which almost continually
doth happen)"; 7. the "Harmonious conspiracy of various Accidents
to one End or Effect," for it "is beside the nature, it is beyond the
reach of Fortune, to range various causes in such order." To these
may be added one found in many sermons, and expressed thus by
Hickes: "Another sign of God's special Providence, and Assistance,
is, when a remarkable Event happens to any, especially to Publick
and Illustrious Persons, upon the same day, in which another Accident, as remarkable, as that, happened to them before."

No themes, perhaps, are more common to such illustrations of
God's intervention in human affairs than those which insist upon
the ways in which good men may be saved by their own mistakes,
defeats, or stumblings and those which stress the way in which evil
men may be overcome by their very successes or hoisted with their
own petards. "When *Man plotteth* to save him selfe, that *plotting*
delivers him unto his *ruine,"* says Owen Feltham, and he adds that
we also "take courses to ruine us, and they prove *meanes of safety."*
He then concludes by quoting St. Jerome: "Providentia Dei omnia
gubernantur; & quae putatur poena, Medicina est."[32] It often
happens, Tillotson states, "that those very means which the wisest
men chuse for their security do prove the occasions of their ruin,
and they are thrown down by those very ways whereby they
thought to raise and establish themselves."[33] Sometimes, says the
Reverend Anthony Tuckney, "we drive on blindfold, and very often
pursue that which would ruin us: and were God as shortsighted as
we, into what precipices should we minutely hurry ourselves."[34]

Life in this world is often described as a condition of "darkness,"
a word, says Archbishop Sharp, "by which Scripture expresseth any

kind of Straits, or Difficulties, or Adversities,"[35] and Sherlock asks
how Providence could "more effectually convince us" that "we live
in the dark, and know not what is good for our selves" than "to let
us see by every days experience, how apt we are to be mistaken, and
to chuse ill for our selves; that our wishes and desires, were they
answered, would very often undo us; and that we are saved and
made happy by what we feared."[36] In illustration of the way God
may work through a very human "mistake," Arrowsmith repeats
the story of how St. Augustine "had appointed to go to a certain
town to visit the Christians there, and to give them a Sermon or
more":

> The day and place were known to his enemies, who set armed
> men to lie in wait for him by the way which he was to pass, and
> kill him. As God would have it, the guide whom the people
> had sent with him to prevent his going out of the right way
> mistook, and led him into a by-path, yet brought him at length
> to his journeys end. Which when the people understood, as also
> the adversaries disappointment, they adored the Providence of
> God, and gave him thanks for that great deliverance.[37]

From the Psalms and the Book of Proverbs came such texts as
maintained that the "Evil shall slay the wicked" (Psalms 34:21)
and that "the wicked shall fall by his own wickedness" (Proverbs
11:5), and the preachers and others exploit to the full the gratifying
ironic justice of such events. What, says Sherlock, "can more become
the Wisdom and Justice of Providence, than to make bad men the
Ministers and Executioners of a Divine Vengeance upon each other,
which is one great End God serves by the Sins of men." A bit later
he comments: "When our very Fears are turned into triumphs, and
that which seemed to threaten us with some great evils, is made the
Instrument of some great and surprizing Blessings; When bad men
are ensnared in their own Counsels, and fall into the Pit they have
digged for others [Proverbs 28:10]; When God turns their Curses
into Blessings, and saves good men by the Ministry of those who
intended their ruin: These, I say, and such like Events, of which
there are numerous Instances, both in Sacred and Prophane Story,
and which our own observation may furnish us with fresh Examples

of, justly gives us great and admiring thoughts of the Divine Wisdom."[38] Where "power is," wrote Nathaniel Wanley, "it is ordinary to be oppressive according to the measure of it; but then many times the Providence of God steps in, and measures out the greatest Insolents the measure they have meted, causing them to fall into the very pits they have digged for others."[39]

III

Other than the words from Matthew 10:29–31, which assured men that not a sparrow's fall would go unnoted and that even the hairs of their own heads were numbered, perhaps no single biblical text was more used to expound God's providential control of worldly events than the one from Proverbs 16:33: "The lot is cast into the lap; but the whole disposing thereof is of the Lord." The *"least, most inconsiderable things,"* even that "which seems most *casual, The disposing of the Lot,"* says Bishop Wilkins, are "not neglected by Providence."[40] The words of Solomon in The Proverbs, says Sherlock, are not to be "confined to the Case of Lots," but are meant to "signify to us, that nothing is so casual and uncertain, as to be exempted from the disposal of Providence. For what seems accidental to us, is not Chance, but Providence."[41] Preaching on the same text, South says that because "there are some Events, beyond the Knowledge, Purpose, Expectation, and Power of second Agents," it is "the Royal Prerogative of God himself, to have all these loose, uneven, fickle Uncertainties under his Disposal." However much things may be "accidental in their Production, and unstable in their Continuance," nevertheless "God's Prescience of them is as certain in Him, as the Memory of them is or can be in us."[42]

A cognate text for that in Proverbs was provided by the entire Book of Esther, and particularly by the events in it which led to the inauguration of the Feast of Purim among the Jews. As the Reverend William Beveridge, bishop of Asaph, told the House of Lords in a sermon preached on the anniversary of the Gunpowder Plot in 1704, the two days of Purim stem from the occasion when Haman, the wicked minister of King Ahasuerus, became "so incensed against *Mordecai* the *Jew,* for not bowing to him as other People did," that he designed "to destroy all the *Jews* that were in all the Empire, reaching from *India* to *Ethiopia*":

> and for that purpose, he cast a sort of Lot, called *Pur,* according
> to the superstitious Conceits of those Times, to find out which
> was the most lucky Day in the Year whereon to bring about
> his Design: And the Lot falling at last upon the thirteenth day
> of *Adar,* the last Month in the *Jewish* Year, he procured the
> King's Decree, That all the *Jews* in his Dominions, consisting of
> 127 Provinces, should be destroyed on that day.

But of course the "King's Mind was altered" by Esther, his Jewish
queen, and Haman was hanged upon the gallows, "fifty cubits high,"
which he had "prepared for Mordecai." Then the king decreed that
on "the thirteenth *day* of the twelfth month, which *is* the month
Adar," the day designed for their own destruction, the Jews would
have the power to "destroy all that were ready to destroy them."[43]
The Bible scarcely offers another story so ironic, or dramatic.

"There are many things, indeed," said Archbishop Tillotson,
"which to us seem chance and accident; but in respect to God, they
are providence and design; they may appear to happen by chance, or
may proceed from the ill-will and malicious intent of second causes,
but they are all wisely designed" and "appointed or permitted by
God."[44] And in illustration of such "providence and design,"
George Hickes not only offers us "The Story of *Esther*" but does so
by way of the pervasive stage metaphor: "that she should be chosen
into the *Seraglio of Ahasuerus* among a Crowd of other Virgins,
seems a Matter of Fortune, or common Providence, and yet it was
contrived by God, for the Deliverance of his People; and the providential Scene, which depended upon it, was perhaps, as miraculous,
as ever was acted upon the Stage of human Affairs."[45]

The fact of the matter, I believe, is that the great majority of persons in the Restoration (including the playwrights as well as the
preachers) would have agreed with Culverwell's statement that *"Fortune* was nothing but a more *abstruse,* and *mysterious,* and *occult*
kinde of *Providence."*[46] Today we may dismiss or smile over Dryden's words when he says he could "easily demonstrate" that "no
Heroick Poem can be writ on the *Epicuraean Principle,*" because the

English people, "better taught" by their "Religion" than the
Romans were by theirs, "own every wonderful Accident which be-
falls us for the best, to be brought to pass by some special Providence of Almighty God; and by the care of guardian Angels."[47] Yet
Dryden's words are perfectly consonant with those of Stillingfleet
when he rebukes Epicurean notions of a fortuitously created universe by asking if we can "imagine" that a Being of "*Infinite power*
should *stand by* and leave things to *chance* and *fortune*?"[48]

From the pulpits, as well as from the playhouses, of the Restoration, there is a vast amount of evidence which suggests that Englishmen of the day were fascinated by that "secret providence of God
which sometimes presents men with unexpected opportunities, and
interposeth accidents which no human wisdom could foresee; which
gives success to very unlikely means; and defeats the swift, and the
strong, and the learned, and the industrious, and them that are best
versed in men and business, of their several ends and designs." They
surveyed, and were intrigued by, a world in which there was "an
unaccountable mixture of that which the heathen called fortune,"
but which they were taught to know "by its true name, the providence of God; which does frequently interpose in human affairs,
and loves to *confound the wisdom of the wise*, and *to turn their
counsels into foolishness.*"[49]

The Restoration stage, like life itself, offers a seemingly "unaccountable mixture" of happy accidents, fortuitous encounters,
unlucky successes, strange coincidences. In our contemplation of
them, we should keep in mind those contemporary aphoristic statements which held that while man may "throw the dice," God
"appoints the chance."[50] We would do well to recall Sherlock's
observation that, "if Providence governs any thing, it must govern
Chance, which governs almost all things else, and which none but
God can govern."[51] We should remember, indeed, that the common
view of chance and fortune in the seventeenth century is that
offered in Thomas Wilson's *A Christian Dictionary:* "Chance.]
Such occurences and events as doe fall out to men beyond their
skill and counsell, through Gods providence, but to us by happe
or chance, Luke 10, verse 31." As Henry Knight Miller has observed, in the traditional view of the universe still predominant in

the seventeenth century, "Chance and Fortune were merely aspects of (indeed, proof of) God's overarching Providence."[52]

IV

Responding to the age-old complaint "that if goodness governed the world, and administered the affairs of it, good and evil would not be so carelessly and promiscuously dispensed," Archbishop Tillotson first assured his listeners that "notwithstanding the rage and craft of evil men, poor and unarmed innocence and virtue is usually protected, and sometimes rewarded in this world; and domineering and outrageous wickedness is very often remarkably checked and chastised." But then he went on to say that even the mixed and apparently inequitable state of affairs in this life is, if rightly considered, "an effect of God's goodness, and infinite patience to mankind, that *he causeth his sun to rise, and his rain to fall upon the just and the unjust;* That upon the provocation of men, he does not give over his care of them, and throw all things into confusion and ruin." The plain conclusion to be drawn from all this, he then says, is that God has designed "this life for the trial of mens virtue and obedience." God therefore "suffers men to *walk in their own ways,*" for "the fuller trial of them, and the clearer and more effectual declaration of his justice, in the rewards and punishments of another life."[53]

The vision of this world as a time of probation, of temptation and trial, is of course fundamental to Christian thought, and in the late seventeenth century the preachers, like their predecessors for centuries before them, commonly took as the appropriate text for the topic the verses from 1 Peter 1:6-7 which state that men "for a season" may be "in heaviness through manifold temptations," in order that the "trial" of their faith, "being much more precious than of gold that perisheth, though it be tried with fire, may be found unto praise, and honour, and glory, at the appearing of Jesus Christ." In their exposition of the theme, the clergy drew upon a rich and commonly shared stock of analogies. Thus it may please God to set a man "up for a mark, and to suffer many and sharp arrows to be shot at him, to try whether his faith and patience be proof; as men set up armour and shoot at it with a double charge, not with a design to hurt it, but to prove and praise it."[54] Similarly, God, may "ordain or permit such Afflictions upon his Servants" as may be a "Tryal of their Virtue, as the best tempered Arms are proved by a Higher Charge than ordinary."[55] The "Potters Vessals are Try'd in the Furnace, and so are Men in their Afflictions,"[56] and as "when the Founder hath cast his bell, he doth not presently hang it up in the steeple, but first try it with his hammer, and beat upon it on every side, to see if any flaw be in it," so "Christ doth not presently after he hath converted a man, convey him to heaven, but suffers him to be beaten upon by manifold temptations."[57]

Most of the objections against the goodness and justice of Providence are seen as the result of a failure to consider "the present State of Mankind in this world" as a "State of Trial and Discipline." However severe the methods used to reform sinners, moreover, they are "as great an Expression of Goodness, as it is to force and to compel them to be happy; as it is to cut off a Hand or a Leg, to preserve Life."[58] If men were properly to consider the benefits and ends God intends for them by his trials, they would come to understand that often mankind is exercised "with trouble and afflictions, with a very gracious and merciful design, to prevent great evils, which men would otherwise bring upon themselves." God may, "as it were, by afflictions, throw men upon their backs, to make them look up to heaven."[59] Most succinctly put, "All Afflictions are advantageous to the godly. They often help to make bad men good, always to make good men better."[60]

In their explications of the fact that it is "in the nature of things a *necessary* and *essential* condition of a *Probation-state,* that there should be some *Tryal* of men's virtue."[61] the clergy failed not to remember and to employ the metaphor of the world as God's great stage. For in His "afflicting Providences" God does not, says Tillotson, send his judgments "upon this theatre of the world for his sport and pastime, nor set on one part of his creation to bait another for his own diversion: he does not, like some of the cruel Roman emperors, take pleasure to exercise men with dangers and to see them play bloody prizes before him." Rather, "if he cast us into the furnace of affliction, it is that he may refine and purify us from our dross."[62] Every man, says Stanhope, "hath a Post appointed him by God, and the Character of a Christian to maintain," and few "arrive to any uncommon Excellencies in their Station except Such, as make their way up to them through Sufferings." Hence it is, "we commonly call Afflictions *Tryals,* because they are the Test of a Man's Vertue, and discover what he really is."[63]

V

We shall not begin fairly to apprehend the vision, the substance, or the design of most late seventeenth-century English drama until we somehow "place" the playwrights and their plays more squarely within the framework of that "world" in which most people of the age considered themselves to live—that larger and providentially ordered theater presided over by an Almighty Dramatist. We must begin to see that, in most if not all cases, a plot on the stage in Drury Lane or Lincoln's Inn Fields may have been designed with a larger "*Plot* of *Divine* Providence" in view. We must begin to see that the lesser and larger stages of the world were brought together in cathedrals as well as in theaters by spokesmen who shared much in their visions and illustrations of human existence. It is not hard, I think, to find a voice and a vision mutual to both priest and playwright in these words by Isaac Barrow:

> Who values the fortune of him that is brought forth upon the Stage to act the Part of a Prince; though he is attired there, and attended as such; hath all the garb and ceremony, the ensigns and appertenances of Majesty about him; speaks and behaves himself imperiously; is flattered and worshipped accordingly; yet, who in his heart doth adore this Idol; doth admire this mockery of greatness? Why not? because after an hour or two the Play is over, and this Man's reign is done. And what great difference is there between this and the greatest worldly state? between *Alexander* in the History, and *Alexander* on the Stage? Are not (in the *Psalmist*'s accompt) *all our years spent as a tale that is told;* or, as a Fable, that is acted?

Does not the greatest "worldly glory" therefore "appear to be no more than a transient blaze, a fading shew, a hollow sound, a piece of theatrical pageantry?"[64]

3

Poetical Justice in the World of the Theater

> To conclude, I approve extremely of your killing *Fredage* and
> *Beron.* Poetical justice requires him; and for her you may easily
> drop a word, to intimate her delivering of *Gustavus* to have
> proceded from some spark of love, which afterwards she may
> repent of, and her character remain as perfect as nature need
> require.
>
> Letter from William Congreve to Catharine Trotter
(November 2, 1703)

> Poetick Justice would be a Jest if it were not an Image of the
> Divine, and if it did not consequently suppose the Being of a
> God and Providence.
>
> John Dennis, *The Usefulness of the Stage* (1698)

In 1699, the "learned and ingenious Dr. Drake," as Dryden called
him, observed that among the "Moderns" (as opposed to the "Antients" of Greece and Rome), "Poetick Justice" had "become the
Principal Article of the Drama";[1] yet in our own time this "Principal Article" has been either largely ignored, or misunderstood, or
much depreciated as a shaping factor in most plays of the late
seventeenth century. Considered by one recent critic as "irrelevant
to the course of tragedy"* during the Restoration period, poetical
justice is, on the contrary, not only aesthetically important for the

---

*Cf. Eric Rothstein, *Restoration Tragedy* (Madison: University of Wis-
consin Press, 1967), p. 158 and n.: "But poetic justice, which would have
had to have been universal in order to have been perceived as anything but
arbitrary, remained a dead issue, disputed but irrelevant to the course of
tragedy." By contrast, cf. E. N. Hooker, *The Critical Works of John Dennis,*
2 vols. (Baltimore: The Johns Hopkins Press, 1939, 1943), 1 : 477: "When
therefore Addison attacked the doctrine of poetic justice in *Spectator,* no.
40, he was assailing a doctrine so far from being peculiar to Dennis that it was
generally accepted in the two decades before he wrote, by critics and dramatists alike."

way it regulated the "Fable" (the plot or design) of most Restoration plays, comedies as well as tragedies, so that vice and folly would be shown as punished or scorned and virtue, even if unfortunate, as approved. Of perhaps even more fundamental importance for our understanding of the concept and its contemporary appeal is the fact that the poetical justice illustrated on the stage was generally accepted as the dramatic equivalent or embodiment of Providential justice. In their punishment of vice, as in their reward or at least approval of virtue, the majority of Restoration plays make either an implicit or an explicit affirmation of a metaphysical order of justice assumed by most persons actually to exist.†

I

First employed, at least in print, by Thomas Rymer in 1677, the phrase "poetic justice" has generally come to mean a rather arbitrary reward of the good and punishment of the wicked, or perhaps an outcome which seems peculiarly or ironically appropriate in a given set of circumstances. But such understandings of the concept are highly reductive and very misleading when set against the actual implications of "Poetick Justice" in the late seventeenth and early eighteenth centuries, and if we are fully to apprehend the strength and import of the concept at the time we must recapture in some sense the way it stood for the mirroring of God's justice in literary form. The playwright observing the concept in this way "does not believe," as Richard Tyre has said, "he is inventing his own version of justice, since he is merely following what he believes to be the pattern of divine order."*

†Again my view is at odds with that of Rothstein: "to the practicing playwright, poetic justice was never a real issue. The didactic and the metaphysical had different theoretical bases during the Restoration, and the two must be unified in theory for poetic justice to thrive" (p. 158).

*"Versions of Poetic Justice in the Early Eighteenth Century," *SP* 54 (1957):29–44. Tyre finds in the period "two different and often totally unrelated concepts" of poetic justice: one, which he considers "literal," is "didactic-ethical" and "bears little resemblance to what actually takes place in the world of reality"; the other he considers "liberal," and represented an attempt to reflect a "Divine Plan." His distinctions seem to me to be erroneous and unnecessary; in my view, employment of the concept nearly always represented an effort to illustrate the workings of Providence.

Leaving aside foreshadowings of the concept in Plato or in such writers as Sidney and Jonson,[2] what became the common inference of "Poetick Justice" may be clearly seen in Bacon's statement that "because true history propoundeth the successes and issues of actions not so agreeable to the merits of virtue and vice, therefore poesy feigns them more just, and more according to revealed providence."[3] Precisely such an emphasis is found in all of Rymer's important statements on the subject. Thus he observes that Sophocles and Euripides found "in History, the same *end* happen to the *righteous* and to the *unjust, vertue* often opprest, and *wickedness* on the Throne," and so

> They saw these particular *yesterday-truths* were imperfect and unproper to illustrate the *universal* and *eternal truths* by them intended. Finding also that this unequal distribution of rewards and punishments did perplex the *wisest,* and by the *Atheist* was made a scandal to the *Divine Providence.* They concluded, that a Poet must of necessity see justice exactly administered, if he intended to please.

Elsewhere Rymer declares that in tragedy "something must stick by observing that harmony and beauty of Providence, that necessary relation and chain, whereby the causes and the effects, the virtues and rewards, the vices and their punishments are proportion'd and link'd together; how deep and dark soever are laid the Springs, and however intricate and involv'd are their operation." And it is a similar concern that any stage justice be "according to revealed providence" that lies behind Rymer's attack on *Othello.* Speaking of the murder of the innocent Desdemona, he complains: "Is not this to envenome our spirits, to make us repine and grumble at Providence; and the government of the World? If this be our end, what boots it to be Vertuous?" Rymer then bitingly proposes an alternative ending, one that would leave Desdemona alive but would have Othello very "honestly cut his own Throat, by the good leave, and with the applause of all the Spectators," who "might thereupon have gone home with a quiet mind, admiring the beauty of Providence; fairly and truly represented on the Theatre."[4]

Rymer coined a phrase, but as the passage from Bacon makes

clear, the assumptions behind the phrase were already established
and very much in evidence in Restoration drama before Rymer had
anything to say about the matter. It would be hard to find a Restoration play that did not affirm some order of justice; and in a
profoundly Christian society, as I believe Restoration society to have
been, it would be highly unlikely to find the order of justice
"feigned" by the poets to be at odds, in Bacon's words, with "revealed providence." Dryden himself believed that the "Ancients"
had not "administered poetical justice (of which Mr. Rymer boasts)
so well" as the English, partly because the English playwrights
had not limited themselves to the passions of "pity and terror."
Since the end of tragedy is to "reform manners," he says, then
"all the passions" (including "joy, anger, love, fear") are to be
"set in ferment," for the purpose of moving "love to virtue and
hatred to vice; by shewing the rewards of one, and the punishments
of the other; at least by rendering virtue always amiable, though it
be shown unfortunate; and vice detestable, tho' it be shown triumphant."[5]

The concern underlying such a view, and such a view's ultimate
rationale, may be best discovered, in my view, in Dryden's reproach
of himself because, as we have seen, the misfortunes of St. Catharine
as represented in his own *Tyrannick Love* might "produce impious
thoughts in the beholders" and perhaps lead them to "accuse the
heavens of injustice, and think of leaving a religion where piety was
so ill requited." A more extreme, but nonetheless revealing, illustration of the contemporary cast of mind may be found in Charles
Gildon's declaration that "no unfortunate Character ought to be
introduc'd on the Stage, without its Humane Frailties to justifie its
Misfortunes: For *unfortunate* Perfection, is the *Crime* of Providence,
and to offer at that, is an Impiety a Poet ought never to be guilty of;
being directly opposite to his duty of *Rewarding the Innocent, and
punishing the Guilty;* and by that means to establish a just notion
of Providence in its most important Action, the Government of
Mankind."[6]

The testimonies of Rymer, Dryden, and Gildon* were all set down

---

*Between the actual wriitng of his preface to *Phaëton* and its publication,
Gildon appended a section where he says he has just "met with a Book, call'd
a short View of the Immorality, and Profaneness of the English Stage."

before Collier, by his sudden assault on the stage in 1698, elicited from critics and playwrights alike their various defenses of the theater. But one immediate consequence of Collier's book was the most forthright declaration, by John Dennis, of what I take to have been, for almost everyone, the generally understood implication of "Poetick Justice." For Dennis, as Hooker has observed, the concept "involved a belief in the possibility of the intervention of a 'particular Providence,' and therefore implied a belief in the immanence of God"—but so it did, I believe, for most other persons in the age. In any event, here is one of Dennis's statements as to the ways "the Stage is useful to the Advancement of Religion":

> First, the things to be believ'd are, 1. The Being of God. 2. Providence. 3. Immortality of the Soul. 4. Future Rewards and Punishments. The Poet, and particularly the Tragick Poet, asserts all these, and these are the Foundations of his Art.

The underlying rationale for the distributive justice so markedly illustrated in plays for decades is then once again insisted upon in Dennis's ensuing words: "Poetick Justice would be a Jest if it were not an Image of the Divine, and if it did not consequently suppose the Being of a God and Providence."[7]

Addison is sometimes represented as having summarily dismissed what he calls, in *Spectator* no. 40, the "chymerical Notion of Poetical Justice," yet as Hooker has pointed out, Addison was really not much different from Dennis in his view that the best tragedies were those in which "the main character ends unfortunately."[8] And while Addison found that "more of our *English* Tragedies have succeeded, in which the Favorites of the Audience sink under their Calamities, than those in which they recover out of them," he also says he "must allow, that there are very noble Tragedies, which have been framed upon the other Plan, and have ended happily," among them Congreve's *Mourning Bride* and "most of Mr. *Dryden*'s." Addison is simply against a theory or concept which would *always* "make Virtue and Innocence happy and successful," and what seems to have been lost sight of is the fact that he in no way wishes the stage to deny or fail to reflect the idea that all earthly affairs are governed by a providential administration. Just the reverse, in fact, for in *Spectator* no. 39 he says that "a well-written

Tragedy" will "soften Insolence, sooth Affliction, and subdue the Mind to the Dispensations of Providence." His earnest concern to make his position utterly clear on this matter is manifest, moreover, in *Spectator* no. 548, where he states that while "good Men may meet with an unhappy Catastrophe in Tragedy," his earlier paper had not held "that ill Men may go off unpunish'd." In a statement utterly consistent with Christian doctrine,* though not as strict as those of Rymer and Gildon, he then states that the "Reason for this Distinction is very plain, namely, because the best of Men are vicious enough to justifie Providence for any Misfortunes and Afflictions which may befall them, but there are many Men so Criminal that they can have no Claim or Pretence to Happiness. The best of Men may deserve Punishment, but the worst of Men cannot deserve Happiness." However dissatisfied Addison was with the more strict construers of "Poetick Justice," he was not willing to surrender the view that stage plays, whichever way they were written, should "subdue the Mind to the Dispensations of Providence."

In 1677 Dryden had responded to Rymer's attack on *The Tragedies of the Last Age* by claiming that the "Antients" had not administered "poetical justice" so well as the English, and twenty years later James Drake, responding this time to Collier's denunciations of the English stage, undertook his "survey" of *The Antient and Modern Stages* to demonstrate, as his title page states, "the comparative [i.e. superior] Morality of the *English* Stage . . . upon the Parallel." It was this work which prompted, the year after it appeared, Dryden's public compliment on Drake's learning and ingenuity,[9] and the substance and purpose of Drake's "survey" prompts me to wonder if he had not been privy to Dryden's unpublished "Heads of an Answer to Rymer." In any event, a major section of Drake's argument is devoted to "notice of two or three things which are apparently the indisputable advantage of the

---

*Cf. the representative words of William Nicholson, Bishop of Gloucester, in his *A plain but full Exposition of the Catechism of the Church of England. Enjoyned to be learned of every Childe, before he be brought to be confirmed by the Bishop* (London, 1662), p. 143: "Trespassers we are all, and therefore had need to pray, *Forgive us our trespasses,*" for "The Lords Prayer teacheth, that we are sinners, and that our whole life ought to be a life of repentance."

Moderns over the *Antients,* in respect of the General *Moral* of
their Fables." The "things" Drake chooses to "notice" reflect,
no doubt, a considerable bias, as well as considerable critical dim-
sightedness, but the terms and substance of his discourse suggest
he expects from his readers a shared understanding as to the ultimate
implications of that "Poetick Justice" they desired, and even demanded, from the stage.

In the first place, Drake says, the Moderns "never are at the expence of a Machine [i.e. a supernatural intrusion] to bring about
a wicked Design, and by consequence don't interest Providence
in promoting Villany; as the Antients have notoriously done in
many of their Plays."* Secondly, the Moderns "never engage Providence to afflict and oppress Virtue, by distressing it by supernatural means, as the Antients have manifestly done, by making
their Gods the immediate Actors in or directors of the misfortunes
of virtuous persons."† Finally, Drake declares that the "Malefactors" in modern plays "are generally punished, which those of the
Antients seldom were"; and even if their malefactors do escape
punishment, "the Moderns don't provide 'em with a miraculous
delivery, or have recourse to such extraordinary Methods as exceed
the reach of Humane Force or Cunning, so as to entitle Providence
to the Protection of 'em, which was the frequent Practice of the
Antients."* From his survey, and for such reasons, Drake concludes
that "we may see with how much more respect to Providence, and
the Divine Administration, our Poets have behaved themselves," as
well as "how far the Ballance of Religion inclines to our side."
Drake's words here, his confidence that "*we* may see" how much
more "*our* Poets" and "*our* side" evince a "respect to Providence,
and the Divine Administration," testify once more to a cosmic
vision mutual to authors and auditors alike.

---

*Here Drake, p. 218, cites "the *Electra* of *Sophocles*; the *Electra, Orestes,
Hippolytus, Ion,* and *others* of *Euripides,* and the *Thyestes* of *Seneca.*"

†Drake cites, p. 218, "the *Prometheus in Chains* of *AEschylus,* the *Oedipus*
of *Sophocles,* the *Hippolytus* and *Hercules furens* of *Euripides,* the *Oedipus* and *Hercules furens* of *Seneca,* and divers others of Antiquity."

*Drake cites, p. 219, "the *Electra* of *Sophocles;* the *Medea,* the *Orestes,*
the *Electra,* and others of *Euripides;* the *Medea* of *Seneca,* &c."

It is in his critiques of two particular plays, one by Shakespeare and one by Congreve, that Drake may best serve, however, to exemplify the "understood" analogies between "Poetick" and "Providential" Justice. Speaking of *Hamlet,* he states that "Nothing in Antiquity can rival this Plot for the admirable distribution of Poetick Justice," for the "Criminals are not only brought to execution, but they are taken in their own Toyls, their own Stratagems recoyl upon 'em, and they are involv'd themselves in that mischief and ruine, which they had projected for *Hamlet.*"

> The Moral of all this is very obvious, it shews us, *That the Greatness of the offender does not qualifie the Offence, and that no Humane Power, or Policy are a sufficient Guard, against the Impartial Hand, and Eye of Providence, which defeats their wicked purposes, and turns their dangerous Machinations upon their own heads.* This Moral *Hamlet* himself insinuates to us, when he tells *Horatio,* that he ow'd the Discovery of the Design against his Life in *England,* to a rash indiscreet curiosity, and thence makes this Inference.
>
> > *Our Indiscretion sometimes serves as [sic] well,*
> > *When our dear Plots do fail, and that shou'd teach us,*
> > *There's a Divinity, that shapes our ends,*
> > *Rough hew 'em how we will.*[10]

The deeds and their consequences which demonstrate, for Drake, the "Moral" of *Hamlet* are the kinds of deeds and consequences used in countless Restoration sermons, as well as in more vulgar literature, to demonstrate the earthly justice of God: the snares that enmesh the snarers, the machinations that catch the machinator, the rashnesses that "prove *meanes of safety,*" the triumphs that are actually ruin and defeat. When Drake comments, moreover, that in *Hamlet* we have "a Murther privately committed, strangely discover'd, and wonderfully punish'd," he touches upon the brother-murder by Cain which inaugurated that most ancient and popular of providentialist themes—"Mordre wol out." It was a theme endlessly, and gruesomely, served up for some readers in such works as John Reynolds's

The Triumph of God's Revenge Against the Crying and Execrable Sinne of (Wilful and Premeditated) Murther. For others, as Rymer noted, there were "every day cried in the Streets, instances of God's *revenge* against *murder,* more extraordinary, and more poetical" than the designs of some stage plays.[11] For later generations there would be, among other works, Henry Fielding's *Examples of the Interposition of Providence in the Detection and Punishment of Murder.*

In his dedication to *The Double-Dealer,* Congreve stated that he first "design'd the Moral" of his play, and then "to that Moral . . . invented the Fable." In this procedure he was merely following a rule of "invention" prescribed by Le Bossu, practiced by many, and endorsed thus by Dryden: "The first rule which Bossu prescribes to the writer of an heroic poem, and which holds too by the same reason in all dramatic poetry, is to make the moral of the work, that is to lay down to yourself what that precept of morality shall be, which you would insinuate into the people." It is "the moral," Dryden continues, "that directs the whole action of the play to one centre; and that action or fable is the example built upon the moral, which confirms the truth of it to our experience: when the fable is designed, then, and not before, the persons are to be introduced with their manners, characters, and passions."[12]

Elusive as a playwright's precise intentions may always remain, such statements as these by Dryden and Congreve, as well as many others, add considerable force to Drake's observation that if "we are to feel the *Poets* Pulse, and find out his secret affections," we must do so by "the temper and disposition" of the "Fable," and for these reasons: "The Fable of every Play is undoubtedly the Authors own, whencesoever he takes the Story, and he may mold it as he pleases. The *Characters* are not so; the Poet is obliged to take 'em from Nature, and to copy as close after her, as he is able. The same may be said for the *Thoughts* and *Expressions,* they must be suited to the Mouth and *Character* of the Person that speaks 'em, not the *Poet's.*"* Drake's observation is the more happy because it follows

*Pp. 219–20. Cf. the words of Rymer, in *The Critical Works,* p. 131: "The *Fable* is always accounted the *Soul* of Tragedy. And it is the *Fable* which is properly the *Poets* part. Because the other three parts of Tragedy, to wit the

close upon his critique of Congreve's *Mourning Bride,* where he
provides us with a good example of the kind of attention a sophis-
ticated theater-goer would have paid to the "Fable" of a contemporary play—as well as of the reflections to which it led. Published
less than two years after the play was staged, Drake's comments at
the very least affirm once more the way in which stage justice was
commonly assumed to be "an Image," as Dennis said, of divine
justice.

The "Fable of this Play," Drake says, "is one of the most just and
regular that the Stage, either Antient or Modern, can boast of. I
mean, for the distribution of Rewards, and Punishments":

> For no virtuous person misses his Recompence, and no vitious
> one escapes Vengeance. *Manuel* in the prosecution and exercise
> of his Cruelty and Tyranny, is taken in a Trap of his own laying,
> and falls himself a Sacrifice in the room of him, whom he in his
> rage had devoted. *Gonsalez* villanous cunning returns upon his
> own head, and makes him by mistake kill the King his Master,
> and in that cut off, not only all his hopes, but his only Prop and
> Support, and make sure of his own Destruction. *Alonzo,* his
> Creature and Instrument, acts by his instructions, and shares his
> Fate. *Zara*'s furious Temper and impetuous ungovernable Pas-
> sion, urge her to frequent violences, and conclude at last in a
> fatal mistake. Thus every one's own Wickedness or Miscarriage
> determines his Fate, without shedding any Malignity upon the
> Persons and Fortunes of others. *Alphonso* in reward of his
> Virtue receives the Crowns of *Valentia* and *Granada,* and is
> happy in his Love; all which he acknowledges to be the Gift of
> Providence, which protects the Innocent, and rewards the
> Virtuous.

"All this," Drake concludes, "as well as the *Moral* is summ'd up so
fully, and so concisely, in *Alphonso*'s last speech, that 'twere injustice not to give it in the Poets own words":

Characters are taken from the Moral Philosopher; the *thoughts* or sense, from
them that teach *Rhetorick:* And the last part, which is the *expression,* we
learn from the Grammarians."

> (*To* Alm.) *Thy Father fell, where he design'd my Death.*
> Gonsalez *and* Alonzo, *both of Wounds*
> *Expiring, have with their last Breath Confest*
> *The just Decrees of Heaven, in turning on*
> *Themselves their own most bloody Purposes.*
>
> (*To* Garcia) —— —— *O* Garcia
> *Seest thou, how just the hand of Heaven has been?*
> *Let us, that thro our Innocence survive,*
> *Still in the Paths of Honour persevere,*
> *And not for past, or present ills despair:*
> *For Blessings ever wait on virtuous deeds;*
> *And tho a late, a sure Reward succeeds.* [13]

The words of Congreve's principal and most virtuous character, along with the "Fable" of his play (and the way that "Fable" was construed at the time by an educated and, I think, representative layman) make it impossible for me to accept the view of a modern critic who would maintain that Congreve only "paid lip-service to the equation of Providence and poetic justice."[14] The "Fable" of *The Mourning Bride,* and its "Moral" as Congreve has it so fully, so gravely, and so straightforwardly "summ'd up" at the end, rather bespeak an author who had invented for his auditors a theatrical representation of justice that would point unmistakably to that divine justice which, they had been assured since childhood, so often manifested itself "when Craft incurreth disappointment, and Simplicity findeth good successs" and "when bloudy Oppressours have *blood given them to drink.*"

II

As Thomas Stroup and Roy Battenhouse have both observed,[15] one of the notable statements indicative of the way earlier English dramatists shaped their plays with the concept of *theatrum mundi* consciously in mind is that by Thomas Heywood in a poem prefatory to his *An Apologie for Actors* (1612). Heywood's succinct and happy phrasing of the analogy between the divine and human playwrights was carried forward with the reissuance of his work in 1658 (and possibly in 1703),* and his words reveal once more how fully reciprocative the metaphoric language of poets and preachers could be:

> The World's a Theater, the earth a Stage,
> Which God, and nature doth with Actors fill,
> Kings have their entrance in due equipage,
> And some their parts play well and others ill.

After citing various other roles (clowns, citizens, courtesans, soldiers, and so on) played in "this Theater," Heywood concludes with these stately lines:

> If then the world a Theater present,
> As by the roundnesse it appears most fit,
> Built with the starre-galleries of hye assent,
> In which *Jehove* doth as spectator sit.
> And chief determiner to applaud the best,
> And their indevours crowne with more than merit.
> But by their evill actions doomes the rest,
> To end disgrac't while others praise inherit.
>
> *No Theater,*   He that denyes then Theaters should be,
> *no world.*   He may as well deny a world to me.

Inherent in the concept of *theatrum mundi,* as in Heywood's particular phrasing of it, is the traditional Christian view of man's earthly existence as a state of probation, a time of "trial" and "judgment" in the eyes of God (the chief "spectator") as well as in the eyes of men. Stroup has demonstrated the pervasiveness of what he defines as a "testing pattern" in English drama before the Interregnum,[16] but we need to recognize also how frequently a principal character's faith or merit is "tried" in Restoration drama,

---

*The issue of 1703 is suggested by Sister Rose Anthony in *The Jeremy Collier Stage Controversy* (Milwaukee: Marquette University Press, 1937), p. 181, though she had not seen a copy. A long passage from Heywood's book is certainly quoted in *The Stage Acquitted,* an anonymous work of 1699, with the suggestion that it was still well known (see pp. 157–59). The reissue of 1658 was under the supervision of William Cartwright, who altered the title to *The Actor's Vindication* and made minor changes in the text.

in comedy as well as in tragedy. Such "trials," besides being inherently dramatic, have the additional virtue of making an individual's reward or punishment seem more "earned" or "deserved." And for contemporary audiences at least, they would have been a reminder and a reaffirmation of what they had learned with their catechism, that "'tis in the nature of things a *necessary* and *essential* condition of a *Probation-state,* that there should be some *Tryal* of man's nature."[17]

A good illustration of the way the concept of "trial" inhered in the concept of *theatrum mundi* is a passage in Dryden's *Tyrannick Love* (1669), where St. Catharine, just before her martyrdom, speaks to Berenice in terms of unmistakably loaded import to an audience fully conscious of itself as audience, and conscious also of playing not only a "spectatorly" but an "actorly" role as well in God's own great drama:

> Heav'n doth in this my greatest Tryal make,
> When I for it, the care of you forsake.
> But I am plac'd, as on a Theater,
> Where all my Acts to all Mankind appear,
> To imitate my constancy or fear.
>
> [IV, i, 535–39]

Angels were traditionally employed by God as "testing" agents and as the "ministers" of His justice, and so in Dekker and Massinger's *Virgin Martyr,* a "stock play at the King's Theatre" throughout the Restoration period,[18] the character Angelo (played, we may recall, by Nell Gwyn in page-boy attire) finally reveals himself as actually being an angel in disguise, and then, addressing himself to Dorothea, the virgin martyr, utters words designed to carry a solemn admonishment to the playhouse audience:

> I tri'd your charity,
> When in a beggars shape you took me up,
> And cloth'd my naked limbs, and after fed
> (As you believ'd) my famish'd mouth. Learn all
> By your example, to look on the poor
> With gentle eyes; for in such habits often
> Angels derive an alms.

The "ministry" of an Angelo in such a context as *The Virgin Martyr*
no doubt will be readily conceded, but still a modern audience, or
critic, may not be prepared to grasp or credit fully the ultimate
dimensions of a comedy like Congreve's *Love for Love,* the "Fable"
of which presents us with a Valentine who is obliged to undergo an
"utmost Tryal" of his "Virtue" at the hands of a young woman
named Angelica. Scarcely, of course, a figure of merely allegorical
signification. Angelica has also not been altogether separated from
a certain vestigial emblematic bearing and import. But while some
today may be reluctant to grant, in a Restoration comedy, such
theological signification as I find in her name and role, I rather believe that Congreve's contemporary audiences would have instantly
accepted, and much delighted in, the way he had fashioned a comic
heroine who should shadow forth an ancient and serious Christian
belief, still retained by many,[19] in "guardian angels," and who at
the same time should "lively" personate the alluring shape and air of
a "real" young woman.

It really should come as no surprise, of course, that the theme of
"trial," so intrinsic to the English dramatic tradition and to received
religious convictions as well, crops up almost everywhere in Restoration drama, whether in plays of martyrdom, plays of heroic conquest and self-conquest, or plays of sexual pursuit.[20] A decade
before Etherege made his Harriet resolve on seeing if Dorimant
could "keep a Lent for a Mistress," he had made the idea of trial
of central import to *The Comical Revenge* (1664), as should be clear
from Graciana's words to Beaufort, "My Love has but dissembled
been to thee,/To try my gen'rous Lover's constancy" (IV, v, 48–49),
and by Beaufort's own later lament over Graciana's seeming perfidy:

> Was there no way [my] constancy to prove,
> By by your own inconstancy in Love?
> To try another's Virtue cou'd you be,
> *Graciana,* to your own an enemy?
>
>   [V, i, 113–16]

Wycherley not only makes Harcourt pass a test of his faith in Ali-
thea's virtue in *The Country Wife,* but in *Love in a Wood* (1671) one
of the significant utterances of the play occurs when Valentine, in a

moment of intense self-realization, comments thus on himself and his beloved Cristina, "S'death, what have I giddily run my self upon? 'Tis rather a tryal of my self than her; I cannot undergo it" (act 5), and in *The Gentleman Dancing-Master* (1672) much of Hippolita's behavior is given a special cast when she confesses to Gerrard in act 5 that she had "had a mind to try" whether his "interest" in her fortune had not swayed him more than love for her person.

The terminology of "trial" may be traced in the bulk of Dryden's plays, in such diverse works as *An Evening's Love* (1668), where Jacinta on at least four occasions (in acts 3 and 4) speaks of her determination to "trie once more," to "make an absolute trial," and to undertake "one more triall" of Wildblood's love for her; in *The Conquest of Granada* (1670–71), where Almahide says she "will refuse no trial" of her love and where a trial by combat establishes her innocence; and, as one would expect, in *The State of Innocence* (1674), where Eve is made to manifest her folly thus: "I know myself secure,/And long my little trial to endure." The "trials" often take the form of temptations, again as one would expect, whether it be a temptation to brother-murder and usurpation of a crown, to which Abdalla succumbs in *The Conquest of Granada* (part 1, act 2); or that in Otway's *The Atheist* (1683), where Beaugard, after some natural and thoroughly comic vacillation, determines to remain faithful to his "widow," Portia, and declares that if the masked lady who has had him abducted should "attempt" him, he will "put on that monstrous Vertue, called Self-denial, and be damnably constant"—and so he proves.

One of the great plays of the 1690s is Vanbrugh's *The Relapse* (1696), and it is also one of the great examples of a play whose central theme is that of temptation and trial. Any approach to the play should be made, furthermore, in full awareness of Christianity's traditionally dual position or attitude toward temptation, a binary union set forth, for example, by Bishop Nicholson, in his exposition of the catechism of the Church of England, where he says there are two kinds of temptation, those of "*Probationis*. Of Triall, Probation," and those of "*Seductionis*. Of Seduction, ruine." By the first, "God is said to tempt, that is to try and prove his children," and such trials are to be welcomed when they come, as come they will.

But the second sort is "A temptation to seduce, to overcome, to destroy, and undo us; and against this we here pray, *Lead us not;* or, as Cyprian reads it, *Ne patioris induci,* Good Father suffer us not to be lead into that *temptation,* by which we may be overcome."[21]

I choose Bishop Nicholson to cite because Loveless, in the opening scene of *The Relapse,* reveals the folly, a reenactment of Eve's original folly, of gratuitously seeking out temptation, or "occasions of sin," and does so in words that actually repeat a phrase of Nicholson's. I would not claim the bishop to be the source for Loveless's speech (though I think his work may well have been read by Vanbrugh at school or elsewhere), but I do believe that when Loveless says these words to Amanda,

> This winter shall be the *fiery trial* of my virtue,
> Which, when it once has passed,
> You'll be convinced 'twas of no false alloy,
> There all your cares will end,
>
> > [I, i, 140–43; my italics]

a peculiarly rich and appropriate context for them is provided by Nicholson when he says that we may compare God's temptations "to a fire which burns out dross and corruption, and makes the mettle the purer," and that because of "this *fiery trial,* the virtues of his children are made the clearer, their vicious inclinations being separated and removed."[22]

Trusting too much in his own strength of will, Loveless has "resolved," he says, "to launch into temptation," in the "uneasy theater" of London, and so he does in spite of all Amanda's fears and her warning that "still 'tis safer to avoid the storm." Seeking out temptation, Loveless succumbs to carnal lust in the form of Berinthia, and becomes emblematic of that "ruin" which may come, "Seductionis"; while Amanda, trial unsought, withstands the passionate importunities of Worthy, and becomes exemplary of that virtue which may be aroused and proved, "Probationis." The most appropriate gloss on Amanda's temptation and trial, and a gloss that has immense relevance, indeed, to many another Restoration play, is provided, I think, by these words of an anonymous critic of 1698:

Virtue cannot very well be brought up to any *Dramatick* Perfection, nor sparkle with any considerable Brightness and Beauties, unless it stands a temptation, and surmounts it. We have a Proverbial Saying, that will hardly allow that Woman to be truly chaste, that has never been try'd.* This I am sure, the noblest Triumphs of Virtue are made by the Assaults it can resist and conquer. Thus the *Relapser*'s *Amanda* crowns her Character even with a double Laurel; not only by Illustrating and (I may, not improperly, say) Aggrandizing her own Invincible Virtue in the Assault she has repuls'd; but likewise, in the Conversion of her Assailing Libertine. 'Tis not supposed therefore that the *Dramatick* Poet must be oblig'd to borrow his Characters of Virtue from Lazy Cells, and Melancholy Cloysters; a Copy from a *Hermit,* or an *Anchoret.* No, his Characters of Virtue must come forth into the gay World, with Levity, Vanity, nay Temptation it self, all round them. They must go to the Court, the Ball, the Masque, the Musick-Houses, the Dancing-Schools, nay, to the very Prophane Play-Houses themselves, (to speak in Mr. *Collier*'s Dialect;) and yet come off unconquer'd. These are the Virtues that, to be Instructive to an Audience, are what should tread the Stage.

And consequently, if our Poets will set forth such Virtue, they must find her all this Worldly Conversation, and furnish the *Drama* accordingly.[23]

Not quite so eloquent a statement as Milton's on the same theme, the writer's purport is the same, and one with which most Retoration playwrights would have agreed; it is difficult to "praise a fugitive and cloistered virtue unexercised and unbreathed, that never sallies out and sees her adversary." Restoration playwrights, after all, were of the same time and, saving some doctrinal details, of the same faith as Milton, and they would have been taught as well as he, that "that which purifies us is trial, and trial is by what is contrary,"

---

*Ovid had written, "casta est, quam nemo rogarit" (*Amores,* 1.8.43), a saying echoed twice in Congreve's *Love for Love,* when Scandal says to Angelica that "she is chaste, who was never ask'd the Question," and when he introduces, a few minutes later, a song whose burden is that "the Nymph may be Chaste that has never been Try'd" (act 3, scene 1, lines 127–28, 208).

and that therefore "the knowledge and survey of vice is in this world" as "necessary to the constituting of human virtue" as is "the scanning of error to the confirmation of truth."

III

Among other things, the Restoration period is notable, even notorious, for those adaptations of Shakespeare then perpetrated by some so that his plays would conform to contemporary notions of poetical justice. But as Christopher Spenser has observed, the structure of plays "is part of an attitude toward life," and in their restructuring of Shakespearean plays the Restoration adapters were really divulging their sense of the "harmony and pattern and consistency and order that they felt art should offer." And because "poetic justice reveals what is felt to be a natural pattern of things rather than accidental exceptions, guilty charcters are regularly punished; and those who are more sinned against than sinning, including Lear, Cordelia, and Gloucester, are usually permitted to live." The result of the application of such poetic justice no doubt may tend, as Spenser adds, to emphasize seemingly "permanent patterns of human relationships with less attention to the depths of individual experience."

So far so good, but the patterns reflected in such plays should not properly be seen as merely "the great pattern of Nature,"[24] for "Nature" is here a weak and evasive alternative term for "Providence." Most Restoration plays, whether adaptations, revivals, or original compositions, were thought to reveal, or were made to reveal, the great patterns of Providence, and they reflect a specifically religious attitude toward life, not a secular respect for something so vague as "Nature." We have seen the way divines and preachers so commonly compared the actions of God to those of the playwright, as in this additional example from Sherlock, the Dean of St. Paul's:

> We seldom know in any measure, what God is doing in the world; and then it is impossible for us to understand the admirable Wisdom of all those intermediate Events, which tend to unknown ends. In the best contrived Plot there will always

be some Scenes full of nothing but Mystery and Confusion, till the End explains them, and then we admire the Skill and Art of the Poet.

Now the great Obscurities and Difficulties of Providence are in such intermediate Events, before we know what God intends by them.[25]

The accordant strain may be found when Dryden, in 1664, writes of the playwright who undertakes to "conduct his imaginary Persons, through so many various Intrigues and Chances, as the Labouring Audience shall think them lost under every Billow; and then at length to work them so naturally out of their Distresses, that when the whole Plot is laid open, the Spectator may rest satisfied, that every cause was with such due order Linck'd together,* that the first Accident would naturally beget the second, till they all render'd the Conclusion necessary." The reciprocative terminology becomes even stronger a paragraph later, when Dryden compliments Roger Boyle for writing a play in which there

is no chance which you have not foreseen; all your Heroes are more than your Subjects; they are your Creatures. And though they seem to move freely, in all the Sallies of their Passions, yet you make Destinies for them which they cannot shun. They are mov'd (if I may dare to say so) like the Rational Creatures of the Almighty Poet, who walk at Liberty, in their own Opinion, because their Fetters are Invisible; when indeed the Prison of their Will, is the more sure for being large: and instead of an absolute Power over their Actions, they have only a wretched Desire of doing that, which they cannot choose but do.[26]

Isaac Barrow had conceded that "if any thing should hit advantageously to the production of some considerable Event, it may with some plausibility be attributed to Fortune, or common Providence," but he added that if "divers Things, having no dependence, or co-

---

*Dryden's phrasing here seems to have been remembered by Rymer when he speaks of the way causes and effects should be "proportion'd and link'd together" so as to observe the "harmony and beauty of Providence" (see above, p. 39).

herence one with another, through several times, should all joyn
their forces to compass" such an event, it must "be ascribed to
God's special Care wisely directing, to his own Hand powerfully
wielding these concurrent instruments to one good purpose. For
it is beyond the nature, it is beyond the reach of Fortune, to range
various causes in such order."[27] A vision, and a terminology, that is
fully complimentary to that of Barrow may be found in Dennis,
when he says that if the "Calamities" of drama "appear to be the
Work of Chance, they might as well have happened to those who
have not committed . . . Faults, as to those who have":

> And therefore a Train of Incidents, which, contrary to our Ex-
> pectation, surprisingly produce one another, is necessary, be-
> cause the more plainly the Punishment appears the result of the
> Fault, and the more clearly we are convinc'd of this, when we
> least expect it, Providence appears the more in the case, and our
> Security is shaken the more, and the more we are mov'd and
> terrified.[28]

Dennis had his peculiarities, his biases, and no doubt a more than
ordinary Christian fervor pervades his critical writings. But he was
also very much a product of the time with which we are concerned,
born in 1657, thirteen years before Congreve, and dying in 1734,
five years after Congreve. In the following passage, I think his words
are as good as may be found to convey the mutually reciprocative
language, and visions, of contemporary poets and preachers:

> But, as in some of the numberless Parts, which constitute this
> beauteous All, there are some appearing Irregularities, which
> Parts, notwithstanding, contribute with the rest, to compleat
> the Harmony of Universal Nature; and as there are some seeming
> Irregularities, even in the wonderful Dispensations of the Su-
> preme and Sovereign Reason, as the Oppression of the Good,
> and Flourishing of the Bad, which yet at the Bottom are rightly
> adjusted, and wisely compensated, and are purposely appointed
> by Divine Fore-Knowledge, for the Carrying on the profound
> Designs of Providence; so, if we may compare great Things with
> small, in the Creation of the accomplish'd Poem, some things

may at first Sight be seemingly against Reason, which yet, at the Bottom, are perfectly regular, because they are indispensably necessary to the admirable Conduct of a great and a just Design.[29]

The stage of the world as seen in the seventeenth century suggested that the justice of God was in itself "poetic," and so the world of the stage could scarcely, at the time, do less than suggest that its own justice was "providential."

4

Priest versus Playwrights, and "Moral Dialogues" versus "Lively Examples"

Comoediam esse Cicero ait imitationem vitae, speculum con-
suetudinis, imaginem veritatis.

Aelius Donatus, *Commentvm Terenti*

For Moral Truth is the Mistress of the Poet as much as of the
Philosopher: Poesie must resemble Natural Truth, but it must
be Ethical.

John Dryden,
A Defense of An Essay of Dramatic Poesy (1668)

A diatribe of 288 pages, Jeremy Collier's *A Short View of the
Immorality, and Profaneness of the English Stage* is the product
of a fiercely demagogic spirit, a fabrication of sensational charges,
specious claims, wild distortions. Taken seriously though it was
by at least a segment of the public in its own time, the wonder is
that so many ever since have believed, or been led to believe, it a
just representation of contemporary stage viciousness and also
the triumphant document in the controversy it generated. The
prevailing view since the time of Samuel Johnson has been that
Collier, in *A Short View* as well as in later tracts, simply overwhelmed the defenders of the stage by the vigor of his rhetoric as
well as by a swarm of devastatingly corroborative citations. At
the same time, the replies to Collier, including not only those of
Congreve and Vanbrugh but also those of a number of other able
critics, have largely been either left unread or been considered in-
trinsically feeble because they were thought to defend the indefen-
sible—plays as licentious and blasphemous as Collier had charged.

Collier proclaimed that the playwrights had discovered a "new
World of *Vice*" and in it had "run through all the Topicks of Lewdness." And he drew his first attack to a close in these terms: "In

short: Nothing can be more disserviceable to Probity and Religion, than the management of the *Stage*. It cherishes those Passions, and rewards those Vices, which 'tis the business of Reason to discountenance."[1] For their part, the playwrights and their defenders proclaimed again and again that their intentions were good and their plays conducive to both private and public morality. We can understand so contradictory a confrontation only by defining, more exactly than has been done in the past, Collier's philosophical as well as critical premises, and then juxtaposing them with the quite opposite premises argued by the playwrights and critics. The opposing premises may be ordered and brought into sharper focus, perhaps, by way of four emphatic critical *postulata* set forth by Congreve near the start of his own answer to Collier's attacks. In examining the premises, as well as the tactics and animadversions of both sides, we may find reason, moreover, to question one current view that Collier, on his own "moral grounds," is unbeatable,* and, more importantly, we may get a better sense of both the ethical and the aesthetic frameworks within which the playwrights, by their own testimony, considered themselves to be fashioning their fables and characters.

I

As the first of the postulates he will use, Congreve desires that he may "lay down *Aristotle*'s Definition of Comedy":

> *Comedy* (says *Aristotle*) is an Imitation of the *worst sort* of People. Μίμησις φαυλοτέρων, *imitatio pejorum*. He does not mean the worst sort of People in respect to their Quality, but in respect to their Manners. This is plain, from his telling you immediately after, that he does not mean Κατὰ πᾶσαν κακίαν, relating to all kinds of Vice: there are Crimes too daring and too horrid for Comedy. But the Vices most frequent, and which are the common Practice of the looser sort of Livers, are the

---

*See Maximillian E. Novak, "The Artist and the Clergyman: Congreve, Collier, and the World of the Play," *CE* 30 (1969):556. Novak notes that the "victory" in the battle between Collier and Congreve "has invariably been given to Jeremy Collier."

subject matter of Comedy. He tells us further, that they must be exposed after a ridiculous manner: For Men are to be laugh'd out of their Vices in Comedy: the Business of Comedy is to delight as well as to instruct: And as vicious People are made asham'd of their Follies or Faults, by seeing them expos'd in a ridiculous Manner, so are good People at once both warn'd and diverted at their Expence.

That comedy "may answer to its true end and purpose," he adds, the "Comick Poets are oblig'd" to "represent vicious and foolish Characters" on the stage.[2]

No issue, it should be stressed, more clearly separates the opposing sides in the Collier controversy than this of the mimetic representation of vice and folly on the stage. And here it is necessary that we recognize what was regarded by his contemporaries as the essentially "Platonic" bias of Collier's premises. James Drake noted, for example, that Collier was "all along a *Platonist* in his Philosophy," while Settle, if Settle it be, observed sharply that "if our Platonick Author is for banishing of Plays," because places of general resort may lead to assignations and attract pickpockets, "he may as justly vote for the rooting up a Garden, for fear the Spider should suck Poyson from the Flowers."[3] And Collier himself, in his *Short View* as well as in subsequent works, makes his "Platonic" bias abundantly clear.* He simply will not tolerate any "lively" (that is, lifelike or realistic) representations of vice on the stage, and he quotes André Dacier to the effect that "a good Poet, who has a mind to bring a Covetous, or Ambitious Person upon the Stage, will choose to form the Image more upon Idea, than Example; and Paint him rather from general Notion, than particular Life." For this, he adds, "is consulting the Original, and the way," in Dacier's words, to "give Truth, and Strength to the Resemblance. Whereas to draw from Particulars in the World, is, as *Plato* speaks, no more than a Second-Hand Likeness,

*Edwin E. Williams noted, but did not develop, the Platonic implications of Collier's views in his "Dr. James Drake and Restoration Theory of Comedy," *RES* 15 (1939):180–91. Kathleen Ressler observes the Platonic affiliations of Collier's *Essays upon several Moral Subjects* in her monograph, "Jeremy Collier's Essays," in *Seventeenth-Century Studies,* 2d ser., ed. Robert Shafer (Princeton: Princeton University Press, 1937), passim.

and but Copying at the best." The extravagance of his idealistic premises is all too evident when he furthermore declares that for a poet "to descend to Particulars, and fall to *Characterizing,* is no better than Libel, and Personal Abuse." In whatever "character-izing" the playwrights undertake, they "should endeavour," he declares, "to abstract the Fault from the *Subject,* to hover in Generals."[4] Any "pretence of *Nature,* and *Imitation*" in stage practice was in his opinion "a lamentable Plea" on the part of a playwright, and so he admonishes the lot of them that "All Characters of Immodesty (if there must be any such) should only be hinted in remote Language, and thrown off in Generals."[5]

Some fifteen years before Collier's attack, the Reverend Anthony Horneck, in a similar "Platonic" vein, had declared that "though Vice must almost necessarily be named in these *living Landskips*" of the stage, "yet it should be only named, and never named but with horror, and the generosity and grandeur of virtue only acted to the life, for indeed nothing is fit for action, or imitation but virtue." Horneck's "Scheme" for "Reformation" of the stage was resurrected in 1698 by a Collierite who pointed out its salubrious consequences thus: "if it took effect, the Playhouses would be little esteemed by those who now frequent them most, for according to this Proposal, the Plays would be perfect Historical Lectures upon the Virtues and Vices of Mankind, without any thing of those Amorous Representa-tions and Intreagues, which now recommend them so much to our Gallants."[6]

Collier's Platonic leanings inevitably led him toward a rigorous idea of decorum in characterization that recalls Thomas Rymer (whom he invokes on several occasions).[7] He thus complains that playwrights make "single Women, and Women of Quality, talk Smuttily," and that this is "a direct crossing upon Nature, and Cus-tom," for "Courage is not reckon'd a Quality so essential to a Man, as Modesty to a Woman."[8] He similarly objects strenuously to the way the clergy and other persons of quality are represented. As to the clergy, they ought to be represented only in the most favorable light, "treated by their best Distinction"; and as for the treatment of the gentry, he asked what necessity there was "to kick the *Coro-nets* about the *Stage,* and to make a Man a Lord, only in order to make him a Coxcomb."[9]

The playwrights and critics in general would not have been so aroused, they testify, if Collier had been content to prune the excesses of the stage, "to Lop off as many of the *Luxurious Branches* as shall not be found worth saving."[10] But they became convinced that his design was not *"Reformation,* but *Eradication"* of the theater, a conviction expressed thus by Dryden in his verses to Peter Motteux:

> The Muses Foes
> Wou'd sink their Maker's Praises into Prose.
> Were they content to prune the lavish Vine
> Of Straggling Branches, and improve the Wine,
> Who but a mad Man wou'd his Faults defend?

And indeed, as Collier made abundantly clear, he considered it his "business rather to kill the *Root* than *transplant* it,"[11] and the ultimate rationale for his eradicative endeavors seems to lie in his own brand of Platonic reasoning about the necessarily pernicious consequences produced, in actors and spectators alike, by stage plays. It is not surprising, therefore, that he welcomed most heartily, in an advertisement at the start of the volume, an English translation in 1699 of *Maximes et réflexions sur la comédie,* by Jacques Benigne Bossuet, bishop of Meaux, a work which includes an account of Plato's reasoning on "imitation" which seems in close accord with his own:

> The Argument of this Philosopher hath its peculiar force upon that Observation, *that* Imitation by degrees turns into Nature, and by counterfeiting other men's Qualities and Vices, men at last come to make them their own. They degenerate into the Spirit and Temper they put on, become Slaves by affecting to appear such, and Vicious by committing Vice in *Effigie;* but especially, when the Vehemence of any Passion is to be represented, there is a necessity of forming and blowing up those Passions in their own Minds, which must be expressed and conveyed to the Audience by outward Gestures. The Spectator likewise, who is pleased with this, must partake of the same temper; . . . Thus all the pomp and preparation of Plays tends

only to make men Passionate; to strengthen that *brutal and un-reasonable part of our Souls,* which is the Spring of all our Weakness and Folly. And from hence he determined utterly to reject and exclude from his Constitution, *that voluptuous and sensual kind of Poetry; which* (he says) *is so dangerous a Temptation, that this alone is capable of corrupting the most, and the best of men.* [12]

By some such reasoning Collier could only conclude that the "imitations" of life to be found on the contemporary stage constituted an attractive contagion that spread to the audiences and prompted them to behave likewise in their personal lives. Speaking of the amours represented on stage, he thus declares that such scenes are "acted over again in the *Scene* of Fancy, and the first Imitation becomes a Model. *Love* has generally a *Party Within;* And when the Wax is prepared, the Impression is easily made. Thus the Disease of the Stage grows catching: It throws its own Amours among the Company, and forms the Passions when it does not find them."[13] In the light of such suppositions and such reasoning, it is no wonder that the first sentence in the preface to *A Short View* is a curt statement that "nothing has gone farther in Debauching the Age than the Stage Poets, and the Play-House." Nor is it any wonder that one of the last sentences in the same book sums up Collier's conviction that the stage "strikes at the Root of Principle, draws off the Inclinations from Virtue, and spoils good Education."

"Imitations" of life on stage, for Collier, offered modes of behavior that would inevitably be "imitated," that is, "emulated," by the spectators in life off stage, and so for him, if there were to be any stage plays at all, their "principal Characters" had to be, as Drake observed, "in all respects exemplary, and without Blemish,"[14] while any vicious or foolish behavior could only be hinted at in "remote" terms. The critics and playwrights, on the other hand, had quite a different view of their "imitations" and the effects of such "imitations" on their audiences. In the first place, they argued that the poets must "shew the world as it is," for if "it were not drawn as it is, it would be of no use, nor cou'd any true measures of Conduct be taken from it."[15] In the second place, their mimetic representations were usually designed, they maintained, as examples to be shunned and scorned: in the words of Vanbrugh, "the Business of Comedy is to shew People what they shou'd do, by representing them upon the Stage, doing what they shou'd not. Nor is there any necessity a Philosopher shou'd stand by, like an Interpreter at a Poppet-Show, to explain the Moral to the Audience: The Mystery is seldom so deep, but the Pit and Boxes can dive into it."[16]

In justification of their mimetic realism, the playwrights and critics commonly employed the traditional idea of the poet's obligation "to hold, as 'twere, the mirror up to nature; to show virtue her own feature, scorn her own image, and the very age and body of the Time his form and pressure." In "their *Theatrical Representations*" the poets must present the spectators "a glass, a mirror of *Truth,* to see their *Deformities* in, as well as *Beauty*": they must "shew the world as it is, that you may know how to direct your self in all states."[17] In Drake's words, "*Dramatick* Poetry, like a Glass, ought neither to flatter, nor to abuse in the Image which it reflects, but to give them their true colour and proportion, and is only valuable for being exact. If therefore any man dislikes the Figures he sees in it, he finds fault with Nature, not the Poet, if those Pictures be drawn according to life; and he might as justly snarl at the wise Providence which governs the world, because he meets more ugly Faces than handsome ones, more Knaves and Fools than Honest and Wise Men in it, and those too, generally more prosperous and fortunate."[18] Collier was informed by Vanbrugh that the "Stage is a Glass for the World to view it self in; People ought therefore to see themselves as they are; if it makes their Faces too Fair, they won't know they are Dirty, and by consequence will neglect to wash 'em."[19] Comedy, it was argued, must be a "Representation of common Conversation; and its Design is to represent things Natural; to shew the Faults of Particular Men in order to correct the Faults of the Public."[20]

Collier's view that the stage itself was the source and wellspring of corruption in the real world was sharply rebutted on all sides. Drake, for example, noted that "Mr. *Collier* observes abundance of Licentiousness and Impurity in the world, and is resolv'd to lay it all at the doors of the Theatres":

He sees up and down a great number of figures like those that are expos'd upon the Stage, and he wisely concludes, that the Models must be taken from thence, and that these men are but the Players apes, which is directly contrary to the Truth. For these are the Originals, of which those upon the Stage are but the Copies, the Images, which that, like a Glass, reflects back upon 'em.[21]

Dryden, of course, made the same point, more wittily, and in verse: Collier "tells you," he wrote,

> That this very Moral Age
> Receiv'd the first Infection from the Stage.
> But sure, a banisht Court, with Lewdness fraught
> The seeds of open Vice returning brought.
> Thus Lodged, (as Vice by great Example thrives)
> It first debauch'd the Daughters and the Wives.
> *London,* a fruitful Soil, yet never bore
> So plentiful a Crop of Horns before.
>
> * * *
>
> Thus did the thriving Malady prevail,
> The Court, it's Head, the Poets but the Tail.[22]

The traditional nature of the critical response to Collier's attacks can be illustrated, somewhat ironically perhaps, from a defense of the stage published nearly forty years before *A Short View* appeared. In 1662 a somewhat belated response to William Prynne's *Histriomatrix* was made by Sir Richard Baker in his *Theatrum Redivivum, Or the Theatre Vindicated,* and in it Baker employs the same authorities and terms later to be used againt Collier. "Horace tells us," he writes, "that *Comoedia est Imitatio vitae, Speculum consuetudinis, & Imago Veritatis:* (a short, but a full Description of the Nature of Plays:) *a Comedy is the resemblance of Life, the mirrour of Custome, the Image of Truth.*" To "think to mend mens *Vices* by taking away *Plays,* is as *idle,*" he says, "as that one should think to mend *ill Faces,* by taking away *Glasses.*" He cites Cicero to the effect that plays "were devised by *Poets* for this purpose,"

that in them, as in a *Glass,* we might see the maners, and very
Image of our daily life. Plays indeed are *Glasses* of the Passages,
and Actions of the world: and it is unhappy for *Glasses,* when
they fall into the hands of *Ill-favoured* faces; for they may
chance to lay the *Illfavouredness* of their faces upon the *Glasses:*
and just so it is with this man [Prynne] ; for he lays all the
blame of the world's bad actions upon *Plays,* where he ought
rather to lay all the blame of *Plays* bad actions upon the world;
for, if the world were *good, Plays* would be *good;* but, if the
world be bad, *Plays* are but the *Glasses,* they do but their kinde
to represent it as it is; and therefore no fault of theirs, if they be
bad too.

As to the idea that an audience is likely to emulate vices witnessed
on the stage, Baker asks whether "goers to Plays are such simple
Ideots; that when they see a beastly, or prophane part acted before
them, they take it to be done for imitation?" When "vices are
really acted" in the larger world, "they stand as *Copies,* and *Examples,* which men are apt to follow; but when they are only *feigned*
on a *Stage,* they stand as *Rocks,* shewn only to be shunned."[23]
    The responses to Collier provide a profusion of examples of the
way the stage "instructed" by offering behavior "to be shunned,"
and in so doing offer us a wide, and fascinating, sampling of the way
stage characters were "read" or interpreted by contemporary critics
and audiences. One anonymous writer of 1698, speaking of *The
Relapse,* says, for example, that: "After all, my Lord *Foppington*
was never design'd to teach People to speak or act like him; nor was
it intended that the Ladies shou'd be byass'd by the Example of
Berinthia to turn Coquetts. These and the like Characters in other
Plays, are not propos'd as a Direction for the *Gallant Man,* or the
Vertuous Lady; but that seeing how such Persons behave themselves on the *Stage,* that they may not make the like Figure in the
World."[24] Addressing himself to the character of the most captivat-
ing and accomplished seducer to be seen on the contemporary stage,
another writer states that: "The finest Gentleman, one of them in all
our Comedies; a *Dorimant* himself is no very tempting Character for
a young Lady to fall in Love with. The veriest Wanton of that Sex

is as much for *Monopoly* as the other; they care not for half Hearts, a Gallant divided between a *Lovet,* a *Bellinda,* and a *Harriet.*" As for "the vicious Characters of Love" generally to be met with in plays, they are set forth with such "Corruptions" as "Levity, Hypocrisie, Infidelity," and the "base Wanton" so characterized by "false Vows, false Oaths, Love for Money, Treason for Love, or some other accumulated Sin," that they are therefore "so far from ensnaring & seducing the unwary Auditor" that they are "rather the Objects of his Aversion."[25] Congreve himself, in response to Collier's attacks on the "lightness" of such characters as Belinda in *The Old Batchelour* and Miss Prue in *Love for Love,* declared he will leave it "to the Judgment of any unpartial Reader, to determine whether they are represented so as to engage any Spectator to imitate the Impudence of the one, or the Affectation of the other; and whether they are not both ridiculed rather than recommended."[26]

Speaking of the "*sinful* part of Love," that "Disease of the Stage" which Collier had found so "catching" by the audience, another writer seems to echo Baker when he argues that "these sort of Amours are never represented on the *Stage,* but to shew the *inquietudes,* the *disappointments,* the *fatigues* and *unhappy Conclusions* of them by lively Examples, which will influence any one of sense to avoid the Rocks and Quick-sands, on which they see others Shipwrack'd"—a judgment that seems fully confirmed by the disquietudes and disappointments so vividly illustrated in Etherege's Belinda and Loveit, Wycherley's Fidget, Squeamish, and Olivia, Congreve's Lady Touchwood, Mrs. Frail, and Mrs. Marwood, along with a bevy of other Restoration ladies tormented by their own lascivious spirits. The same writer contends, moreover, that "since there are *designing Jilts, cunning wheadling Pimps,* and *Bawds, fluttering Beaux, Sharpers, false Coquets,* &c. that make it their business to ruine young men, and young women, that have not bought Wit yet by their own Experience," it is "absolutely necessary that they shou'd be discover'd, and shewn to *all,* that all may know how to avoid them."[27]

Another writer contended against Collier that any "Disease is rather cured than catch'd from the Stage," for in exposing the way "The Country Squire or the Knight, the Prodigal or the Bubble" may be "Cozen'd by Sharpers, Spungers, Dicers, and Bullies; or Jilted by Jades, or snared into any other Ruinous Folly," the "Stage does the Work of a *Philosophy School,* it carries the whole Force of *Precept* and *Instruction* to warn unwary Youth from the Snares and Quicksands of Debauchery. It points him out the several Harpies that would devour him, and instead of taking Taint from the Stage, the very Sight of the Plague-spots not gives, but expels the Contagion."[28]

Determined as they were to defend a faithful and "lively" representation of life as they saw it, the playwrights and critics rejected Collier's opinion that the pulpit could give better warnings against the wicked practices of the world than could the poets. The pulpit, they retorted, "*tells* you there are such Vices, but gives you no view of the vicious, nor how subtly they disguise themselves in borrow'd shapes of Virtue, to do the more mischief, while the *Stage* draws you the Picture to the life, gives you so many *Characteristic* marks, by shewing their *practice* and their deceits, their Hypocrisies, and gaudy outsides, that one must be very blind indeed, that is not instructed to know 'em where-ever they are seen; the *Stage* exposing their Tricks teaches to avoid their Imposition; for 'tis impossible to escape them without so perfect a *description* of their rogueries."[29] In this view, Shadwell's "*Squire of Alsatia* gives more effectual Instruction to the Country Gentleman, for the evading his Ruin both in Person and Estate by the Town Sharpers, by exposing their Shifts and Cheats, than the best Advice of the ablest Divines."[30]

Collier's notion that vicious behavior should only be "hinted in remote Language," and that a proper "Dramatick Justice" could be accomplished by punishing someone who is merely *said* to be "Profane in General," and "without Instance, and Particularity,"[31] was thus sharply rebuked by Edward Filmer:

> what in Nature can be more ridiculous, than this Piece of Dramatick Justice of his? How is it possible to distinguish the Character of an Atheist, from that of a Man of Piety and Religion, but by something in his Discourse, plainly inconsistent with either? Or shall we fix a Paper on his Forehead, that shall give the Lie to his Tongue, and in spite of all outward Appear-

ance, declare him a very Atheist in his Heart? This indeed is one way of shewing the Monster, but withal a very scurvy one at best; and therefore Mr. *Collier,* as you see, has found out another; he must have an ill Name given him, it must be said by some body that somewhere, or at some time or other, he had been prophane in his Discourse; and then there's no more to be done, but away with him presently to Execution. And that is making an Example, without Instance or Particularity; in plain *English,* judging without Process, and condemning without Proof; which is certainly the greatest Injustice imaginable.[32]

Drake agrees, for he observed that Collier seemed "to think, that there is no other way of encouraging Virtue, and suppressing Vice, open to the Poets, but declaiming for or against 'em, and wou'd therefore have *Plays* to be nothing but meer *Moral Dialogues,* wherein five or six persons shou'd meet, and with abundance of Zeal and Rhetorick preach up Virtue, and decry Vice." Therefore, he continues, Collier "falls upon the Poets with all the Rage and Fury imaginable, for introducing in their Plays vicious Characters, such as in *Tragedy, Tyrants, Treacherous Statesmen, Crafty Priests, Rebellious Subjects, &c.* In *Comedy, Libertines, Whores, Sharpers, Cullies, Fops, Pimps, Parasites,* and the like."[33] In the words of one of the speakers in John Oldmixon's dialogues on the stage, a "man must appear wicked, before he can be punish'd for his wickedness; and how can he appear so but by his words and actions?"[34]

By no means ready to have plays reduced to "meer *Moral Dialogues,*" or converted into "perfect Historical Lectures upon the Virtues and Vices of Mankind," the evidence is everywhere abundant that critics and playwrights alike were determinedly eager to justify the stage in terms of a moral purpose and seriousness that is often denied it in our time. It is not sufficient, moreover, to dismiss their justifications as merely ingenious or expediential responses to Collier, for they rather bespeak the traditional emphasis on the two-fold function of poetry: instruction as well as delight. Thus Drake rebuts Collier's notions of the contagiousness of plays by saying that "by making Folly and Knavery ridiculous to the View, Comedy gains her end, stops the Contagion, and presents the imitation more effectually than even Philosophy herself, who deals only in Precept can do, as *Horace,* and before him *Aristotle* have observ'd."[35] Dennis certainly goes further than most in insisting that every "legitimate Dramatick Poem, either of the Comick or Tragick Kind, is not a meer Diversion," but "a philosophical and moral Lecture, in which the Poet is Teacher, and the Spectators are his Disciples,"[36] but he is supported by a chorus of others who also insist that "'tis the Property both of Tragedy and Comedy to instruct: The Characters in both are to be Natural; and the Persons concern'd in the whole Action, are to be such whose Vertues ought to provoke us to an Emulation, or whose Vices ought to deter us from imitating their Example."[37] The "end of the Drama," says one, is "the *Correction,* punishment of *Vice,* and reward of *Virtue,*"[38] while another argues that it is the "Expectation" of seeing "Virtue made Comely, and Vice made odious" that brings people to plays. And if lewdness is represented on stage, it is not "the Lewdness it self in a Vicious Character, that recommends it to the Audience, but the Witty Turns, Adventures and Surprises in these Characters that give it Reception":

> The Jilt for Instance, with her Windings and Turnings, her Wheadles to draw in her *Cully,* and her Artifices to secure and Manage him; The False Wife with her Fawnings and Flattery, to lull her Husbands Jealousie. Her Starts and her Fears at every Danger and Alarme, her whole Arts to cover the Hypocrite; and her Surprize and Confusion at her Detection and Discovery (for Comedy itself does that Dramatick Justice to bring her to Shame, if no other punishment) as they afford plot, design, and contrivance, *&c.* are the highest Jest of Comedy. And 'tis for that, and that only Charme that these Characters find so general a Reception on the Stage.

As an example of "Matter of very good Instruction" to be found "in the Cuckolding of Aldermen and Quality in our Comedies," the same writer cites Congreve's *The Old Batchelour,* where the character of Isaac Fondlewife may be considered "a very seasonable Monster to Reverend City Sixty, to warn against the Marrying to Sixteen":

> Nor can I think it such a scandalous part of the Dramatick Poet;
> but rather a true Poetick Justice, to expose the unreasonableness
> of such Superannuated Dotage, that can blindly think or hope,
> that a bare Chain of Gold has Magick enough in the Circle to
> bind the Fidelity of so unequal a Match, a Match so contrary to
> the Holy Ordinance of Matrimony; and an Itch at those Years
> that deserves the severest Lash of the Stage.[39]

In some instances writers justified the realistic portrayal of vice as
a foil, by means of which the brightness of virtue could be enhanced.
One author, for example, quotes Sir Philip Sidney on comedy as
"an Imitation of the common Errors of our Life, which the Poet
represents in the most ridiculous and scornful sort that may be,"
and that furthermore, "as in Geometry the Oblique must be known
as well as the Right, and in Arithmetick the Odd as well as the
Even; so in the Actions of our Life, who seeth not the Filthiness of
Evil, wanteth a good Foil to perceive the Beauty of Virtue."[40] A
composition in which all the characters are virtuous, says another,
could not "truly reach the whole Instructive Ends of the *Drama,*"
for "*Contraria juxta se posita magis elucescunt,* is a very great
Maxim, *The Foyl sets off the Diamond.* And that Foyl . . . is wanted
in the Comedy, to make the Virtue shine the brighter."[41]
Against the Platonic premises invoked by Collier to deplore the
contagious effects of plays, the defenders of the stage also appealed
to Aristotle. Noting that Collier had quoted Plato to the effect
that "*Plays* raise the Passions, and pervert the use of them, and by
consequence are dangerous to Morality,"[42] Dennis exclaimed: "But
what can be concluded from thence? That they ought to be ex-
pell'd from the *English* Government? When every body knows that
the Commonwealth of *Plato* is a meer Romantick Notion, with
which human nature, and human life, and by consequence Dramatick Poetry, cannot possibly agree." Acceding that the raising
of the passions was that which had "exasperated *Plato* against the
Drama," Dennis then counters by calling upon Aristotle, who had
seen "as far into human nature as any man" and who had believed
"that Tragedy, by exciting the passions purges them, and reduces
them to a just mediocrity, and is by consequence a promoter of
virtue."[43]

Other writers also maintained that while passions were indeed aroused, they conduced to virtuous effects and purposes. The "Disposition" of plays "is to be such that all the Characters have a proper Effect with us," so that we "are there instructed to Love, Hate, and Fear within measure, how we may be Men without debasing our Souls; and all this by moving Examples, which in spite of Stubborness, will force its [*sic*] Impression; and 'tis our own Fault if they are not lasting."[44] It was Settle's view that "*Tragedy* indeed does raise the Passions," but that "its chief work is to raise *Compassion*."[45] A similar opinion is expressed by another vindicator of the stage: in viewing tragedy, he asked, who "can express the Charms of a Well-wrought Scene lively Represented?" For what "Heart can forbear relenting to see an unfortunate Person, for some unhappy mistakes in his Conduct, fall into irreparable Misfortunes? This strikes deep into our Breasts, by a tender insinuation steals into our Souls, and draws a Pity from us; . . . And who that sees a Vitious Person severely Punish'd, will not tremble at Vice?" If "Tragedy scares us out of our Vices," moreover, "Comedy will no less shame us out of our Follies," for who "can forbear blushing, that sees some Darling Folly expos'd?" Though "its ridiculousness tickles him into a laughter, yet at the same time he feels a secret shame for the Guilt."[46]

Collier's ideas on strict decorum in characterization met, for the most part, a most scornful response. Dennis asked him "what Fools a Comick Poet may lawfully allow" on the stage, and whether a playwright could go "no further than Squire," and thus make "Fool and Squire continue to be terms synonimous." He then added that "since Follies ought to be expos'd, the follies of the great are the fittest, as being most conspicuous and most contagious."[47] Settle agreed, saying that "as the greatest and best part of our Audience are Quality, if we would make our Comedies Instructive in the exposing of Vice, we must not lash the Vices at *Wapping* to mend the Faults at *Westminster*."[48] Collier's notion that "Modesty is the distinguishing Virtue" of women, "wrought into the Mechanism" of their bodies, and "design'd by Providence as a Guard to Virtue,"[49] was thus exploded by Filmer:

Very likely indeed! and that no doubt of it is the Reason, that there are so very few impudent Women in the World; and that they are as rarely to be met with in this our Island, as Wolves, Bears, or Tygers. But to be serious; I must confess, I ever looked upon the great Modesty of the generality of our Women, to have been the happy Effect rather of a pious, careful, and wary Education, than of any thing extraordinary in the Contexture of their Bodies.[50]

Drake refined the question thus:

If Dignities conferr'd true Merit, and Titles took away all Blemishes, the *Poets* were certainly very much in the wrong to represent any Person of Quality with failings about her. But if Birth or Preferment be no sufficient Guard to a weakly Virtue or Understanding. If Titles be no security against the usual Humane Infirmities; I see no reason, why they mayn't as well appear together upon the lesser Stage of the Theater, as upon the grand one of the World.[51]

Congreve, who took most seriously and answered at unusual length Collier's charge that he had abused the clergy in his plays, responded at one point to the idea that divines "should be exempted from the Correction of the Drama" by asking the simple question as to "whether a Man, after he has receiv'd holy Orders, is become incapable of either playing the Knave, or the Fool?"[52]

In his exaggerations of the power of the stage to corrupt, Collier appeared as merely ridiculous to many of his opponents. Drake found him so "implacably enrag'd at the *Poets*" for reflecting blemishes as well as beauties in their stage "glasses" that he fell "into a Pannick Fear, lest the Beauty of the whole shou'd tempt Folk to Ape the Deformities of it." But whatever Collier's fears, Drake considered "the Understanding of our Youth" not to be "so depress'd and low, but they can very readily distinguish between the obvious Beauties, and Defects of a Character, and are not to be fool'd like *Dottrels* into a vicious Imitation."[53] It was Filmer's view that, "let the Poet represent Virtue never so charming, let him render Vice never so deform'd," Collier would nevertheless insist that we are all so "strangely prone" to infectious wickedness that, "in spight of Education, Sense, Reason, or Religion, our Youth

must needs reject Virtue, and run after Vice, slight Heaven, and
fall in Love with Hell and Damnation; and all this, as the *French*
express themselves, *de gaité de Coeur,* without any manner of
Temptation, Hope, or Prospect, either of Pleasure, Praise, or Profit:
Nay, at that very Nick of time too, when the Poet is actually em-
ploying all his Skill, all his Art, to divert and dissuade them from
it."[54]

A recent study of Restoration comedy has it that "it cannot be
anything but misleading to suggest" that "the plays of Etherege,
Wycherley, and Congreve" are "essentially corrective comedies—
that their heroes, like many of those in earlier and later romantic
comedy, are in the course of the action in some way educated or
'tamed.'"[55] Such a judgment flies straight in the face of not only
what happens in the plays of the authors named, as well as in those
of a host of others, but also runs head on into what contemporary
playwrights and critics were actually saying about the ordinary
course of the comic "hero." In the preface to *An Evening's Love*
(1671), for example, Dryden states that "the first end of Comedy
is delight, and instruction only the second," a priority established
by the need of first moving laughter "by the representation of
deformity" so that "the shame of that laughter" then secondly
"teaches us to amend what is ridiculous in our manners." Because
of the nature of the "heroes" proper to comedy, he goes on, their
"faults and vices are but the sallies of youth, and the frailties of
humane nature," such "to which all men are obnoxious" [i.e. sus-
ceptible], and thereby "such, in short, as may be forgiven, not such
as must of necessity be punish'd." Then, "lest any man should
think" he writes "to make libertinism amiable," Dryden says he
"must farther declare," both for himself and "better Poets," that
"we make not vicious persons happy, but only as heaven makes
sinners so: that is, by reclaiming them first from vice. For so 'tis
to be suppos'd they are, when they resolve to marry; for then
enjoying what they desire in one, they cease to pursue the love
of many."

Dryden's account of the "reclamatory" course of the comic
protagonist is reasserted years later by Drake and others in their

responses to Collier: both the fallible nature of comic characters as well as the corrective nature of their experiences is affirmed once more. To put "a Gentleman of sound Sense and perfect Morals into a Comedy," says Drake, "wou'd be as unnatural, as to draw *Cato* dancing among the Boors of a Dutch Wedding." And while a "Gentleman of Wit and Honour may be judiciously introduced into it," he "must be a man of wild unreclaim'd honour, whose Appetites are strong and irregular enough, to hurry him beyond his discretion, and make him act against the Conviction of his Judgment, on the return of his Reason. Such a Character as this no more is unnatural, than to see a drunken Gentleman frolicking with the Mob, or kissing a Link-Boy."

Nothing is more frequent, Drake continues, "than to meet in our common Conversation, and affairs of Life, with Gentlemen of this Sort, who, tho they may be Men of excellent Parts, Temper and Principles, yet in the heat of their Blood, and Pride of their Fortunes, are apt to be byassed a little towards Extravagance, and not to consult the severity of Reason, or the exactness of Justice, on many occasions, especially in matters relating to their Pleasures." What "therefore is so common and obvious in the World, can't be unnatural upon the Stage," and so if "the Poet employs any of this Character, he is obliged to give him Success, notwithstanding the Blemishes of his Character":

> For, with all his Faults, he is the best, as well as the most considerable Person, that 'tis lawful for him to make bold with. And if he is at last brought to a Sense of his Extravagance and Errours, and a resolution of amendment, the Poet has exerted his Authority to the utmost extent of his Commission; and the Laws of Comedy exact no more.[56]

Such views about the characters proper to comedy, along with the "success" awarded such characters, were of course repugnant indeed to Collier, for to him they represented a blotting of the "Distinctions" between virtue and vice and an effort by "the Stage" to make pleasure "grow absolute" and "Madness carry all before it." If this is not its aim, he asks, "why is *Lewdness* so much consider'd in Character and Success," why "are their Favourites Atheistical, and their fine Gentleman debauched," and "to what purpose is *Vice* thus prefer'd, thus ornamented, and carress'd, unless for Imitation?" To "sum up the Evidence," he says, a "fine Gentleman" of the stage "is a fine Whoring, Swearing, Smutty, Atheistical Man."[57]

Collier's opinions are not much different from those of the critic who recently has argued not only that "From Dorimant in *The Man of Mode* to Mirabell in *The Way of the World* the man on whom fortune smiles lacks the marks of Christian goodness" but also has maintained that "It is surely because the evil of characters like Marwood [in *The Way of the World*] is matched by no saintly goodness on the other side" that Congreve's plays "cannot embody any transcendental moral doctrine."[58]

Leaving aside the issues raised by a "transcendental" moral doctrine, the idea that evil can only be matched by characters of a "saintly goodness" is as much at odds with traditional Christian views of man's fallen nature and besieged existence on earth as it is with the contemporary theories of comedy which argued for both a "lively" and "instructive" representation of so fallible a creature in so precarious a state. Dryden, we should recall, believed that the "perfection" of "stage-characters consists chiefly in their likeness to the deficient faulty nature, which is their original," a view with which Drake and others are in agreement. Because comedy deals "altogether in Stratagem and Intrigue," it "requires Persons of Trick and Cunning on one hand, and easie credulous Folks on the other, otherwise the Plot will but go heavily forward."

In consequence, "all Characters absolutely perfect are excluded the *Comick* Stage. For what has a Man of pure Integrity to do with Intrigues of any kind?" And while it is not proper that "all the Characters in *Comedy* shou'd be vicious," Drake adds, "they ought all to have some failing or Infirmity, to qualifie 'em for the business of the Place":

> Men of Honour may be made use of to punish Knaves, as Knaves to cure Fools, but their honour ought not to be too strait-laced, too squeamish and scrupulous. They must be Persons of some Liberty, that out of an over-niceness will not balk a well laid design, and spoil a Project with too much honesty. Men of

Honour may be men of Pleasure; nay, and must be so too, or we do 'em wrong to make 'em appear in such Company, as *Comedy* must bring 'em into.[59]

Settle agrees, arguing that because "no over-reach or defeat in Comedy can well be performed, but by some Fraud or Cheat or other," therefore he "that carries on the Cheat, cannot reach to the full heights of a perfect Character, *viz.* wholly unblemish'd." At the same time, "'tis the work of the Poet" always "to raise those just Provocations for every Cheat, especially in the prosperous Characters of the Comedy; that their Successes, in the Catastrophe of the Play, may seem the Reward of some *Virtue* and *Justice* even in the Cheat himself, comparable to the *Vice* and *Injustice* they punish."[60]

But Collier could only regard the playwrights, in their imitations of the actual imperfections of human nature, as bent on debauching the youth of an entire age and nation, as offering examples of "Worshipful Things" which were enough "to give Credit and Countenance to Vice, and to shame young People out of all Pretences to Conscience, and Regularity." The extremity of his outrage, and a concrete sample of his interpretations of stage character, may be provided by his glossing of Valentine in Congreve's *Love for Love.* This "Spark," he says, "the *Poet* would pass for a Person of Virtue," although he "is altogether compounded of Vice":

He is a prodigal Debauchee, Unnatural and Profane, Obscene, Sawcy, and Undutiful; And yet this Libertine is crown'd for the Man of Merit, has his wishes thrown into his Lap, and makes the Happy *Exit.* I perceive we should have a rare Set of *Virtues* if these *Poets* had the making of them![61]

Congreve's retort discovers an instructive purpose, and intimates a mode of artifice, that Collier could not, or would not, admit. Conceding that Valentine was a prodigal, and shown as suffering "under hard Circumstances" because of his prodigality, Congreve nonetheless stated flatly that to say Valentine "is *profane* and *obscene,* is a false Accusation, and without any Evidence." Valentine's, he then adds, "is a mix'd Character; his Faults are fewer than his good Qualities; and as the World goes, he may pass well enough for the best Character in a Comedy; where even the best must be shewn to have Faults, that the best Spectators may be warn'd not to think too well of themselves."[62] In spite of such words, however, there have been many besides Collier who have been unable to see how Restoration comedy may, in Dryden's words, "resemble Natural Truth" and "*be* Ethical" at the same time.

II

Having insisted that the ends of comedy can only be achieved by the representation of "vicious and foolish Characters" on stage, Congreve advanced as his second postulate the thesis that nothing should be "imputed to the Persuasions or private Sentiments of the Author, if at any time one of these vicious Characters in any of his Plays shall behave himself foolishly, or immorally in Word or Deed," for "it were very hard that a Painter should be believ'd to resemble all the ugly Faces that he draws."[63] A reasonable enough repudiation of the intentional fallacy, one would think, but made the more necessary by Collier's stubborn insistence that "'tis the Poet that speaks in the *Persons* of the Stage," and that when a playwright ventures any representation of "Smut and Profaneness" his own "*private Sentiments* fall under Censure."[64] And when Drake protested that Collier should not confuse the poets' "private or real sense" with the "Sentiments, which they are obliged sometimes to furnish Villains and Extravagants with in conformity to their Characters," because in such characters the poet is "frequently necessitated to make use of Thoughts and Expressions very contrary to his own proper person,"[65] Collier countered by invoking Quintilian, "who lets us know, that *Afranius,* a Vitious Comick Poet, discover'd his Practice in his Plays." Apparently convinced such testimony was overwhelming in itself, Collier then declared that "Indeed nothing is more natural than for a Man's Fancy to flow into his Ink."[66]

In *A Short View,* Collier had declared that the "Poets are of all People most to blame" for their use of profanity onstage. They lacked, he said, "even the Plea of *Bullies* and *Sharpers.* There's no Rencounters, no starts of Passion, no sudden Accidents to discompose them. They swear in Solitude and cold Blood, under Thought and Deliberation, for Business and for Exercise: This is a terrible Circumstance; It makes all *Malice Prepense,* and enflames the Guilt, and the Reckoning" (p. 58). Such upbraiding drew from Filmer the response that the poets neither "speak their own Sense, or mean any Ill," and he then asked: what "shall we say of Sir *John Denham,* Sir *William D'Avenant,* and My Lord *Orrery,* who when they laid their scenes among the *Turks,* or *Persians,* were oblig'd to make their Persons speak many things unfit for a Christian to utter as directly contrary to his Faith?"[67] Oldmixon put the issue thus: "Has not *Milton* in the best and most Religious Poem that has been writ since our Saviours days, made the Devil say of God Almighty?

> *Sole reigning holds the Tyranny of Heaven.*

And who, that should light on this Verse, would not think the Author guilty of horrid Blasphemy, unless he read what went before, and consider'd who spoke it?"[68]

As noted in the previous chapter, Drake had contended that the characters in a play do not so much reflect the private sentiments of a playwright as does his "Fable," the "Temper and Disposition" of which enable us, he said, "to feel the Poets Pulse, and find out his secret affections." If the poets had "any such lewd Design" as Collier attributed to them, he went on, it would appear in the fable and in the success, or rewards and punishments, handed out to the principal characters. It is the "Fable" that

> discovers most of the Poets proper Opinion, and gives him the fairest Opportunity of stealing it artificially in, and poys'ning the Audience most effectually with least Suspicion. For tho' the Fable, if skilfully contriv'd, be the Part which operates most powerfully, yet it works after a manner least sensible. We feel the effects without suspecting the cause, and are prejudiced without looking after a reason. If the *Poets* had any such villanous Plot against Virtue and Religion, they are certainly the most negligent Fellows, or the most unexperienc'd in the world to overlook the only place of advantage upon the whole Stage for their mischievous purpose, where they might work their Mines unmolested, and spring 'em undiscover'd to most. But they make War like *Dutchmen,* and sell their Enemies Ammu-

nition to spend upon themselves. For all their Fables are contriv'd and modell'd for the service of Virtue and Religion.[69]

Oldmixon, among others, would have concurred, stating that the
"Fable" and the "Moral" of a play differ, "in a Poetick sense,"
from the "Manners," and that the "Moral of a Play may be good,
when the Manners of part of the Characters are naught."[70]

In defense of the moral "Intention" of his own plays, Congreve
reminded Collier of the "common Expedient, which is made use of
to recommend the Instruction of our Plays; which is this":

> After the Action of the Play is over, and the Delight of the
> Representation at an end; there is generally Care taken, that
> the Moral of the whole shall be summ'd up, and deliver'd to
> the Audience, in the very last and concluding Lines of the Poem.
> The Intention of this is, that the Delight of the Representation
> may not so strongly possess the Minds of the Audience, as to
> make them Forget or oversee the Instruction. . . .

And in his more specific defense of *The Mourning Bride,* he said
that "if a fair-dealing man, or a candid Critick had examin'd that
Tragedy, I fancy that neither the general Moral contain'd in the two
last Lines; nor the several particular Morals interwoven with the
success of every principal Character, would have been overseen
by him."[71] Congreve's position is the same as Drake's, and Drake's
recalls Dryden's view that the "action or fable" of a play is "built
upon" that "precept of morality" which "you would insinuate into
the people." (See Chap. 3, p. 45.)

But Collier would have none of such reasoning, nor would he take
seriously Congreve's statement that the "Moral of the whole" play
is usually made evident in its concluding lines. "When a Poet has
flourished on an ill Subject for some Hours," he fumes, and "has
Larded his *Scenes* with Smut, and play'd his Jests on Religion; and
exhausted himself upon Vice; what can a dry Line or two of good
Counsel signify?" And he concludes: "A Moral Sentence at the Close
of a Lewd Play, is much like a pious Expression in the Mouth of a
dying Man, who has been wicked all his Life time."[72]

The extremes of the conflict between Collier and the poets may be summed up on the one hand by Drake's contention that "the *Poet's Morals* may be very good, yet the Man's stark naught, that is, that a man may be a good *Moral Poet,* yet a bad Man."[73] Collier, on the other, would have maintained a Quintilian-like view that only a good man can be a good orator—or a good poet. Drake, to say the least, has the example of *The Pardoner's Tale* on his side.

III

In setting down his third postulate, Congreve desired "the impartial Reader, not to consider any Expression or Passage cited from any Play, as it appears in Mr. *Collier's* Book; nor to pass any Sentence or Censure upon it, out of its proper Scene, or alienated from the Character by which it is spoken; for in that place alone, and in his Mouth alone, can it have its proper and true Signification."[74] But Collier utterly dismissed the idea that dramatic utterance be judged in dramatic context, and demanded to know, "if the Passage be truly cited; if the Sentence be full and determin'd, why mayn't we understand it where 'ere 'tis met with? Why must we read a Page for a Period? Can't a Plant be known without the History of the Garden?" He then told the world he had already informed Congreve that "no pretence of Character, or Punishment, could justify Profaneness on the Stage," and he also declared roundly that "provided Mr. *Congreve* is fairly cited for Smut, or Profaneness, *Sentence may be passed* without having recourse to *Scene* or *Character.*"[75] Congreve nevertheless felt it necessary to restore "to their primitive Station" those passages in his plays Collier had attacked and "transplanted." "I will remove 'em," he said, "from his Dunghil, and replant 'em in the Field of Nature; and when I have wash'd 'em of that Filth which they have contracted in passing thro' his very dirty hands, let their own Innocence protect them." It was his further opinion that Collier, "in the high Vigour of his Obscenity," had first committed a "Rape" upon his words, and then denounced them for immodesty: "he has Barbarity enough to accuse the very Virgins he has deflowr'd, and to make sure of their Condemnation, he has himself made 'em guilty." Collier's strained "Artifice to make Words guilty of Profaneness," he added, "is of the same nature; for where the Expression is unblamable in its own clear and genuine Signification, he enters into it himself like the evil Spirit; he possesses the innocent Phrase, and makes it bellow forth his own Blasphemies."*

Other critics agreed that Collier had mangled or sullied the passages he handled. And while Dryden conceded that he had been taxed justly in certain instances, and gave handsome confession of his regret for whatever passages in his plays could be truly convicted of "obscenity, profaneness, or immorality," he also declared that it would not be "difficult to prove that in many places" Collier "has perverted my meaning by his glosses, and interpreted my words into blasphemy and bawdry of which they are not guilty." Collier, he said, mixes his "truth with falsehood, and has not forgotten the old rule of calumniating strongly, that something may remain." And, he continued, "I will not say, *The Zeal of God's House has eaten him up;* but I am sure it has devoured some part of his good manners and civility."[76] The author of *The Stage Acquitted* complained, along with others, that although Collier "charges the *Stage* with obscenity," the "instances he gives when fairly represented are pure and innocent." In his course of searching out immorality, Collier "wrests, screws, and tortures words so manifestly from the Poet's Sense, that nothing can be plainer."[77]

But the best way to savor, and to judge, of Collier's fairness and acumen as literary censor is by concrete examples, here drawn from some of his aspersions on Congreve's plays. In *A Short View* (p. 27), for instance, he alleges that Congreve "runs Riot" in the betrothal scene which concludes *The Double-Dealer* and declares that Lord Touchwood's blessing of the young couple ended the play with "a mixture of Smut and Pedantry." For his "Proof of this," as Congreve himself noted, Collier did no more than direct "the Reader in his Margin to the 79th Page, which is the last of the Play." And Congreve went on:

Amendments, pp. 3–5. The author of *A Farther Defence of Dramatick Poetry,* p. 42, judged that Collier's "Work is not so much to *find* the Devils upon the Stage, as to *raise* 'em there," and Gildon (preface to *Phæton*) considered Collier to have conjured up "Ten Thousand Devils" of his own and then laid them "at the Expence of the Theatre."

He has made no Quotation, therefore I will do it for him, and transcribe what Lord *Touchwood* says in that place, being the concluding Lines and Moral of the whole Comedy. *Mellefont* and *Cynthia* are to be married, the Villainies of *Maskwell* having been detected; Lord *Touchwood* gives 'em Joy, and then concludes the Play as follows.

Lord *Touch.* — *be each others Comfort:* — *let me join your hands.* — *unwearied nights, and wishing Days attend you both; mutual Love, lasting Health, and circling Joys tread round each happy Year of your long lives.*

> *Let secret Villany from hence be warn'd;*
> *Howe'er in private, mischiefs are conceiv'd*
> *Torture and Shame attend their open Birth;*
> *Like Vipers in the Womb base treachery lies,*
> *Still gnawing that whence first it did arise;*
> *No sooner born but the vile parent dies.*

This, in Mr. Collier's polite Phrase, *is running Riot upon Smut and Pedantry.*[78]

Undaunted, Collier returned to the attack by saying it was the "*Prose* part" of Lord Touchwood's speech to which he objected, and that he still found that prose to be "foul in the Image, Embarrass'd with trifling Epithites, and ill suited to the Character."[79]

Collier's discovery of smut in Lord Touchwood's blessing is a typical example of the way his mind converts the tenderest language of love into terms of raw concupiscence. His reasoning may be better understood, perhaps, in the light of a passage by Bossuet, where the bishop quotes "a Modern Author" in a "Treatise upon Plays" as having "ingeniously observed" that "all Marriage presupposes Concupiscence." Therefore, says Bossuet, anyone who "publicly exposes and recommends that sensible Impression of Beauty which compells and provokes men to Love, though this be done in order to Marriage, yet, at the same time that he labours to render such Impression agreeable, he does also render Concupiscence agreeable, and supports Sense in its Rebellion against

Reason and Religion."* Collier's strong endorsement of Bossuet's book (he may have written the preface, as well as the "Advertisement" to the English translation of it),[80] along with his judgment that Lord Touchwood's blessing is "foul in the Image," may indicate that for him, too, "all Marriage" not only "presupposes Concupiscence," but that there is little distinction between conjugal love and mere lust. And if this is true, there simply was no way an English playwright, however moral his design and however virtuous his intentions, could escape his castigation for dramatizing those "sensible Impressions of Beauty" which must necessarily accompany any "lively" or realistic representation of even the most honorable sexual relationship.

One more instance of Collier's critical bent may be taken from his chapter on "The Immodesty of the Stage," where he reproves Congreve's *Mourning Bride* for "Smut and Profaneness." Even today, nearly three hundred years later, some of Congreve's astonishment at the charge breaks through when he states that, if it could be proven, "I must of necessity give up the Cause. If there be Immodesty in that Tragedy, I must confess my self incapable of ever writing any thing with Modesty or Decency."[81] The passage which most excited Collier's indignation occurs in act 3, where Almeria, the mourning bride, visits her husband Osmyn in prison. Her marriage to Osmyn as yet unconsummated, she is doomed the next day to a forced wedding with the son of the tyrant Manuel, and as the moment arrives when they must part, Osmyn rages thus at the coming event:

> Then *Garcia* shall lie panting on thy Bosom,
> Luxurious, revelling amidst thy Charms;
> And thou perforce must yield, and aid his Transport,
> Hell, Hell! have I not Cause to rage and rave?

Maxims and Reflections Upon Plays, p. 24. The "Modern Author" cited by Bossuet is apparently Pierre Nicole, whose thought (in the third volume of his *Moral Essays,* London, 1680) is translated thus: "'Tis needless to say in justification of Plays and Romances, that therein is only represented lawfull Passions, and which have Marriage as the end they aim at. For tho Marriage may make good use of Concupiscence, 'tis nevertheless in it self always ill, and it is not lawful to excite it, neither in our selves nor in others" (p. 222).

> What are all Racks, and Wheels, and Whips to this?
> Are they not soothing Softness, sinking Ease,
> And wafting Air to this? O my *Almeria*,
> What do the Damn'd endure, but to despair,
> But knowing Heav'n, to know it lost for ever?

Declaring that Osmyn's "Rant of Smut and Profaneness" might "have been spared," Collier quoted only the last portion of his speech, a procedure he later defended by saying that he had been unwilling "to furnish the Reader with a Collection of Indecencies."[82] But his tactics, and the construction he put upon Congreve's passage, prompted one defender of the stage to state that "Mr. *Collier*'s Reproofs"

> seem inveterate; he writes with Animosity, as if he had an Aversion to the Man as well as his Faults, and appears only pleas'd when he has found a Miscarriage. Who, but Mr. *Collier* wou'd have ransack'd the *Mourning Bride,* to charge it with Smut and Prophaneness, when he might have sate down with so many Scenes where in even his malicious Chymistry cou'd have extracted neither? But against this Play, as if the Spirit of Contradiction were his delight, he musters all his Forces; and having passed Sentence as the Divine, commences Critick, and brings the Poetry to his severe Scrutiny, transcribes half Speeches, puts the beginning and end together.[83]

As Ben Jonson once remarked, and as Congreve recalled, "There be some Men are born only to suck the Poison of Books."

IV

Because Collier in his chapter on "The Profaneness of the Stage" had "founded great part of his Accusation upon the Liberty which Poets take of using some Words in their Plays, which have been sometimes employed by the Translators of the Holy Scriptures," Congreve desired as his fourth postulate that "the following Distinction may be admitted, *viz.* that when Words are apply'd to sacred things, they ought to be understood accordingly: But when they are otherwise apply'd, the Diversity of the Subject gives a

Diversity of Signification."[84] Such a distinction was again one that Collier was unwilling to grant; for what, he demanded, "can be more outrageously Wicked, than to expose Religion to the Scorn of Atheism, to give up the Bible to *Rakes* and *Strumpets,* and to make Impudence and Inspiration to speak the same Language?" Ignoring the possibility that religion and the Bible may be found applicable, and even perhaps beneficial, to "Rakes and Strumpets," as to publicans and other sinners, he then declares that when religious language is employed on stage "the Wisdom of God is burlesqu'd, his Omnipotence play'd with, and Heaven's the Diversion of Hell."[85]

As an example of such wickedness of stage language, Collier cited Congreve's *The Old Batchelour,* where Vainlove asks Bellmour, "Could you be content to go to Heaven?" and the latter replies: "Hum, not immediately, in my conscience not heartily." On this exchange, Collier comments: "This is playing I take it with Edge-Tools. To go to Heaven in jest, is the way to go to Hell in earnest."[86] But as Congreve pointed out, "Mr. *Collier* concludes this Quotation with a dash, as if both the Sense and the Words of the whole Sentence, were at an end. But the remainder of it in the Play" is "in these words—*I would do a little more good in my generation first, in order to deserve it.*" And then he went on, "I think the meaning of the whole is very different from the meaning of the first half of this Expression. 'Tis one thing for a Man to say positively, he will not go to Heaven; and another to say, that he does not think himself worthy, till he is better prepared. But Mr. *Collier* undoubtedly was in the right, to take just as much as would serve his own turn."

Congreve then stresses the generally accepted view of the kind of characters suitable for comedy, and stresses also the way ethical instruction may be imparted by such dramatic imitations: "The Stile" of Bellmour's "Expression is Light, and suitable to Comedy, and the Character of a wild Debauchee of the Town; but there is a Moral meaning contain'd in it, when it is not represented by halves."[87] To Congreve's words of self-defense we may add those of Oldmixon, who was prompted by Collier's tactics to exclaim: "I beseech you, we'll have no more of Mr. *Collier's Interpretations;* who knows but *Bellmour* might mean he would live and grow better;

this is nearest the original, and if [Collier] had not come in with his helps, it might not have been hit off into Profaneness."[88] Collier, however, would in no way be appeased, and shot back that the real meaning of the passage was that Bellmour "would gladly be a Libertine somewhat longer, and merit Heaven by a more finish'd course of Debauchery."[89]

Leaving aside the more trivial and absurd conplaints made by Collier against other passages in Congreve's plays, we may notice one instance where, to devout believers at least, his indignation may have seemed justly aroused. Recalling that "Our Blessed Saviour affirms himself *to be the Way, the Truth, and the Light; that he came to bear Witness to the Truth, and that his Word is Truth,*" he then commented tartly that Congreve in *Love for Love* remembered these expressions "to good purpose," for there Valentine "in his pretended Madness tells *Buckram* the Lawyer; *I am Truth,—I am Truth.—Who's that, that's out of his way, I am Truth, and can set him right.*" Now a poet, Collier then went on, "that had not been smitten with the Pleasure of Blasphemy, would never have furnish'd Frenzy with Inspiration; nor put our Saviour's Words in the Mouth of a Madman."[90]

In his rebuttal to this indictment Congreve gave three reasons in justification of Valentine's "Counterfeiting in that manner." First, it conduced "to the design and end of the Play"; it also made "a Variation of the Character; and has the same effect in the Dialogue," as if "a new Character were introduc'd"; and finally it gave "a Liberty to Satire," authorizing a "Bluntness, which would otherwise have been a Breach in the Manners of the Character." Madmen, he observed, "have generally some one Expression which they use more frequently than any other. *Valentine* to prepare his Satire, fixes on one which may give us to understand, that he will speak nothing but Truth; and so before and after most of his Observations says—*I am Truth.*" And as a further disclaimer of any blasphemous intent, he records that in his first draft of the play, he had made Valentine say, "*I am Tom-tell-Troth,*" but that "the sound and meanness of the Expression displeas'd" him, and therefore he "alter'd it for one shorter, that might signify the same thing."[91] While one should not rule out the possibility that Congreve anticipated that a "Tom-tell-

Troth" would evoke recollections of the Fool and Poor Tom in *King Lear,* the veracity and appropriateness of his stated original intention would seem to be supported by the fact that proverbial references to "time" as "Tom Telltruth" abound in the sixteenth and seventeenth centuries, as in Giovanni Torriano's *Proverbial Phrases* (1666), "To tell the truth, playing fair, to be Tom-Tell-troth," and also by the fact that between 1593 and 1680 were published in England at least ten works (some running to many editions) written by anonymous authors who gave themselves the pen name "Tom-Tell-Truth" or in whose titles the same sobriquet is prominent (as in, to name only a few, John Lane's *Tom Tel-Troths message, and his pens complaint,* 1600; Anon., *Tom-Tell-Trouth, or a free discourse touching the manners of the tyme,* 1642; Tom-Tell-truth, *All You,* 1670; Anon., *Tom-Tell-Troth; or, a dialogue,* 1679; and so on).

But for Collier the word *Truth* is applied by Christ "in a most solemn and peculiar manner" to Himself, "sometimes to the Holy Ghost, and sometimes to the Revelation of the Gospel." Therefore it is "as it were appropriated to the greatest Persons, and Things, mark'd as the Prerogative of God," and so what could be a "more intolerable Boldness" than for Congreve "to usurp the Regal Stile, to prostitute the Language of Heaven, and apply it to Drollery and Distraction?"[92] A much more charitable interpretation of Valentine's expressions was put forward by Gildon, who wrote that he dared assert, "in Mr. *Congreve*'s name," that "the impious design which this Author [Collier] has coin'd out of his own head, was far from his thoughts" (preface to *Phæton*). And another defender of Congreve wrote that "Words may be wrested to a quite contrary Sense of their Author, and that made to appear ill in a Quotation, which is not so of it self." How could Collier "be sure that Mr. *Congreve* intended to ridicule Religion, when he made Valentine in his Madness say that *he was Truth*? 'Tis very probable Mr. *Congreve* intended no such matter; and if he did not, Mr. *Collier* is guilty of Falsehood and Slander."[93]

Collier of course made no attempt to understand the way Valentine's words and actions are finally contributory to the larger design and meaning of *Love for Love;* as in his dealings with other plays and playwrights, he is simply unwilling to consider matters of context, of characterization, of dramatic purpose. But if, as Congreve testified, Valentine's language does conduce "to the design and end of the Play," and if that play presents him as finally "mad" enough to "ruin" himself out of love for another, then it may well be that his language of madness is fully serviceable to an order of "truth" that Collier himself, had he read in the same spirit that the author writ, perforce should have honored.

V

Anyone who reads through the scores of books, tracts, poems, and prefaces that make up the Collier controversy may well question some of the accepted opinions about it and about its consequences. For too long Collier has been considered the victorious and virtually unchallenged champion of decency who changed the course of English dramatic history. Undoubtedly he had a strong impact upon the stage and those who wrote for it, but both he and his supporters frequently lamented the inefficacy of their protests, while many of the plays he censured the most held their place in the theater for decades.[94] In 1706, we may note, a clergyman of Bristol, the Reverend Arthur Bedford, produced a book whose title promised "Two Thousand Instances" of immorality "taken from the Plays of the two last Years" in spite of "all the Methods lately used for their Reformation." Thirteen years later the same Reverend Bedford came forth with another volume for which he had been able to collect, he said, "almost Seven Thousand Instances" of the ways the stage showed a "plain Tendency to overthrow all Piety, and advance the Interest and Honour of the Devil in the World." These instances of impiety, he said, were taken from "out the Plays of the present Century, and especially of the five last Years, in defiance of all Methods hitherto used for their Reformation."[95]

Collier's rebutters, more read about than read, and more numerous and astute than generally thought, almost without exception considered his charges to be ill-founded and intemperate, yet he apparently stamped them upon the minds of at least a segment of the population at the time—as well as upon one version of English literary history. The trouble, then as now, is that the playwrights pursued their instructive purposes in the lively and mimetic terms that many besides Collier, with his idealistic bias and straitlaced spirit, have been unable to accept. Collier was not the first, nor the last, to confuse art and life and to assume that stage viciousness, however portrayed, is bound to be "catching."

5

Incognita and "the Extraordinary Care of Providence"

A man's heart deviseth his way: but the Lord directeth his steps.

Proverbs, 16 : 9

Appraisal of Congreve's first published work, *Incognita: or Love and Duty Reconcil'd* (1692), has been mixed and thoroughly insipid in any vein. Though it was reprinted at least four times by 1743, Johnson dismissed it by saying he would "rather praise it than read it." Macaulay and Sir Leslie Stephen considered it to be of inconsiderable esteem, but Sir Edmund Gosse at least observed that the "sallies and rallies" of the novel's young lovers have an air of "courteous impertinence" and "read exactly like what we should expect in the first lispings of a comic dramatist." Twentieth-century criticism, usually of a highly vague and "appreciative" nature, has been generally favorable, especially since H. F. B. Brett-Smith called it "probably the most important as well as the most deliberate achievement of the English novel between *The Unfortunate Traveller* in 1594 and *The Life and Strange Surprising Adventures of Robinson Crusoe* in 1719." For Bonamy Dobrée *Incognita* "shows style and critical acumen"; for F. W. Bateson it is "a fresh and, in its own mannered way, a delightfully written little thing"; for D. Crane Taylor no one who would understand Congreve's "development as a dramatist can pass over this novel with a glance"; and for H. Norman Jeffares it is "an impressive piece of work for a young man to produce." Somewhat more extensive, but scarecely less jejune are the comments of Irène Simon, for whom *Incognita* is "indeed a pretty contrivance" and "a delightful arabesque" whose "unity of contrivance is no more than a useful

compositional device." Most substantive has been a chapter by
Maximillian Novak, who argues that "Congreve shows a precocious
insight into the irrational processes of behavior that underlie a
rational exterior" and part of whose thesis is the idea that Congreve
also builds "a world in which art imposes its own pattern upon the
flux of nature."[1]

To put the matter most baldly, one looks in vain through such
critics to find any discussion of what *Incognita* is really "about,"
or exactly why it is to be considered important in the development
of the English novel—much less as to what bearing on and relation it
may have to Congreve's dramatic work. Criticism at its most idle
may be witnessed when we are told that "the plot of *Incognita* is
well enough handled, but it is a formal plot, and the merit of the
book lies elsewhere." Just as otiose appear declarations that the
novel's "plot is conventional, and carries us along with plenty of
incident," or that it "handles a conventional theme with a quiet
success which was not lost upon its own age"[2]—particularly when
both the "conventional" plot and the "conventional" theme seem
to have been either mistaken or left undefined.

The plot, or "Fable," of *Incognita* is indeed "conventional." But
far from being "no more than a useful compositional device," as
Simon thinks, the plot of *Incognita* would have been recognized as
an instructive emblem, as well as an "entertainment," a diverting
parable, in romance terms, of the way man's wandering footsteps,
amidst his living darkness, may be guided by Providence: a fanciful
parable, indeed, in its most crucial episode and in almost fairy-tale
terms, of the way man's very "stumblings" may be providentially
directed for his salvation. And far from "building a world" in which
his "art imposes its own pattern upon the flux of nature," as Novak
argues, Congreve in his art rather accepts and reflects the Providentialist pattern thought to prevail not merely in nature itself but in
all human affairs, even the most amorous and gallant, a pattern
which affirmed, among other things, that when we are filled "with
the apprehension of some great evil which is just ready to fall on
us, either the evil does not come as we feared, or it proves no Evil,
but a very great Good to us."[3]

The existence of such an instructive pattern in so slight and charming a fiction as *Incognita* may come as a surprise to some today, especially to those who would separate the art of the age from the faith of the age. It nevertheless is present, the contextual frame as well as the informing design which will be seen as assuring that two sets of lovers, after a multitude of mistakes and rash designs of their own contriving, will in the end find their "Love and Duty Reconcil'd."

I

In the preface to *Incognita,* Congreve emphasized his resolve "to imitate *Dramatick* Writing, namely, in the Design, Contexture and Result of the Plot." And he went on:

> The design of the Novel is obvious, after the first meeting of Aurelian and Hippolito with Incognita and Leonora, and the difficulty is in bringing it to pass, maugre all apparent obstacles, within the compass of two days. How many probable Casualties intervene in opposition to the main Design, *viz.* of marrying two Couples so oddly engaged in an intricate Amour, I leave the Reader at his leisure to consider: As also whether every Obstacle does not in the progress of the Story act as subservient to that purpose, which at first it seems to oppose. In a Comedy this would be called the Unity of Action; here it may pretend to no more than an Unity of Contrivance.

Most notable here is the way Congreve stresses the elements of "Design" and "Contrivance" in his "intricate" story, and more particularly stresses the way by which "Obstacles" and "Casualties" (i.e. mishaps, accidents, unforeseen events) of themselves seem in the end to "act as subservient to that purpose, which at first" they seem "to oppose." This stress in the preface, along with the insistent illustration of it both by the actual events of the novel and by the highly specialized vocabulary which accompanies these events, should be taken, I believe, as hinting that the vision of life which provides the shaping purpose of *Incognita* is not to be discovered in the "sallies and rallies" of amorous repartee nor in the amused authorial asides about young lovers. Congreve seems rather to be hinting that the "Unity of Contrivance" to be found in his novel may itself be the best clue he will "leave the Reader at his leisure to consider."

Since *Incognita* is seldom read today, it seems necessary to give here at least a sketch of the elaborate "Obstacles" and "Casualties" which make up its narrative. The story opens in Siena, where Aurelian, a young Florentine, and Hippolito di Saviolina, a young Spaniard, have for some time pursued their studies. The time having come for Hippolito's departure, Aurelian persuades him to go first to Florence in the hope he can there gain his own father's permission to accompany him on his travels. Arriving in Florence, they find a grand festival about to begin in honor of the nuptials of a young kinswoman of the duke. They decide to keep their arrival a secret, so as to enjoy the festivities with less restraint, and provide themselves with masks and habits, Hippolito obtaining his from the valet of a Florentine gallant who has been mortally wounded in a duel.

The pair proceed to the Masquing Ball at Court, where Aurelian's eyes become captivated by a lady of a particularly agreeable air, and where, "as Providence would have it," he is granted what he "so zealously pray'd for," the favor of "her Conversation." Utterly charmed by the wit and person of the Lady, Aurelian is given the choice, at the end of the evening, of knowing her name or seeing her face. Naturally he chooses to see her face, which is so beauteous, Congreve says, as to defy description, but which he proceeds to describe nevertheless. The description provides time for Aurelian to recover his senses, for "Admiration had suppress'd his Speech, and his Eyes were entangled in light," but when he then entreats her name she says he must be content to know her, for the present, only by the name of "Incognita." For his part, Aurelian, in order that his father not know of his arrival in Florence, had already presented himself to the young woman in "the Name and Character" of his friend Hippolito.

While Aurelian has been dancing himself "into a Net which he neither could, nor which is worse, desired to untangle," Hippolito has been approached by a young woman who mistakes him, because of his habit, for her cousin Lorenzo, the wounded duelist. She warns Hippolito that kinsmen of the man slain by Lorenzo had also recognized his habit and might set upon him after the ball. While he stands "mute, and contemplating the hazard he had ignorantly brought himself into," she pulls "off her Mask, and discovered to Hippolito (now more amaz'd than ever) the most Angelick Face that he had ever beheld." Resolving to continue the lady's mistake, Hippolito learns that her name is Leonora and that, in order to resolve the feud brought about by Lorenzo's duel, a match had been arranged for his friend Aurelian with one Juliana, "the Marquess's Daughter." Pretending faintness from his supposed wounds, Hippolito leaves the ball with Leonora, and contrives to get both her handkerchief and a means of communicating with her the next day. Then, "with a Heart full of Love, and a Head full of Stratagem," he returns to his lodgings to compose a letter which will excuse his deceit and declare his devotion.

Aurelian is returning to the same lodgings when he sees a man in his friend's apparel violently beset by two others. Chasing off the assailants, he finds their victim to be Claudio, Hippolito's governor, who had donned his master's habit to join in the festivities and in consequence had been attacked by servants of the man "whom Lorenzo had unfortunately slain." Having seen the wounded Claudio cared for, Aurelian goes to the bed-chamber he shares with Hippolito, who is so totally abstracted in thoughts of Leonora that he seems asleep at his writing table. Startled and disordered "with the Appearance of a Man at his Elbow (whom his Amazement did not permit him to distinguish)," Hippolito overthrows the candles. Here "were they both left in the Dark, Hippolito groping about with his Sword, and thrusting at every chair that he felt oppose him," and when Aurelian takes a "step back toward the Door that he might inform his Friend of his Mistake, without exposing himself to his blind Fury," Hippolito makes "a full thrust with such Violence, that the Hilt of the Sword meeting with Aurelian's Breast beat him down." At this point Congreve writes: "But *such was the extraordinary Care of Providence in directing the Sword,* that it only past under his Arm, giving no wound to Aurelian, but a little Bruise between his Shoulder and Breast with the Hilt" (my italics).

Recovering from so dark and dangerous a misadventure, and congratulating themselves upon "their fortunate Delivery from the Mischief which came so near them," the lovers then confide their

new-found loves to one another, and in due course Aurelian also
learns of his father's plan to marry him to Juliana. With his beauteous Incognita "rooted in his heart," Aurelian is confounded at the
news, while Hippolito is chagrined to learn that Aurelian had taken
possession of his name for his own amour. They decide to continue
their deceptions, however, and so Hippolito sends a note to Leonora,
over the name of Aurelian, which beseeches forgiveness for his deceit
of the night before, declares his "inviolate Love," and announces his
resolve never to place himself "in the Arms" of the Juliana designed
him by his father. The note is such an intriguing expostulation of
love that Leonora proceeds from mere curiosity about its author
into a day-dream of prepossession in favor of his person and gallantry—in spite of the fact that she had not had so much as a glimpse
of his face, and the fact also that Juliana is one of her very best
friends.

The next day, having spent an utterly sleepless night, the two
lovers carry off most of the honors in a tournament, in obscure
ways "identifying" themselves to their ladies (Hippolito wears
Leonora's handkerchief in his plumes and Aurelian gives Incognita
a salute "after the Spanish mode") and inadvertently giving Aurelian's father reason to suspect their presence in Florence. Ordering
their lodgings to be sought out, Don Fabio now presses the young
men in time and place, while Juliana's father orders her to be ready
to marry Aurelian the next day. Since Juliana, of course, is really
the beauteous Incognita, and supposes herself in love with the
Spaniard Hippolito, she is "confounded at the haste that was imposed upon her," while Leonora, who had overheard the marquess's
command, is "ready to swoon" at the thought of losing her "Aurelian." In her dilemma, Incognita (Juliana) takes a coach to her
lover's lodgings, where Aurelian mistakes it for that of his father
and rushes out the back way. Since he is a long time gone, Incognita
composes a note to her "Hippolito," only to tear it up, and leave
in disguise and confusion, when she hears the noise caused by the
actual arrival of Aurelian's father. Aurelian eventually returns to
an empty apartment, picks up what fragments of her note he can
find, and, when he pieces them together, finds that his Incognita
"earnestly desired him (if there were any reality in what he pre-

tended to her) to meet her at Twelve a Clock that Night at a Convent Gate." But "unluckily," Congreve adds, "the Bit of Paper which should have mentioned what Convent, was broken off and lost."

Pouring forth an "Abundance of Curses on his Stars," Aurelian walks "unwittingly" through the dark, until his "unguided Steps" eventually lead him "among the Ruines of an Old Monastery." There he hears the voice of a woman in distresss, and when he "demanded what was the Matter, he was answered with the Appearance of a Man, who had opened a Dark Lanthorn which he had by him, and came toward him with a Pistol in his Hand ready cock'd." Congreve then describes the way Aurelian's life is saved, for the second time and again in the dark of night: "Aurelian seeing the irresistable advantage his Adversary had over him, would fain have retired; and, *by the greatest Providence in the World,* going backwards fell down over some loose Stones that lay in his Way, *just in that Instant of Time,* when the Villain fired his Pistol, who seeing him fall, concluded he had shot him" (my italics). Recovering himself, Aurelian runs the villain through, unbinds the unknown woman, and finds her to be (*mirabile dictu*) his own Incognita. She, it seems, had entrusted a servant to take her to another monastery, "about four Leagues" from where they find themselves at the moment, in order to avoid a forced marriage to the very Aurelian who has just rescued her. But the perfidious servant, pretending to take her "a short and private way," and with designs upon her life and honor, led her, she tells Aurelian, into the "old ruined Monastery, where it pleased Heaven, by what Accident I know not, to direct you." While each then continues to confound truth with fictions as to their actual identities, the supposed "Hippolito" persuades "Incognita" to stay that night at his lodgings.

While all this has been going on, the real Hippolito has himself "wandered" through the night in search of Aurelian, only to arrive at another religious house, the Convent of St. Lawrence, situated, we should not be surprised to hear, immediately adjacent to the home of Leonora. The timing here is important, as Congreve makes pointedly clear. For while the convent is the place actually appointed for a meeting between Hippolito and Aurelian, it is astir at so very "unseasonable an hour" with friars at prayer for the wounded Lorenzo, now at the point of death. And because the convent gates have been opened earlier than usual, Hippolito gains access to the garden of Leonora's house, which he enters at a moment Congreve celebrates with a remarkable specificity: "By Computation now (which is a very remarkable Circumstance) Hippolito entered this Garden *near upon the same Instant,* when Aurelian wandred into the Old Monastery and found his Incognita in Distress" (my italics).

Any doubt as to the significance of so pointed a comment on so remarkable a coincidence* is dispelled a few moments later when Hippolito, having overheard Leonora confess her love for him in a highly agitated soliloquy, approaches her to exclaim: "be not disturb'd at my appearance, but think that *Heaven conducted me* to hear my Bliss pronounced by that dear Mouth alone, whose breath could fill me with new Life" (my italics). Hippolito persuades Leonora to an immediate marriage, and together they then cajole her old confessor into performing a ceremony which is barely concluded before Leonora's father appears. Greatly outraged at first, Don Mario is so moved when Leonora faints at his feet, that he is finally appeased, and the more readily so when he is led to believe that his daughter has married the young "Aurelian."

All the confusions are finally sorted out when the principal characters gather at Aurelian's lodgings. There Aurelian begs his father's approval of his own choice for marriage, only to find that the Juliana he had sought so strenuously to avoid is really the Incognita he had so strenuously wooed and so "miraculously" saved. Juliana discovers that her lover is the Aurelian to whom she had already been contracted by her father, and Leonora and her father are happy with the fact that Hippolito comes of a distinguished Spanish house. Loves and duties are reconciled.

II

The narrative language of *Incognita* is dominated by a small set of terms which are completely responsive to the novel's intricacies

*For the significance of remarkable coincidences in providentialist thinking, see chapter 2, section II.

of plot and are also highly suggestive of that plot's essential import. The four main characters are repeatedly involved in "designs" or "contrivances" of their own invention which operate to frustrate the very ends they most desire. At the same time they are also continually involved in "errors" and "mistakes," in "stumblings" and in "wanderings," some of which bring about a most fortunate escape, or a rescue from rape and death, and all of which terminate in a happy solution totally unanticipated in their own schemes and deceptions. All such self-defeating contrivances and designs, along with all such happy errors and fortunate wanderings, are most dramatically exemplified in those most crucial, and most emblematic, scenes where characters are seen as "groping" in darkness. In two such scenes, "in the Dark," or when a character has "wandred both into the Dominions of Silence and of Night," there occurs an escape from death which is specifically attributed either to "the extraordinary Care of Providence" or to "the greatest Providence in the World."

The grain of the novel's language is everywhere apparent. Leonora first approaches Hippolito because "she had mistaken" him for her cousin Lorenzo, and in the ensuing conversation Hippolito quite "forgot his design of informing the Lady of her mistake." Then, though he "was in a hundred Minds, whether he should make her sensible of her Error or no," he finally resolves "to humour the mistake a little further," and all of a sudden, while thinking of how to get the lady away from the ball, he finds "the success of his design had prevented his own endeavours." Later, "after so many Contrivances as he had formed for the discovery of himself," he decides to wait till next day to "inform her gently of her mistake."

Aurelian's departure from the ball is followed almost immediately by two remarkable deliveries that occur in complete darkness. Turning "the Corner of a Street," he sees "the glimmering of Diamond Buttons" on the habit of a man defending himself against two assailants. Fancying the habit that of Hippolito, Aurelian drives off the two men who later confess "their Design to have been upon Lorenzo" and had grounded "their Mistake upon the Habit which was known to have been his." Of course, the person delivered is Claudio, the governor, fortunately "mistaken" by Aurelian for

Hippolito, but it is only by Aurelian's "timely Assistance" that he escapes death in a dark alley. This episode, moreover, is followed immediately by that other "fortunate Delivery from Mischief," when Hippolito and Aurelian are "both left in the Dark" of their apartment, with "Hippolito groping about with his Sword, and thrusting at every Chair that he felt oppose him." Before Aurelian can "inform his Friend of his Mistake," he receives the blow which beats him down and which causes Hippolito, once a light is brought, to believe he has committed "the most Execrable Act of Amicide"— as indeed he would have, but for "the extraordinary Care of Providence in directing the Sword."

The next day, at the tournament, the two friends "mistake" a merely honorific challenge on behalf of the guest of honor, "the Bride and Duke's Kinswoman," as the real thing—while in truth it "was only designed for show and form." Here citations from one paragraph alone may suggest how heavily Congreve stresses the theme of "mistake" in his narrative: "our Cavaliers were under a mistake"; one attendant on the duke demands "His Highness's Permission to inform those Gentlemen better of their mistake, by giving them the Foyle"; when they are informed "of their Error," the pair confess it and beg pardon of the bride "for not knowing her Picture"—a curious analogue to the obscured identities among the lovers themselves. From out of all these "mistakes" and "errors," however, they emerge triumphant, winning in the lists the right to serve as champions of that bride whose beauty they had so wrongly disputed.

The "Two Cavalier-Lovers" next steal back to their lodgings, where for some time they sit "fretting and contriving to no purpose." Although they "rack'd their Invention till it was quite disabled," they "could not make discovery of one Contrivance more for their Relief," and so "Night came upon them while they sate thus thoughtless, or rather drowned in Thought." When Hippolito, with a "profound Sigh," asks what they must do, Aurelian replies faintly, "We must suffer," and then goes on to utter a high-flown and vastly exaggerated complaint which, in spite of the comedy of the situation, serves to recall all the traditional outcries made by man since Adam when a seemingly insoluble predicament causes him to question the order of justice in his world: "Oh ye unequal Powers," he exclaims, "why do you urge us to desire what ye doom us to forbear; give us a Will to chuse, then curb us with a Duty to restrain that Choice! Cruel Father, will nothing else suffice! Am I to be the Sacrifice to expiate your Offenses past; past ere I was born?"

The rhetoric, for such a slight and mannered tale, is so grandiloquent as to be absurd, but nevertheless it is brimfull of reminders of man's first disobedience and the fruits thereof, along with references to free will, suffering, sacrifice, offenses past, and the expiation thereof. At the same time, Aurelian's protest is ironically undercut and rendered utterly foolish by our knowledge that he is far from being "doomed to forbear" that which he has been "urged to desire." Just the reverse, in fact; for his father, as well as those "unequal Powers" he rails against, are all working together to bring about the consummation he so passionately wishes but frustrates by his deceptions and an impatience which, in the context created by Aurelian's own terms, would likely have been seen as a refusal to undergo and sustain the "adversities and crosses disposed to us by Providence."[4] The folly of Aurelian's complaint, and the self-defeating nature of his own impatience, is vividly illustrated the very moment after his declamation, for on being told a coach is at the door, he "concluded immediately it was his Father in quest of him; and without saying any more to Hippolito, than that he was Ruined if discovered," he rushes out the back way—and so misses the entrance of Incognita.

Aurelian's impatience is matched almost instantly by that of Incognita and by another nearly fatal "Mistake." She, "impatient" at Hippolito's "long stay" in search of Aurelian, takes "a Pen and Ink and some Paper which she found upon the Table, and had just made an End of her Letter, when hearing a Noise of more than one coming up Stairs, she concluded his Friend had found him, and that her Letter would be to no purpose, so tore it to pieces, which she repented; when turning about, she found her Mistake, and beheld Don Fabio and the Marquess of Viterbo just entring at the Door." The marquess, "thinking they had been misinformed, or had mistaken" the location of Aurelian's lodgings, "made an

Apology to the Lady for their Errour," but Incognita rushes past
them to her coach, "which hurried her away as speedily as the
Horses were able to draw."

It is immediately after these incidents that Congreve presents us
with the most remarkable and most decisive, as well as the most
improbable, episode of his story—the delivery of Incognita, amidst
blackest night and in the remotest place, from rape and death.
The circumstances of her delivery, moreover, are so contrived, and
so spelled out, as to admit of only one overriding intention on
Congreve's part—illustration of the way man may be led by his
heart and yet have his steps directed by God. We are presented with
an Aurelian who is unable to find the "Bit of Paper" naming the
convent at which he should meet his Incognita "at Twelve a Clock
that Night" and who in consequence is so earnest in "the Contemplation of his Misfortunes" that "he walk'd on unwittingly" in
the darkness until he finds that his "unguided Steps" have caused
him to "wander" among "the Ruines of an Old Monastery." There,
and not at the convent to which the bit of paper would have led
him, his life is first spared "by the greatest Providence in the World,"
and he is next able to effect the rescue of the unknown woman who
turns out to be his Incognita and who considers herself to have been
preserved "by miracle" and because "it pleased Heaven" to "direct"
his way to her. Yet immediately after all these blessed events, they
continue their deceiving of one another with small falsehoods as
to their real identities.

In the last few pages of the novel, we see how Hippolito has also
"wandred much" during the night, in search of Aurelian, before
finding himself, "sooner than he thought for," amidst yet another
religious setting, the Convent of St. Lawrence. He wonders much
to see the gates of the convent opening "at so unseasonable an
Hour," and when he enters to inquire the reason, a friar not only
tells him that the inmates are all up "to pray for the Soul of a
Cavalier, who was just departing or departed this Life," but also that
he is about to open a "private door out of the Garden" of the house
next door so that the family there "might come and offer up their
Oraisons for the Soul of their Kinsman." And so in a religious
setting and by a religious man, Hippolito finds the way opened for

him into Don Fabio's garden. There, in the darkness, he overhears Leonora's confession of her love for him, and when he falls upon his knees before her startled and frightened eyes, he entreats her thus: "be not disturb'd at my Appearance, but think that *Heaven conducted me* to hear my Bliss pronounced by that dear Mouth alone, whose Breath could fill me with new Life" (my italics).

Here the reader may have "leisure to consider," as Congreve said in his preface, "whether every Obstacle does not in the progress of the Story act as subservient to that purpose which at first it seems to oppose." And as to there being "any thing more in particular resembling" the dramatic writing he "imitates," and which he says "the Curious Reader will soon perceive," he will "leave it to show it self, being very well satisfy'd how much more proper" it is for such a reader to find "out this himself," than "to prepossess him with an Opinion of something extraordinary in an Essay began and finished in the idler hours of a fortnight's time." For a modern reader, even the most "curious," it may be more difficult to perceive "something extraordinary" in a story of how two sets of lovers repeatedly frustrate their own desires and purposes by a multitude of "designs," "contrivances," and "mistakes" and are yet preserved by "the extraordinary Care of Providence" and finally "directed" or "conducted" by "Heaven" to one another's arms. For the modern reader, therefore, it may be useful to consider a representative exposition of a biblical text, frequently cited during the late seventeenth century, where Isaac Barrow writes that when men, "without regard unto God's providence, do rely upon themselves and their own abilities, imagining that, without God's direction and help, by the contrivances of their own wit and discretion," they "can arrive to the utmost of their desires, and become sufficiently happy," they fail to consider that God "manageth and turneth all things" and that "nothing can be achieved without the concurrence of his providence," for "although, *a man's heart deviseth his way, yet the Lord directeth his steps.*"*

---

*Works, 2:1. Preaching on the text of Proverbs 16:9, and especially recommending it to the attention of his congregation, the Reverend John March noted that "of all those three thousand Proverbs, which are Recorded as the products of *Solomon*'s Wisdom, there is not any one the Holy Ghost has

III

About a third of the way through *Joseph Andrews,* in the open countryside off the main road from which he had wandered, and somewhere between London and his home parish in Somersetshire, on a night of the greatest darkness and in a most lonely place, Fielding's Parson Adams arrives "near some Bushes: whence, on a sudden," he hears "the most violent Shrieks imaginable in a Female Voice." Brandishing his crabstick, Adams knocks out a man attempting to ravish a young woman who turns out to be, a few pages later, Fanny Goodwill. Having heard of her beloved Joseph's misfortunes, she had set out in search of him and subsequently had "accidentally" met a man who said he would show her "a nearer way" to a night's lodging "than by following the Road." Not having recognized his own parishioner as yet, Adams asks by "what Misfortune she came, at such a time of Night, into so lonely a Place," and Fanny replies that upon meeting the stranger who offered to be her guide, she had no reason to suspect him of evil, and that even if she had, she "had no human Means to avoid him," being "alone on those Downs in the dark," and so she had "put her whole Trust in Providence." Adams then praises her "for saying she had put her whole Trust in Providence," and adds that "He doubted not but Providence had sent him to her Deliverance, as a reward for that Trust."

Such an episode is a common occurrence in Fielding's novels, and indeed all of them, from *Joseph Andrews* and *Jonathan Wild* to *Tom Jones* and *Amelia,* proceed by way of the most strange and startling coincidences, the most amazing and fortuitous mishaps, the most extraordinary encounters and intrusions of persons necessary to the relief or deliverance of a hero or heroine.[5] The majority of the encounters, moreover, occur by the most improbable intersections, in time as well as in space, of intimately related characters.

---

thought fit to repeat so often, or inculcate more frequently, than this of the Text; for it is repeated thrice in this one Chapter, besides what it is in other places of this Book of *Proverbs.* In all which places, the Wise man gives us to understand, that the wonderful Providence of God does rule and govern all the Actions of Men" (*Sermons Preach'd on Several Occasions,* 2d ed., London, 1699, pp. 241–42; 1st ed., 1693).

When one considers the geography involved in the encounter between Adams and Fanny (the space between Somerset and London),
the fact that it occurs off the main road in complete darkness, and
also the nice requirements of an exact timing, then the probability
of such a conjunction seems incalculable and practically unthink-
able. Nevertheless, such encounters are a major substantive element
in the narratives of Fielding (as well as in those of Defoe, Richardson, Smollet, and others), they are nearly always encounters intended for the relief of a distressed innocence or a deliverance from
sin, and they are for the most part explicitly attributed to an interposing Providence. They are so commonplace, moreover, because
they reflect the common view of the world as a place where Providence does interpose directly and continuously in human affairs,
manifesting itself by events of a strange or startling or coincidental
nature, working through accident and mishap (we may recall the
story of St. Augustine's escape from murder because his guide
"mistook, and led him into a by-path"; see chap. 2, p. 30).

An argument for a providentialist structure (and the vision it
entails) in so "little" a "thing" as *Incognita* may seem odd or merely
eccentric to some. But the real oddity is the argument that *"Incognita* relies heavily on chance," and that Congreve in it constructs
"a world in which art imposes its own pattern upon the flux of
nature."[6] It is not chance which directs that Hippolito's thrusting
sword, in the utmost darkness, shall go under Aurelian's arm instead
of into his heart; it was, says Congreve as plainly as can be said,
"the extraordinary Care of Providence in directing the Sword, that
it only past under his Arm." It is not by chance that Aurelian
stumbles and falls in the darkness at the moment when a pistol is
fired at him: it is "by the greatest Providence in the World" that,
"going backwards," he "fell down over some loose Stones that lay
in his Way, just in that Instant of Time, when the Villain fired his
Pistol." It is not chance that directs Aurelian to the "Ruins of an
Old Monastery" or Hippolito to the Convent of St. Lawrence: in
both instances they are said to have been directed, through the darkness in which they wander, by "Heaven."

The emblematic character of such episodes would have been un-
mistakable to readers reared in literature and fed by sermons which

maintained that in "innumerable" instances of life "we drive on blindfold, and very often impetuously pursue that which would ruin us: and were God as shortsighted as we, into what precipices should we minutely hurry our selves."[7] Such readers would have had minds well stocked with the idea and the image and the advice that "We ought always to appear before [God], like blind Men, who stretch out their Hands, to be conducted by Providence."[8] Just as familiar and easily decipherable to them would have been the "sign" of God's providential interposition when an event "which in it self is not ordinary, nor could well be expected, doth fall out happily, in the nick of an exigency, for the relief of innocence."[9] When the "relief of innocence" occurs in an old monastery, they would have seen it, moreover, as deliberately placed on God's own ground.

Such considerations as these are not put forward, of course, with the aim of overwhelming a sprightly story under a load of providentialist lumber. *Incognita* is a witty and charming and ingenious "Essay," as Congreve called his first work. But it is certainly worth remembering that it has its more somber content: two deaths by dueling, the near death of Claudio, two escapes from death by Aurelian, the near rape and death of Juliana. When we consider such elements, along with the multiple mistakes and mishaps and cross-purposes which characterize its "Fable," we may admire all the more the way Congreve gave to his novel the "Unity of Contrivance" he sought. We also may see, however, that his own admirable contrivances are closely reflective of a world where, it was assumed, there could be discovered another "admirable (though unsearchable) contrivance" in the "obscure administrations," by Providence, of even the most "casual, negligent, promiscuous Events."[10]

Incognita is important in the history of the English novel, but not for the reasons usually given. It is also important as a prologue to the plays Congreve was so soon to write. There he would again illustrate, though in more subtle and complex terms, the ways in which men and women, even the most witty and urbane, may be thwarted by their own ingenuity, be delivered or defeated by seemingly casual or negligent events, find a guerdon, or meet disaster, through a "mistake."

6

The "Apocryphal" Scene: "Natural Vizors" and "Wordly Faces"

> *Qui nescit dissimulare, nescit vivere.*
> Old Latin tag

> They little guess, who at our arts are grieved,
> The perfect joy of being well deceived.
>
> Rochester,
> *A Letter from Artemesia in the Country
> to Chloe in the Town* (1679)

Probably written in 1689, when Congreve was only nineteen, the manuscript of *The Old Batchelour* was brought in 1692 to the attention of Dryden, who is supposed to have said that "he never saw such a first play in his life" and that "the stuff was rich indeed" but lacked "the fashionable cutt of the town." According to this story, Dryden also thought "it would be pity to have it miscarry for want of a little Assistance," and so "putt it in the order it was playd." This account, as recollected by Thomas Southerne some forty years later,[1] is slightly at variance with the testimony, barely six years after the play's first performance, of Charles Gildon, who says he had "been assur'd [it] was writ, when our Author was but Nineteen Years Old, and in nothing alter'd, but in the Length, which being consider'd, I believe few Men that have writ, can shew half so good at so unripe an Age."[2]

The brilliance of wit in the new play was immediately acclaimed, and Congreve was also instantly hailed as the only worthy "Successor" to Dryden, a judgment the older playwright himself was to endorse a year later in his generous, and poignant, verses "To My Dear Friend Mr. Congreve, On His Comedy, call'd *The Double-Dealer.*" With Wycherley in "wise Retreat," with Etherege "in wild Pleasures tost," with "*Lee* and *Otway* dead," as Southerne wrote in

a commendatory poem before the play, a new "Age of Wit" was
seen by some as having arrived on the English stage. And even
though Congreve's reign over the new "Age" would span a mere
seven years, it was impossible then and later to withhold the "blaze
of admiration" Johnson felt due one whose "efforts of early genius
were over by the age of thirty."[3]

Amidst the acclaim, Congreve showed himself very sensible of
what he considered the "good Nature of the Town" in receiving his
play "so kindly, with all its Faults," and confessed, in his dedication
of it, a youthful "Ignorance of the Town and Stage" that he hoped
would be pardoned. Years later, in his response to a "dreadful
Comment" by Collier on a portion of the Fondlewife episode, he
declared he could not "hold Laughing" when he reflected "how
young a beginner, and how very much a Boy I was when that Comedy was written,"[4] a statement that may be merely disingenuous—or
may indicate, as Van Voris has suggested, that he "wanted his first
play to be read as the work of a young man, and not as a statement
of mature conviction."[5] It does seem fair to say that *The Old
Batchelour* lacks the more discriminating ethical configurations
discoverable in the plays that so quickly followed it. Compared to
subsequent plays, where words and deeds, and their consequences,
seem more closely correlative with motives and moral worth, *The
Old Batchelour* offers characters whose motives at times are dubious
or inexplicable, if not downright perverse. The problems seemingly
raised in the play may be due to the fact that its "wit," in Johnson's
words, is "so exuberant that it 'o'er-informs its tenement.'"[6] But
whatever such dubieties, the play is a rich and spicy exhibition of
the "cloaks" and "coverlets" that may be used to "Cover Carnal
Knavery," as well as a tantalizing illustration of the proposition,
announced by Bellmour near the start of the play, that human
"Wisdom," in a world where appearances may be "Apocryphal,"
may be "nothing but a pretending to know and believe more than
really we do."

I

Recent critics have stressed the thematic presence in *The Old
Batchelour* of such ideas as appearance versus nature, sight versus

blindness, delusion versus reality.[7] More particularly, in my view,
Congreve seems to exploit, in the most teasing fashion, the age-old
idea of mankind as "actors" who "play a part" on the world-stage.
Such exploitation seems most clearly manifested when Bellmour,
attired in the "habit" of a "Fanatick one-ey'd Parson," enters at the
beginning of act 4 and inquires thus of a pimping servant: "Well and
how Setter hae, does my Hypocrisy fit me? Does it sit easy on me?"
In these words Congreve seems deliberately to invoke the root as
well as the common meaning of "Hypocrisy," that is, *hupokrisis,* the
"playing of a part on the stage,"* as well as the pretending or
feigning of beliefs, virtues, feelings one does not actually possess.

A few minutes later, moreover, Bellmour, having "out-fac'd Suspicion" in his "Fanatick Habit" and gained access to the chamber of
Fondlewife's young wife, is made to signal the audience another
reminder of the "actorly" import of hypocrisy; striking a pose in
his black cloak, he exclaims, "Methinks I am the very Picture of
Montufar in the *Hypocrites"*—referring to the popular novel by
Scarron in which the mountebank Montufar, pretending to be one
Friar Martin and always wearing a black cassock and coat, hood-
winks the entire populace of Seville into thinking him a "saint."
Deliberate recall of the "actorly" roles played by men and women
in the real world is even more apparent in act 3 when Lucy "Puts
on her Masque" to accost Setter, and he demands of her: "Why
how now! prithee who art? lay by that Worldly Face and produce
your natural Vizor."† The correspondence of world-stage life to
stage-world art could not be more succinctly, or more piquantly,
phrased.

A view of human nature in terms of the world-stage metaphor
implies at least some understanding, and acceptance, of the ways

---

*A similarly deliberate reminder of the root meaning of *hypocrisy* occurs
in *Love for Love,* act 4, scene 1, lines 706–08, when Valentine says to Angelica: "Nay faith, now let us understand one another, Hypocrisie apart,—The
Comedy draws toward an end, and let us think of leaving acting, and be
our selves."

†Perhaps a recollection of Dryden's *An Evening's Love,* act 1, scene 1,
lines 179–80, where Beatrice says: "By that Face of thine, which is a Natural
Vizor: I will not tell thee."

men and women prudently, even necessarily, may wear their faces as the "natural Vizors" given them to meet the faces that they meet. And indeed, one of the more popular sayings of the period was that *qui nescit dissimulare, nescit vivere.* As a writer of advice to the female sex observed, the "World is too full of *Craft, Malice,* and *Violence,* for absolute *Simplicity* to live in it."

> It behoves therefore our Sex, as well as the other, to live with so much caution, and circumspection in regard to their own Security, that their Thoughts and Inclinations may not be seen so naked, as to expose 'em to the *Snares, Designs,* and *Practices* of *Crafty Knaves,* who wou'd make a property of 'em; . . . For this reason it is that it has been Proverbially said of Old, that, *He that knows not how to Dissemble, knows not how to Live.* The Experience of all Ages since has confirm'd this Observation, and ours no less than any of the preceding.[8]

Or, as the writer of a contemporary courtesy book (for which the Latin tag served as an epigraph on the title page) declared:

> *Dissimulation* is part of the essence of *Complaisance,* without which 'tis impossible that a Courtier or any other person should be able to conduct himself with safety amidst the malice and contrivances of men, for he who knows not how to conceal his game, gives great advantage to those he plays with, not only against himself, but against his friends whose affairs and interests are twisted with his.[9]

While dissimulation "is indeed oftentimes criminal," it is, like "most other good Qualities," only "accidentally so," according "to the Ends and Purposes to which they are misemploy'd." And given "the present Constitution of the World," dissimulation "is many times absolutely necessary, and a main ingredient in the Composition of Human Prudence."[10]

The idea that dissembling may be a necessary, prudent, and even "natural" human trait is churlishly rejected by George Heartwell, the old bachelor. A self-proclaimed despiser of gallants and gallantry, as well as of marriage and womankind, he is "for having every body be what they pretend to be; a Whoremaster be a Whoremaster." He boasts that his own "Talent is chiefly that of speaking truth," but he is so unfit for society that he would entertain "company like a Physician, with discourse of their diseases and infirmities." The "truths" he blurts out are such "odious Truths" as would put a "fine Lady" out "of conceit with herself" by persuading her that "the Face she had been making all the morning was none of her own." Such a truth-teller as he is "as unwelcome to a Woman, as a Looking glass after the Small-pox."

Playing the part of the blunt and honest man, and unwilling to grant to others the right of even a little dissembling, Heartwell all the while frantically attempts to cover up the ridiculous passion he has conceived for Sylvia, the young woman whose own experience may exemplify the difficulties of distinguishing a "true" lover from a "false" one: having agreed to an assignation with Vainlove, Sylvia is taken in the dark by Bellmour, "acting" in his friend's place. Having "lost" her "innocence," Sylvia is then advised to "put on" an innocence. "Strike *Heartwell* home," her maid Lucy urges: "receive him pleasantly, dress up your Face in Innocence and Smiles; and dissemble the very want of Dissimulation." And when Sylvia expresses doubt that she has the "Art" to "Counterfeit Love," Lucy exclaims, "Hang Art, Madam, and trust to Nature for Dissembling."

And so she may, for Heartwell is so urged and blinded by his lust that he takes her face of innocence for innocence itself: "Pox," he exclaims in an aside, "how her Innocence torments and pleases me!" Looking upon Sylvia as a "Child," as "a beauteous Changeling," the old bachelor becomes, in his own turn, "a bearded Baby for a Girl to dandle." Regarding Sylvia as a "Fool," Heartwell himself decides to "play the Fool," even though he thinks that "to Marry, is playing the Fool all ones Life long." As for Sylvia, she finds, in her own words, that "dissembling to our Sex is as natural as swimming to a *Negro;* we may depend upon our skill to save us at a plunge, though till then we never make the experiment."

Sneering at those who would fawn "upon a little tawdry Whore," Heartwell himself engages in the most abject fawning upon just such a creature. Unable, moreover, to "see the Miscarriages obvious to every Stander by," he is blind to the fact that his friends have detected his "Love," and, in the words of Bellmour, believe that "a little time will swell him so, he must be forc'd to give it birth, and the discovery must needs be very pleasant, to see what pains he will take, and how he will strain to be deliver'd of a Secret, when he has miscarried on't already." Such imagery of birth and miscarriage is a notable element in several of Congreve's plays (particularly in *The Double-Dealer* and *The Way of the World*), and for him seems to have been expressive of a basic fact of human experience: truth, the old saying went, is the daughter of time (*veritas filia temporis*), and for Congreve time, even "a little time," was apparently the great revealer of reality, of truth—though perhaps only to those with the eyes to see and the ears to hear. Even so little time as the three hours of a play could be used to illustrate the way a burden of the past, or a person's true nature, would eventually be disclosed.

At the same time, Congreve's plays suggest that for some the truth may be too much to be borne: there are always those who cannot or will not accept the evidence of their own senses; and indeed, given the ways in which the plays so often illustrate the unreliability of the senses, such refusal is not at all times to be contemned. In the final analysis, moreover, Congreve's work suggests that even the most discerning, such as Bellmour in *The Old Batchelour* or Mirabell in *The Way of the World,* must learn to regard the ordinary failings of human nature much as they would their own—that is, with considerable forbearance.

In *The Old Batchelour* it is well for George Heartwell not only that his friend Bellmour regards his surliness and folly with considerable forbearance, but also highly ironic that Bellmour should deliver him from his folly by means of the very dissembling he so much despises. So "impatient" is Heartwell for marriage to Sylvia that he readily accepts Bellmour, in the guise of the one-eyed parson Tribulation Spintext, as the minister to perform the ceremony. And when Lucy, "through Mistake," goes to solicit Bellmour about the "Business," he tells her that it is a "Mistake" she "must go through with"—a reminder of the fortunate "mistakes" so pervasive in *Incognita,* as well as of providential "mistakes" to come in later plays. "Look you," Bellmour says to Lucy, "*Heartwell is* my Friend; and tho' he be blind, I must not see him fall into the Snare, and unwittingly marry a Whore." A comment by Holland seems especially discerning here: "we feel that Heartwell trapped himself but was saved by the charity that a pretending person like Bellmour may actually have. (The gallant's disguise as a minister, while a common device, is in this case meaningful.)"[11] It is not the last time Congreve was to use clerical garb as the visible instrument of deliverance from vice or folly.

Thinking himself "irrecoverably married," Heartwell is finally reduced to the conscious and deliberate dissembling he had so denounced in others. Invited by Sharper to visit the "Corner House" where lives "a young Creature that *Vainlove* debauch'd, and has forsaken," Heartwell is racked by the thought of his marriage to such a creature becoming known: "Hell, and the Devil," he says in an aside, "Does he know it? But, hold:—If he shou'd not, I were a Fool to discover it.—I'll dissemble, and try him." Unable, finally, to let Sharper "go and whore" his supposed wife, he groans forth the supposed fact of his marriage, and when Sharper regards his plight as "a Jest" he rages from the scene with these bitter words: "Death: D'ye mock me? Heark-ye: If either you esteem my Friendship, or your own Safety;—come not near that House,—that Corner-house,—that hot Brothel. Ask no Questions."

The idea that one person's "Afflictions" may be another person's "Jest" is recurrent in *The Old Batchelour.* "My Affliction is always your Jest," Laetitia Fondlewife says to her husband, and the hapless Sir Joseph Wittol speaks better than he knows when he says to Sharper that he would "have lost a good Jest for want of knowing me." Several times, however, it is suggested that a jest may be carried "too far," and such almost seems the case near the end of the play when Heartwell, much like an old bear at a baiting, is surrounded by younger friends who take their turns in teasing and goading him into a fury, making him, he thinks, their "Laughing-stock." Galled beyond endurance, especially after Belinda has nastily observed that he will have need of a "Fly-flap" because his "Wife has been blown upon," he breaks out in a retort so dark and anguished that their jestings at his afflictions seem anything but comic. "Damn your pity," he says:

How have I deserv'd this of you? Any of ye? Sir, have I im-
pair'd the Honour of your House, promis'd your Sister Marriage,
and whor'd her? Wherein have I injured you? Did I bring a
Physician to your Father to prolong his life, and you One-and-
Twenty? Madam, have I had an Opportunity with you and
bauk'd it? Did you ever offer me the Favour that I refus'd
it? Or——

The scene is not pretty, and one's discomfort with it may arise in
part because the jestings at Heartwell's expense come from characters, particularly Belinda, who have throughout the play exhibited a
thoroughly callous disregard for the feelings of others. And even
though Heartwell, in Bellmour's words, had "sold [himself] to
Laughter" by way of his lechery, there remains the paradoxical
fact that his observations on the more base and silly dimensions
of human nature are shrewd and telling: were it not for his uncivil
bluntness and silly infatuation with Sylvia, he might well stand as
a legitimate censor of the society around him. But with all his years
and knowledge of the town, and even with all his evident self-
knowledge, he is yet brought to a condition of torment from which
he can only be rescued by Bellmour's more cool and inventive
manipulation of appearances. His faults no doubt warrant the affliction into which they lead him, though his virtues are such that
they also warrant his release from it. As Araminta comments at
one point, "there are few Men, but do more silly things, than they
say."

II

Somewhat apart from the old bachelor stand the two contrasted
young gallants, Vainlove and Bellmour, the first of whom is accurately perceived by Heartwell as "one of Loves April-fools,"
always "upon some errand that's to no purpose, ever embarking
in Adventures, yet never comes to harbour." The inconclusiveness,
the bootless and barren nature, of Vainlove's amorous enterprises
is also stressed by Lucy when she terms him "a Mumper" (a slang
word for a beggar) "in Love, lies Canting at the Gate; but never dares
presume to enter the House." He is so "Capricious a Lover," so

"capricious in his Love," that he breaks off an amour the instant
a woman gives the slightest hint of a serious response, or else turns
her over to Bellmour once her susceptibility has been established.
In Bellmour's words, each has his "share of sport": "'tis his diversion to Set, 'tis mine to Cover the Partridge." While almost all the
characters are compared to animals at one time or another (as if,
Birdsall suggests, they were figures in beast fables),[12] Vainlove's
pleasure solely in the pursuit itself seems chiefly expressed in imagery of the hunter: he is "continually starting of Hares" for Bellmour to run down, and his main complaint is that "there's not a
Woman, will give a Man the pleasure of a chase: My Sport is always
balkt or cut short—I stumble ore the Game I would pursue.—'Tis
dull and unnatural to have a Hare run full in the Hounds Mouth; and
would distaste the keenest Hunter—I would have overtaken, not
have met my Game."

Critics have sometimes seen Vainlove as "the romantic dreamer
for whom real life can offer, he fears, no fulfillment equal to his
dreams,"[13] or as one who refuses "the acceptance of something less
than ideal."[14] A much better, and more disparaging, view of his
disposition is offered by various characters in the play. Thus, when
Bellmour says that Vainlove "takes as much always of an Amour as
he cares for, and quits it when it grows stale, or unpleasant," Sharper
glosses his words as "An Argument of very little Passion, very good
Understanding, and very ill Nature." Lucy, indeed, is not far wrong
when she calls him "the head Pimp to Mr. *Bellmour,*" while Sharper
regards his forsaking of Araminta as "a kind of a Mungril Curs trick"
and wonders he can "be so great a Brute as to slight her."

Most typically, however, Vainlove's temperament is revealed in
imagery of taste, or palate, or stomach. Sharper, for example, considers his capriciousness a kind of "damn'd illnatur'd whimsey"
which proceeds from "a sickly peevish Appetite" that can only
"chew Love" and not "digest it." Vainlove himself says, "I hate to
be cram'd," and "Faith I hate Love when 'tis forced upon a Man; as
I do Wine." Heartwell scorns him as one who will "kiss a Lap-Dog
with passion, when it would disgust him from the Lady's own
Lips," and Lucy knows full well that her counterfeit note to him
will "disgust his nicety, and take away his Stomach" for Araminta.

The folly, and the "very ill Nature," of Vainlove's squeamish disposition is most apparent in his relations with Araminta, the one woman of dignity and good sense in the play. Aware of his finicky temperament, she keeps herself "a kind of floating Island," sometimes "seems in reach, then vanishes" to keep him "busied in the search." But when he first affronts her with "a Kiss which he forced," and then mistakes as hers Lucy's counterfeit note of abject apology for the offense she took, he instantly judges her to be like other women: "lost" and only worthy of his contempt. And when Sharper, to whom he shows the note, advises him that Araminta is "A delicious Mellon pure and consenting ripe" and that she "has been breeding Love" to him "all this while" and "just now" is "deliver'd of it," Vainlove callously replies: "'Tis an untimely Fruit, and she has miscarried of her Love."

When he proceeds, on so slight grounds as the note, to treat Araminta with a cold insolence, she responds to his words with amazement and indignation, rightly seeing that behind his behavior lies "Some villainous Design" to blast her honor. She uses, moreover, an image that most appropriately turns Vainlove's own imagery of miscarriage back upon him: "How time might have deceiv'd me in you, I know not; my Opinion was but young, and your early Baseness has prevented its growing to a wrong Belief.—Unworthy, and ungrateful! Be gone, and never see me more." Vainlove comes to regret his "sawcy Credulity" in accepting too readily an appearance of frailty in Araminta, but here his history of aborted amours culminates in a most poetic revenge on himself.

If Heartwell, with all his experience and observation of human frailty, allows his lust for Sylvia to urge him into a bad marriage, Vainlove seems so contrary and delicate in temperament as to lack appetite for any sexual union whatever, much less that to be found in marriage (more than has been realized, he fully lives up to Lucy's denomination of him as a "Mumper in Love," for in *A New Dictionary of the Terms Ancient and Modern of the Canting Crew,* by B. E., Gent., London, 1699, *Mumpers* are defined as "Gentile [i.e. heathen] Beggars, who will not accept of Victuals, but Money or Clothes"). His squeamish overnicety toward woman, along with his excessive self-esteem, scarcely suggest an idealist or romantic dreamer: rather, they declare a narcissism so complete as to bar him utterly from the giving of self customarily expected, and required, of a good marriage.

III

Set against the overnice temperament of Vainlove is that of Bellmour, the self-described "Cormorant in Love," who "not contented with the slavery of honourable Love in one place, and the pleasure of enjoying some half a score Mistresses" of his "own acquiring," must "yet take *Vainlove*'s Business" upon his hands, "because it lays too heavy upon his." Even his sexual voracity seems to have its limits, however, for he ends the inventory of his mistresses by saying to himself: "I must take up [i.e. get married], or I shall never hold out; Flesh and Blood cannot bear it always." Strikingly enough, moreover, this accomplished seducer so knowledgeable in the ways of women and the world is the only character in the play who enters the marriage state fully resolute and also fully cognizant of its pitfalls. When Heartwell, at the close of the play, tries to dissuade him from falling "into the same snare, out of which" he had just been delivered, Bellmour gives him thanks for "good intention," and adds: "But there is a fatality in Marriage.—For I find I'm resolute."

Critics from Collier to the present have questioned the creation of so licentious a character as the "hero" of *The Old Batchelour*. We have noted, in chapter 4, Collier's attack on what he considered an instance of Bellmour's irreverence, along with Congreve's rejoinder and concession that "The Stile of [his] Expression is Light, and suitable to Comedy, and the Character of a wild Debauchee of the Town." In more recent years a critic has wondered how "such a debauched character" could "be the hero, even the comic hero," of a play, and suggested as a partial answer that "the moral standards of the audience were very different from our own"[15]— a presuming opinion that takes much too much for granted, and one that ignores completely the contemporary theories of comic characterization, which held that persons of "perfect Morals" were to be "excluded the Comick Stage." At the very least, any consideration of Bellmour's character should keep in view Dryden's belief that the comic playwright may reward persons whose "faults and vices are but the sallies of youth, and the frailties of human nature," though only after "reclaiming them first from vice," which "is to be supposed they are, when they resolve to marry; for then enjoying what they desire in one, they cease to pursue the love of many." (See the discussion of comic characterization in chapter 4, pp. 74ff.)

His sexual profligacy notwithstanding, Bellmour stands out in the play as not only the character with the clearest insight into his own and others' natures, but also as the one with the greatest decency of nature—a decency evinced on the two major occasions when he is shown preserving others from the consequences of their own folly. The most important of these, of course, is his rescue of Heartwell from the madness of marriage with a strumpet. But also indicative of his nature, and of his adroitness of mind, is his decision to clear Laetitia Fondlewife, at his own expense, from her husband's all too justified suspicions as to their adultery. Utterly discomfited at the aged alderman's premature return home, and with coition barely accomplished, Bellmour is at first so much at a loss for words that he can only come out with a weak "Soh" when Fondlewife demands to know who and what he is. But when Laetitia twice equivocatingly declares she never saw him "before," Bellmour collects himself, and makes this aside: "Well, now I know my Cue.—That is very honourably, to excuse her, and very impudently accuse my self." And so the next time Fondlewife demands to know who he is, and also what he is, he comes out with the forthright reply: "A Whore-Master." Not only does he then proceed to convince Fondlewife of Laetitia's innocence, in spite of all appearances to the contrary, but does so, ironically enough, by living up to that ill-tempered and unconscionable demand by Heartwell in act 1 that "every body be what they pretend to be; a Whoremaster be a Whoremaster."

In the main, however, any assessment of Bellmour (with all his "faults and vices" upon him) cannot be made apart, in Dryden's words, from his "resolve to marry"—a resolution he announces, moreover, before he leaves Fondlewife's house and with Laetitia's example of wifely guile and frailty fully before him: "For my part," he says to Fondlewife, "I am so charm'd with the Love of your Turtle to you, that I'll go and sollicite Matrimony with all my might and main." And so he does, in the very next act.

Unlike Heartwell, who is so blinded by lust that he thinks Sylvia a compound of "so much Tenderness and Beauty—and Honesty" as to be "a Jewel," Bellmour approaches his own marriage undeluded. He seems to acquiesce fully in Sharper's opinion that Belinda is "too Proud, too Inconstant, too Affected and too Witty, and too Handsome for a Wife," agreeing that "'Tis true she is excessively foppish and affected"—but reminding Sharper at the same time that "she can't have too much Mony" and brings "twelve thousand Pound" with her. Knowing as he is, Bellmour, moreover, fully understands that a stomach like Vainlove's is too delicate and squeamish for ordinary intercourse, and much the more so for marriage and the ultimate purposes of life. When he says that Vainlove is "of a temper the most easie to himself in the World," taking only as much "of an Amour as he cares for" and quitting "it when it grows stale, or unpleasant," he not only assesses his friend correctly but also obliquely expresses his own awareness of, and preparation for, the uneven daily fare attendant on even the best of marriages. And when he tells Sharper that he believes "the Baggage loves me" and that "Give her her due, I think the Woman's a Woman, and that's all," he seems to acknowledge, and accept, the less than perfect human reality to be expected from anyone.

We may recall that in the first moments of his meeting with Laetitia Fondlewife, she is momentarily chagrined at Bellmour's being "privy to a weak Woman's Failing," a comment we may enlarge upon to suggest a privity he enjoys with all the sex. But we should also recollect that when Bellmour put on the garb of Tribulation Spintext he not only donned the "swinging long Spiritual Cloak, to Cover Carnal Knavery" but also the "Black Patch" with which the fanatic parson covers "one Eye," for, as "some say," it was "with that Eye, he first discover'd the frailty of his Wife." However open-eyed his view of Belinda's faults and short-comings, Bellmour nevertheless seems to recognize the necessity, even the wisdom, of closing at least "one Eye" to them. The "part" he "plays," even though it be that of a "fanatic" nonconforming parson, becomes pointedly suggestive of a choice he makes. And grotesque as Tribulation Spintext may seem, Congreve nevertheless has Lucy say, "He has been lawfully ordain'd," and seems himself utterly nonsectarian in his willingness to use his "stalking Form of Godliness" to send a message of Christian forbearance.

We may remember that Collier had objected to Bellmour's saying he would not wish to go to heaven "immediately," but would do "a little more good" in his "generation first, in order to deserve it" (see chap. 4, pp. 86–87). Certainly, the last scene of the play shows him resolute for the work of generation, if not regeneration. There, immediately after Heartwell has called down all sorts of curses on himself if he ever weds again, Bellmour declares: "Well; 'Midst of these dreadful Denunciations, and notwithstanding the Warning and Example before me, I commit myself to lasting Durrance." And when Belinda gives him her hand and says, "Prisoner, make much of your Fetters," Congreve seems to stress once again how knowingly and deliberately Bellmour has chosen the enjoyment of one rather than the pursuit of many. Having accepted his fetters, Bellmour is moreover shown, at the very end of the play, as able to "dance" within them.

IV

Perception of truth in a world of surfaces, soundness of judgment amongst inscrutable faces both "natural" and "worldly," these are commonplace themes, and scarcely a character in *The Old Batchelour* fails to illustrate the riddling nature of existence. Sylvia lies with Bellmour in the dark, thinking all the while he is Vainlove, and thus has been, in the latter's mocking words, as "true as Turtle—in imagination." Thinking he has a fawning note from Araminta "in his pocket," Vainlove is shocked by her indignation at his presuming insolence, and exclaims, "Did I dream? Or do I dream? Shall I believe my Eyes, or Ears," while on her part, Araminta finds his behavior "mystically senceless and impudent." Approached by Lucy in a mask, Setter demands of her, "who the Devil could know you by instinct," while Lucy herself, having mistaken Bellmour for Spintext, tells him "I shou'd not believe my Eyes," for "you are not what you seem to be." Captain Bluffe, Bellmour explains to Sharper, "is a Pretender, and wears the habit of a Soldier, which now a' days as often cloaks Cowardice, as a Black Gown does Atheism." Sir Joseph Wittol mistakes Sharper for the man who had "rescued him" in the dark from "the hands of some Nightwalkers," and so is bilked of a hundred pounds. And of course Bluffe and Wittol, seeking to "undermine" and "countermine" each other, find they have married women whose identities must be "unriddled" for them.

Corollary to the perception of life as enigmatic is another issue: the degree to which faith or trust is not only possible but necessary in human relationships, particularly as these may be represented by marriage. To put the issue another way, how willing must one be to lay aside suspicion, to doubt the evidence even of one's own senses, to accept a large measure of dubiety even in one's most intimate relationships? In a world of certainties, no trust or faith would be called for. In an apocryphal world, too much or too little faith may be equally self-destructive. Such matters, pervasive in *The Old Batchelour,* are raised most pointedly perhaps in the Fondlewife episodes, where the old banker is faced with the quandary of his young wife's innocence or guilt.

Their marriage is typically January and May, and was considered by one contemporary critic, as we have seen before (see chap. 4, pp. 70-71), as offering "Matter of very good Instruction" by exposing "the unreasonableness of such Superannuated Dotage, that can blindly think or hope, that a bare Chain of Gold has Magick enough in the Circle to bind the Fidelity of so unequal a Match, a Match so contrary to the Ordinance of Matrimony." Quite apart from their satiric illustration of senile folly and impotence, however, the Fondlewife scenes are fully integral to the play's larger concerns with a world in which faces are often a "False-Witness" and in which one may commit an act of infidelity and yet be "true as Turtle—in Imagination." It is a world in which, to use the words of Laetitia Fondlewife, "We are all liable to Mistakes."

The very means by which Bellmour is "discovered" by Fondlewife in his wife's bedchamber is a brilliant insinuation of the issues. Having taken along a copy of "trusty *Scarron*'s Novels" as his "Prayer-Book," and having "forgot" in his haste to take up the volume at Fondlewife's knocking at his wife's door, Bellmour's intrusion is exposed when the old man notices the book and, in spite of Laetitia's desperate claim that it is only "Mr. *Spintext's* Prayer-Book, Dear," opens it to the novel entitled *The Innocent Adultery*—a work whose plot turns on the scheme by which a base fellow so well impersonates his brother, in a darkened bedchamber, that a woman mistakes him for her husband and thus "innocently" allows him to enjoy her. Congreve's strategy in repeatedly raising the issues of his play may be better appreciated if we recall here Bellmour's earlier defense of Sylvia, in the very opening scene of the play, when he tells Vainlove that "her Soul was true to you; tho' I by treachery had stoll'n the Bliss—."

The conundrum before him is instantly stated by Fondlewife, who exclaims: "Adultery, and Innocent! O Lord! Here's Doctrine! Ay, here's Discipline!" Rejecting Laetitia's suggestion that the book is "a good Book, and only tends to the Speculation of Sin," Fondlewife demands, "Where is this Apocryphal Elder," and so proceeds to hale Bellmour out of his bedchamber. But then, with all the circumstantial evidence as to his own cuckolding placed squarely before him, he also proceeds, from his initial conviction that he has been "brutified," into a state of bafflement before Bellmour's brazen and yet crafty "confession" that he had "a long time designed" him the "favour" of a set of horns but had been hindered by his coming home "so soon." So plausible, indeed, is Bellmour's explanation of the situation that Fondlewife is finally brought to exclaim: "Ha! This is Apocryphal; I may chuse whether I will believe it or no." From here on the scene is best recalled in its own terms. Fondlewife, already weakening, asks Laetitia: "Art thou not vile and unclean, Heh? Speak."

> *Laetitia.* No—h. *Sighing.*
> *Fondlewife.* Oh, that I could believe thee!
> *Laetitia.* Oh, my heart will break!
>
> > *Seeming to faint.*
>
> *Fondlewife.* Heh. How? No, stay, stay, I will believe thee, I will—Pray bend her forward, Sir.
> *Laetitia.* Oh! Oh! Where is my Dear?
> *Fondlewife.* Here, here, I do believe thee.——I won't believe my own Eyes.

The aging Fondlewife's favorite ejaculation is "I'feck" ("in faith"), and in his exchange with Bellmour the vocabulary of "faith" and "belief" is obtrusively iterated. The scene, moreover (like the earlier one between Heartwell and Sylvia), is a marvelously ludicrous exemplification not only of deception but of the most willing self-deception: man all too apparently at times chooses to "believe" rather than to "know," chooses to be "blind" rather than to "see," chooses not to bear too much reality. Throughout the play, indeed, Congreve seems to be suggesting that marriage, or life itself perhaps, even so wretched a marriage and life as that of the Fondlewifes, or that of Bellmour and Belinda yet to come, could not go on if the full "truth" were insisted upon, if all appearances were stripped away.

Act 4, and the Fondlewife episodes, end with Laetitia's "monster" saying to her, "Come, my Dear. Nay, I will believe thee, I do, Ifeck," and with Bellmour's pointed observation and aphoristic couplet: "See the great Blessing of an easy Faith; Opinion cannot err.

> No Husband, by his Wife, can be deceiv'd:
> She still is Vertuous, if she's so believ'd."

Fondlewife has decided, to his own satisfaction at least, that an actual adultery never happened, that whatever did happen was "innocent," and the full irony of the situation may come through the more if we ponder the meaning of the name of his Laetitia (i.e., the quality or condition of great joy or gladness). In the light of the "great Blessing" he receives by his "belief" in "her Vertue," we may also ponder, for its relevance to the whole play, the multivalent and riddling implications of Bellmour's remark, made in the very opening lines of the play, that "Wisdom's nothing but a pretending to know and believe more than really we do." At the very least we may question whether Fondlewife's "faith" as to his wife's "Vertue" is any more fatuous and absurd than Vainlove's "credulity" as to Araminta's "guilt."

V

The Old Batchelour is a brilliant first play, one wherein a surpassing insight into human frailty is surpassingly displayed. If it seems a bit uncertain in its final ethical impress, this may be in part because, as Novak has said, Congreve "had not yet developed those ideal couples whose intelligence and sensibility seemed to promise an ideal match."[16] Indeed, the couples of the play all seem curiously mismatched. Love is certainly inexplicable, but never again will Congreve stage a pairing so inexplicable as that of Araminta and Vainlove, where a woman so chaste, witty, honest, and above all, sensible, is presented as being in love with so self-regarding a man. It seems just as odd that Bellmour, the superior male of the play, should be yoked with a woman whose head, as Araminta drily understates the matter, is "a little out of Order." Marriages made on earth may not have been designed by heaven, but what seems unsatisfying about these pairings is their dramatic unaccountability: Araminta's love for Vainlove, and Bellmour's for Belinda, seem incongruous with their temperaments as established in the play.

Somewhat troubling also is the treatment accorded Heartwell. However much he is inclined to a surly pride, and however much his lust for Sylvia has turned him infatuate and hypocritical, his faults seem rather those of the rude plain-dealer and malcontent than anything else, more harmful to himself than to anyone else. Compared with Bellmour's deceitful debauching of Sylvia and his successful attempt on the honor of Fondlewife's house, the old bachelor's passion for Sylvia seems innocuous, no matter how absurd and unbecoming, and even more innocuous when set against Vainlove's narcissism and cold disdain for all women. Yet with his comparatively mild follies and failings, he is treated the most unmercifully of any character in the play. And while he is saved from his folly, it is not before he has undergone insufferable taunts from a circle of his "friends." As several critics have noted, the tormenting he receives "is in danger of becoming too serious for comedy,"[17] and though Congreve quickly restores a sense of mirth, one may still feel, when Heartwell is so provoked as almost to be ready to "draw upon a Woman," that the narrow verge between tragedy and comedy is nearly crossed—as it will continue to be; for Congreve's comedies, mirthful as they may be, are always turning up the darker undersides of life.

The conclusion of *The Old Batchelour* is unlike that of any subsequent Congreve play, all of which in the end impart a stronger sense of couples blest and harmony restored, and all of which, either explicitly or implicitly, suggest the eventualities of a most poetic justice. *The Old Batchelour,* instead, ends by giving George Heartwell the last word, a disturbing intimation to Bellmour, on the eve of his marriage to Belinda, of

> What rugged Ways attend the Noon of Life!
> (Our Sun declines,) and with what anxious Strife,
> What Pain we tug that galling Load, a Wife.

A coming "Affliction" in store for Bellmour, perhaps, that in its own turn may be deserving of a very fine "Jest."

7

Catoptromancie, or Discovery of "the Monster in the Glass"

Colubrum in sinu fovere: To bring up a Snake in ones bosome, viz. to entertain one, thinking him to be a Friend, who afterwards proves a mortall Enemy.

Torriano, *Proverbial Phrases* (1666)

"if they will not hear the Serpent's hiss, they must be stung into experience, and future caution."

Maskwell, *The Double-Dealer,* act 5

It may have been *The Double-Dealer* which prompted Coleridge to say that "*Wickedness* is no subject for comedy" and that this "was Congreve's great error, and almost peculiar to him."[1] The play certainly provoked Macaulay to the declaration that "there is something strangely revolting in the way in which a group that seems to belong to the house of Laius or Pelops is introduced into the midst of the Brisks, Froths, Carelesses, and Plyants,"[2] and more recently Herbert Davis has suggested that the reason "the play did not take" at first was perhaps because it was felt Congreve "had strained the limits of comedy to the utmost in those scenes where Mrs. Barry made Lady Touchwood a character of almost tragic intensity."[3]

Such statements delimit the comic mode much too narrowly, for it is a genre, after all, which at times has reflected, in its own particular mirror, a darker and more unlovely view of humanity than has many a "tragical" play. Congreve obviously felt no qualms himself about the generic substance of his play: he not only stamped it "A Comedy" on its title page, but also there quoted Horace to the effect that "at times even Comedy lifts up its voice." Dryden also apparently found nothing strange or "revolting" in the material of the play, for it inspired his magnanimous commendatory poem printed with the play, as well as a letter to William Walsh in which he states that although the "Double-Dealer is much censured by the greater part of the Town," it is defended "by the best Judges, who, you know, are commonly the fewest."

> Yet it gains ground daily, and has already been acted Eight times. The women thinke he has exposed their Bitchery too much; and the Gentlemen, are offended with him; for the discovery of their follyes: and the way of their Intrigues, under the notion of Friendship to their Ladyes Husbands. My verses, which you will find before it, were written before the play was acted. But I neither alterd them nor do I alter my opinion of the play.[4]

In his dedicatory epistle to Charles Mountague, Congreve obviously prides himself on his play's design; "for the Mechanical part of it," he says, "is perfect," a claim he feels can be made "with as little vanity, as a Builder may say he has built a House according to the Model laid down before him; or a Gardiner that he has set his Flowers in a knot of such or such a Figure." He amplified this statement, moreover, by declaring, "I design'd the Moral first, and to that Moral I invented the Fable," pointing us thereby to the "very last and concluding Lines of the Poem," where, as he was later to remind Collier, "there is generally Care taken, that the Moral of the whole shall be summ'd up, and deliver'd to the Audience." The very last lines of the "Poem" before us are these:

> Let secret Villany from hence be warn'd;
> Howe're in private, Mischiefs are conceiv'd,
> Torture and Shame attend their open Birth:
> Like Vipers in the Womb, base Treach'ry lies,
> Still gnawing that, whence first it did arise;
> No sooner born, but the Vile Parent dies.

"Strange!" says Brisk at one point in the play, "To see how Love and Murder will out." Strange indeed, no doubt; but also, Congreve seems to insist, strangely true. Brisk's words, taken along with other passages of the same drift, as well as with the concluding "Moral," clearly associate the events of *The Double-Dealer* with that most ancient and most popular of providentialist themes—"Mordre will out." The imagery of conception and birth in the play's closing statement, along with the burden of meaning it carries, should furthermore be set beside the accordant statements wherein a multitude of other seventeenth-century Englishmen use the same imagery of birth to declare, as in a typical passage, that "All Histories afford us strange examples in their several kinds," of "ambitious spirits" who

> have ventured upon very *desperate* and almost *impossible attempts:* and yet by the strength of their *wits* have so laid *the Scene* before-hand, and so carried on the *design* all along; that they have very many times; either wholly accomplished what they intended, or brought their *conceptions* so near to *the birth,* that nothing but a visible hand of an *over-ruling providence* from above, could render them abortive.[5]

The Double-Dealer presents us with just such an "ambitious spirit," one who so lays "the *Scene* before-hand" that his "very *desperate* and almost *impossible attempts*" are brought so "near to *the birth*" that they are only at the very last instant rendered "abortive"—by the narrowest of margins and, I believe, by a "hand" that is indeed "over-ruling." Coleridge, if wrong in his conclusions, was at least right in his perception that Congreve's subject, in *The Double-Dealer* at least, is "wickedness"—and of a very special kind.

I

In his letter to Mountague, Congreve stated that he had preserved "the three Unities of the Drama" to "the utmost severity"; and in truth a remarkable feature of *The Double-Dealer* is announced immediately below the list of dramatis personae: "The SCENE, A Gallery in *Lord Touchwood's House*," "The Time, from Five a Clock to Eight in the Evening." Once the play starts, the very place and time of events seem thereafter to become prime components of its total meaning. Thus, while all the scenes take place in the "gallery" (except the one in Lady Touchwood's immediately adja-

cent bedchamber), we are so frequently reminded, usually by Maskwell, of "private passages," "back ways," "back stairs," "private
stairs," that the house itself seems to become a veritable maze of
hidden "ways," suggestive not only of the hidden motives and
schemes of many of the characters but reflective also of the baffled
state to which Mellefont is reduced, by Maskwell's stratagems, and
which he thus bewails: "I am confounded in a maze of thoughts,
each leading into one another, and all ending in perplexity."

Van Voris has observed that Maskwell "knows better than the
owners every door and every chamber" of the house, as "surely as
he knows every emotion and every stupidity of the persons in
it."[6] An even better way of perceiving Maskwell's utter command
of Lord Touchwood's household, I think, is to regard him as having
taken "possession" of the place, as surely as he has taken "possession," in more ways than one, of Lord Touchwood's own wife. On
his very first appearance his almost total usurpation of authority in
the household is openly declared by Lady Touchwood herself, when
she bitterly demands of him, in the last scene of act 1: "have not I
in effect made you Lord of all, of me, and of my Lord?"

Having been constituted "Lord of all," Maskwell thenceforward
seems to become a malevolent Prospero, both stage director and
actor in scenes and plots of his own contriving, a deviser who so lays
"*the Scene* before-hand" that he appears to command both place
and time, directing the principal characters in and out of rooms
and passages in maneuvers requiring the most exquisite coordina-
tion. As he does so the play seems to build, in the most tense and
insistent fashion, toward an outcome completely dependent upon
the intersection, or the nonintersection, of characters in the most
exact locations and at the most critical moments. The mounting
intensity of the play's action may have been heightened for a contemporary audience, furthermore, by the fact that toward the end
of the seventeenth century, stage performances generally concluded
"by eight o'clock, suggesting a curtain time of from four to five
o'clock."[7] With a marvelous sense of stagecraft, which may have
had the audience looking, almost minutely, at their own watches,
Congreve seems to have attempted to match stage-time with clock-
time, preparing everyone, by eight references to eight o'clock in

the last three acts,[8] for the momentous events to occur then and shortly thereafter.

Congreve's "severe" observance of the unities of time and place in *The Double-Dealer* is thus readily verifiable, but the precise nature and import of the play's "unity of action" has proved elusive, in spite of the hints offered by his concluding lines. Dobrée, for example, has said that "the difficulty is to arrive at that very subtle and elusive thing, the 'idea' of the play, the dominating mood that led to its creation,"[9] a confession which reflects the general critical inability to perceive the way in which any "Moral" in the concluding lines may be embodied in the "Fable" Congreve said he had "invented" for it.* Put in seventeenth-century terms, and in the words of Dryden, what is in question here is "that precept of morality" which a playwright "would insinuate into the people" and which "directs," furthermore, "the whole action of the play to one centre" (see p. 45 above). If we are to come by a clearer sense of any such "precept of morality," or "idea," by which Congreve may have shaped his play's unity of action, we must begin, I think, with Maskwell, the character who gives the play its title, and whose private "plots" actually comprise much of the play's larger "plot"— so much so that at times the "invention" of the playwright seems, in however illusory a fashion, the mere issue of the brain of the villain he has created.

Previous assessments of Maskwell have varied widely, from Van Voris's view that he is simply "another of Congreve's ordinary men, a young bachelor turned predatory,"[10] to Dobrée's opinion that "he is villainy itself" and that "there is something tremendous about him."[11] Closer to the mark is Birdsall, who observed Maskwell's kinship with the medieval Vice and with Iago, as well as the many instances when he is associated with the devil.[12] At the same time, however, Birdsall seems unable to grasp the full implications of the diabolism Congreve made so much a quality of Maskwell's character—mainly, I think, because she considers the events of the play

---

*I ignore here the more ambiguous uses of "Fable" and "Action." For some discussion of these, see H. T. Swedenberg, Jr., *The Theory of the Epic in England: 1650-1800* (Berkeley and Los Angeles: University of California Press, 1944), pp. 166 ff.

to take place in a "deceitful, naturalistic world" where one survives only by one's own wits and by "whatever possibilities luck or chance may bring his way."

It is my own view that *The Double-Dealer*, in spite of its Restoration esprit and gloss, is a genuine descendant of the English morality play tradition, and so I wish to give a rather heady measure of import to the way Maskwell's diabolism seems to recapitulate that of all the other incarnations of evil who appear, in one shape or another, at one or another time and place, in the English literary tradition, who there work their malevolent and destructive ends, and who are finally unmasked—only to reappear, we may be sure, in still another guise on still another stage. The satanism so insistently imputed to Maskwell by Congreve, along with a dazzling amount of demonological allusion hitherto unnoticed in critical discussions of the play, carries with it intimations of a world that simply cannot be reduced to the "naturalistic." On the contrary, the repeated association of Maskwell with "Hell" and "Damnation," along with all the occasions when Lady Touchwood not only is specifically categorized as a "Witch" but also is said to be "possess'd," would have been, to a contemporary audience, more than casual reminders of an ancient Adversary and of the human agents he might enter and subdue to his purposes—reminders, indeed, of an order of existence which for many still pressed closely upon the "natural" world.

How is it likely to have been otherwise in 1693, the year of the play's first performance, in an England where, in the Western Circuit alone, there were fifty-two trials for witchcraft between 1670 and 1712;[13] where men so learned and astute as Henry More and Joseph Glanvill had registered, only a few years previously, their personal belief in the reality of witches and witchcraft; where, on February 4 of the same year (the year, we should recall, of the Salem witch trials) John Evelyn wrote in his diary of "Unheard of stories of the universal increase of Witches, men women Children devoting themselves to the Devil, in such numbers in New England, that it threatened the subversion of the Government"? We may smile, or perhaps wince, at the idea that men, among them the best minds of the period, would take such goings-on seriously, but the fact is that such matters were a part of everyday consciousness. And while belief in demonology and witchcraft was on the wane, there is no question in my mind that the demoniacal attributes and behavior accorded Maskwell would have prompted, in a contemporary audience, a sense of old acquaintance with a maleficent intelligence somehow still at large in the world.

We at least should not ignore (though we seem to have done so) all those times in the play when it is clearly suggested that Maskwell's possession of Lady Touchwood is far from merely sexual in nature. Thus, though she is incensed enough, at their first appearance together, to defy him as an "Insolent Devil," a "sedate, a thinking Villain, whose Black Blood runs temperately bad," he so manipulates her spirit as to become, only moments later, that "mollifying Devil" before whom, as she despairingly confesses, she cannot hide the innermost secrets of her soul: "O *Maskwell*," she cries, "in Vain I do disguise me from thee, thou knows't me, knows't the very inmost Windings and Recesses of my Soul." It is something more than adultery, something akin to a most rank idolatry, spiritual as well as carnal whoredom, she confesses when she bitterly admits that she has in effect made Maskwell "Lord" of herself, "Lord of all"—"Lord," she says to him in words of a larger and more malevolent import than we have understood, even of her own "Lord, who has been a Father to you in your wants, and given you being." If her abject demonolatry is not apparent when she tells Maskwell that she has "subjected" her "Person" to his "Pleasure" and that he can "wind" her "still'd Soul" one moment and then, a moment later, "unwind it," then surely it emerges clearly two acts later when Maskwell, as is his "way," disingenuously confides to Mellefont that he has entered into a pact with his aunt to get him disinherited and that, "as an earnest of that Bargain," he is "to have full and free possession of the person of" her ladyship. This piece of news causes the stunned Mellefont to speak more meaningfully than he knows: "Hell and the Devil," he exclaims, "is she abandon'd of all Grace—Why the Woman is possess'd—."

It is not the first time Mellefont is so dumbfounded, nor the first time he speaks in words bearing a dramatic signification greater, no doubt, than he realizes. For when Lady Touchwood, at Maskwell's instigation, has worked Lady Plyant into a belief that "*Mellefont* Loves her" and is only wooing her stepdaughter Cynthia as a blind

to her own seduction, Mellefont is put into such a distracted state
by his future mother-in-law's coy but gushing encouragement of a
liaison she obviously relishes as incestuous, that he can only exclaim
helplessly, in two asides Congreve gives him: "Hell and Damnation!
this is my Aunt; such malice can be engendred no where else"; and
"Incest! O my precious Aunt, and the Devil in Conjunction." In
"Conjunction," indeed, but with Lady Touchwood as the devil's
bondswoman, for, as Maskwell tells Mellefont a few minutes later,
his "precious" aunt "does but Journey-Work" under his direction.

One of the more notable features of the play, as the above citations suggest, is the way Maskwell's machinations are repeatedly
identified by other characters, in a way beyond their actual ken,
as the work of a "hellish" agent—and yet never connected with
Maskwell personally. Such a procedure not only suggests, in dramatic terms, the traditionally shifty nature of evil; it also has the
dramatic virtue of keeping Maskwell from being too grossly a merely
allegorical figure of evil: it preserves the verisimilitude of a character
who exhibits a quite human mendacity and lust, but also one whose
very smile "speaks in Ambiguity" and who, Iago-like, seems finally
inexplicable in a consecration of self to evil for its own sake. Manifest "Villain" (as he is bluntly declared to be in the Dramatis Personae), Maskwell also bears about his person the dark but still
visible lineaments of another presence entirely, one that seems to
justify Lady Touchwood's furious understanding of him, near the
end of the play, as "Damnation Proof, a Devil already," whose
native "Element" is "Fire."

Perhaps the best illustration of the way Congreve has his characters quite unwittingly identify Maskwell's workings with those of
the devil incarnate occurs when Cynthia and Mellefont reflect upon
all the lets and hindrances posed to their marriage by the incestuous
lust, and also the resentful hatred, with which Lady Touchwood
regards Mellefont ("Let him but once be mine," she says, "and
next immediate Ruin seize him"). Having agreed that they marry
only for "Love, Love, down right Villanous Love," Cynthia nevertheless insists on a "trial" of Mellefont's "Wit," arguing that "'tis
but reasonable that since I consent to like a Man without the vile
Consideration of Money, he should give me a very evident demon-

stration of his Wit: Therefore let me see you undermine my Lady
Touchwood, as you boasted, and force her to give her Consent,
and then—." To this Mellefont responds by vowing that "this very
next ensuing Hour of Eight a Clock, is the last Minute of her Reign,
unless the Devil assist her in *propria persona.*"

> *Cynthia.* Well, if the Devil should assist her, and your Plot
>   miscarry—
> *Mellefont.* Ay, what am I to trust to then?
> *Cynthia.* Why if you give me very clear demonstration that it
>   was the Devil, I'll allow for irresistable odds. But if I find it to
>   be only chance, or destiny, or unlucky Stars, or any thing but
>   the very Devil, I'm inexorable: Only still I'll keep my word,
>   and live a Maid for your sake.

Of course, Mellefont's "Plot" does "miscarry," and if we are not
given a "very clear demonstration that it was the Devil" who, "in
propria persona," caused the "Mine" he had planted beneath his
aunt's feet to blow up under his own, neither are we given the
assurance that his utter defeat and discomfiture have been accomplished by the exercise of a strictly human intelligence. Thinking
he has Lady Touchwood "on the hook," and that he has reduced
her to tears "of the purest kind—Penitential Tears," Mellefont
suddenly finds himself entrapped, for the second time in one evening, in another apparently incestuous design, this time against his
uncle's wife. And with Lord Touchwood convinced that Maskwell
has given him "Ocular Proof" of his nephew's "impious Design"
on her ladyship, Mellefont is reduced to the most bootless appeals
that his uncle hear the wrongs done them both by a woman who,
he expostulates helplessly, "has all the Host of Hell her Servants"
and who, like the "noon-day devil" of Psalm 91:6, "can wear more
shapes in shining day, than fear shows Cowards in the dark—."

The episode at eight o'clock, while not the climax of *The Double-
Dealer,* is undoubtedly its dramatic centerpiece, a counterpart in
its way to a major scene in *Hamlet,* and sharing with the Shakespearean scene a striking use of mirror imagery. Not all the similarities
need be noted here, but we must at least set certain words of Lady
Touchwood, when confronted in her bedchamber by Mellefont,

against certain words of Gertrude, when confronted in her bed-chamber by Hamlet. Lady Touchwood, having collected herself enough to "dissemble" a contrite spirit, feigns a sudden recognition of all her sins, and tells her nephew, "O the Scene was shifted quick before me," and "I was surprised to see a Monster in the Glass, and now I find it is my self." Gertrude, with Hamlet having "set up" a "glass" by which she may see her "inmost part," utters words of apparently sincere remorse:

> O Hamlet, speak no more.
> Thou turns't mine eyes into my soul,
> And there I see such black and grained spots
> As will not leave their tinct.

There seems little doubt that in both scenes we are to recall pro-verbial ideas of a glass or mirror as the medium by which one may be told unwanted truths about one's self: "He that beholds himselfe in a glas, may see himself well," and "What your Glass tells you will not be told by counsel"[14] (in a more recent version, "Mirror, mirror, on the wall, who is fairest of us all?").

Behind such homely sayings as these, however, ramifies an ancient and occult kind of diablerie (still well known and practiced in the seventeenth century) which Congreve's language, more particularly than Shakespeare's, seems to invoke, and by means of which the more dark and chthonic level of his play may be probed. I refer to the practice of divination by mirrors, variously known in the seven-teenth century as "Catoptromancie," "Catoptricks," "Capyroman-cie," or to use a more common term, "Crystallomancy."[15] And while mirrors could be used by sorcerers and magicians for a variety of discoveries, their employment was at times particularly revela-tory, it was supposed, of shapes and spirits from another world. Thus, in Samuel Purchas's very popular *Pilgrimage,* a reader would have learned that the ancient Persians "had a tradition of two *Genij,* which attend every man, one good, the other euill; proceeding (in likelihood) from diuine truth, concerning good and euill Angels, which are either *ministring spirits* for mans good, or *tempters* vnto euill." From this belief among the Persian people, their Magi, or "Curious men," took "occasion to deuise new Artes," among which was "Catoptromancie," by which they could call up the good or evil genius of a person and receive their "resemblances in cleare glasses."[16] The skeptical Robert Burton, describing various kinds of delusion, comments that "'tis ordinary to see strange uncouth sights by Catoptricks," and adds that by use of "concave and cylinder glasses we may reflect any shape of men, Devils, Anticks, (as Magicians most part do, to gull a silly Spectator in a dark room)."[17]

In 1659 Meric Casaubon published *A True & Faithful Relation of what passed for many Years Between Dr: John Dee . . . and Some Spirits,* a work which detailed at length the great and famous Elizabethan mathematician's contacts with spirits by way of crystal-lomancy—and which the government wished to suppress but could not because it "was so quickly published & spread & so eagerly bought up as being a great & curious Novelty." For the rest of the century, and into the next, indeed, a debate continued over the merit of Casaubon's charges that Dee, in his experiments, had been the victim of "diabolic deception."[18] (Dee's principal "Shew-stone," or crystal, by which he thought he received divine intelligence, is now in the British Museum). As late as 1697, William Turner, in his *A Compleat History of the Most Remarkable Providences, Both of Judgment and Mercy, Which have Hapned in this Present Age,* in a chapter "Of Divination, Soothsaying, Witchcraft," not only cites the "several Ways of Divination *Satan* hath invented" (among which is "Capyromancy, by Looking-Glasses") which are "still used" by "some superstitious People among us," but also lists over twenty persons, many of some note, who had testified to a successful divinatory experience.*

Such information is only a small part of what could be set forth to indicate how likely it is that a seventeenth-century audience would have been familiar with a practice most of them would have condemned as an attempt to communicate with or by way of evil spirits—and to enrich our sense of the way certain proverbial commonplaces do seem to lie behind Congreve's mirror imagery

*See pp. 59–60, especially example "19. *James Harrington,* Author of *Oceana,* told me that the Earl of *Denleigh,* then Ambassador to *Venice,* did tell him, *That one did shew him there several times in a Glass, things past, and to come.*"

and help to shape his play's meaning. For example, if we now recall that when Lady Touchwood sees "a Monster" in her "glass" it is shortly after eight o'clock at a season in England when it would have been dark, then we may the better understand what she sees there if we recall such proverbial utterances as "The Devil appears when a woman looks at herself in a mirror after sunset," along with "He that looks in the mirror at night sees the devil there." And if we consider also that in their first scene together Lady Touchwood angrily denounces Maskwell to his face as "one, who is no more moved with the reflections of his Crimes, than of his Face; but walks unstartled from the Mirror, and straight forgets the hideous form," then we may have reason to suspect that the mirror Congreve is holding up to nature in *The Double-Dealer* is being used in a kind of "catoptrick" way to reveal a "hideous form" not given us otherwise to see.

Lady Touchwood's glimpse of a monster in her glass may have a signification that complicates the matter even further, for there is another well-known tradition of mirror imagery, one which held, and holds to this day, that a woman might, especially on All-Hallow's Eve, or Hallow-e'en, behold her lover in her glass. Now the date of the first performance of *The Double-Dealer* is not precisely known, but the editors of *The London Stage* find the evidence "suggests that the premiere was near the end of October or early in November."[19] Could the first performance of Congreve's play have been on Halloween, the night of the year set apart from all others, it was thought, for a universal moving abroad of evil spirits, and the time when divination, and the art of summoning up evil spirits by various means, was thought most feasible? Perhaps not, but even if the occasion of first performance was not actually October 31, the date seems close enough to have made the play's manifold allusions to demonology and witchcraft especially meaningful to an audience of that period. And in light of the tradition that a woman might see her lover in a glass on All-Hallow's Eve, the teasing question arises as to whether the "Monster" in Lady Touchwood's glass is the image of her own iniquity, or the "hideous form" of Maskwell, her lover as well as her tutelary spirit.

It may not be possible to demonstrate beyond cavil that Congreve intended, in his mirror imagery, so thick and sinister a coalescence of meaning as I have suggested, but such imagery does provide us with a medium, unavailable to the more innocent characters in the play, by which an accursed spirit may be descried. A similar kind of insight is of course provided by Maskwell's soliloquies, to which the other characters again are not privy, and in two of these Congreve has Maskwell use imagery which further defines his emblematic role in the more allegorical dimensions of the play.

In the first instance, in a soliloquy where he promptly disposes of duty, piety, gratitude, and other such onerous traits, Maskwell then asks himself: "Ha! but is there not such a thing as honesty?" His answer, "Yes, and whosoever has it about him, bears an Enemy in his Breast," is an utterly malignant twist on an age-old proverb, *Colubrum in sinu fovere* ("To bring up a Snake in one's bosome, viz. to entertain one, thinking him to be a Friend, who afterwards proves a mortall Enemy"), and yet also an identification of the way such a serpent has been nurtured in the Touchwood household.

The second instance is even more explicitly suggestive of the figurative undercurrent of the play, and occurs when Maskwell has put his last stratagem in motion and is musing on another old Latin tag: "Why, *qui vult decipi decipiatur.*——'Tis no fault of mine, I have told 'em in plain terms how easie 'tis for me to cheat 'em; and if they will not hear the Serpent's hiss, they must be stung into experience, and future caution." A serviceable analogue to Maskwell's words may be provided by some words from Robert South when he warned his Westminster congregation, in 1676, that "Men are generally credulous at first" and will not learn certain truths "at the Cost of *other* Mens Experience, till," having admitted "the Serpent into their Bosom," they "come to be bitten into a Sense of it by their own."[20]

II

In the dedication of his play Congreve "hearkened after" several complaints made against it, including a "very wrong objection" made "by some who have not taken leisure to distinguish the Characters":

The Hero of the Play, as they are pleas'd to call him (Meaning *Mellefont*) is a Gull, and made a Fool and cheated. Is every Man a Gull and a Fool that is deceiv'd? At that rate I'm afraid the two Classes of Men* will be reduc'd to one, and the Knaves themselves be at a loss to justifie their Title: But if an Openhearted Honest Man, who has an entire Confidence in one whom he takes to be his Friend, and whom he has obliged to be so; and who (to confirm him in his Opinion) in all appearance, and upon several tryals has been so: If this Man be deceived by the Treachery of the other: must he of necessity commence Fool immediately, only because the other has proved a Villain? Ay, but there was Caution given to *Mellefont* in the first Act by his Friend *Careless*. Of what Nature was that Caution? Only to give the Audience some light into the Character of *Maskwell*, before his appearance; and not to convince *Mellefont* of his Treachery; for that was more than *Careless* was then able to do: He never knew *Maskwell* guilty of any Villainy; he was only a sort of Man which he did not like.

All too conscious himself, one may suppose, of the demoniacal attributes he had given his villain, Congreve then went as far as would be seemly in an effort to put his critics on the right scent, and advised them to look once again "into the Character of *Maskwell*, before they accuse any Body of weakness for being deceiv'd by him."

Yet the critics, by failing to see, or credit, the magnitude of the evil Maskwell was designed to represent, have continued to fault *The Double-Dealer* for what they consider to be Mellefont's inadequacies as a "hero." Holland thus states that "Ultimately, of course, the play fails because Mellefont is so woefully inadequate as a hero," and Birdsall finds that what "little pertinence" the play has for her study "lies, strangely enough, in its villain rather than in its hero, the latter being after all of very slight inherent interest"[21] (if we recall Congreve's words quoted above, we may suspect he would have grimaced weakly at the use here made by such

*I.e. knaves and fools, traditionally.

critics of the word *hero*). Preoccupied, like so many others, with
the wholly specious notion that the "hero" of a successful Restoration comedy is or must be a totally successful Machiavel, such
critics simply overlook the basic fact that in no Congreve play after
The Old Batchelour does the "hero" (whether Mellefont, Valentine,
Alphonso, or Mirabell) succeed to a final reward as a result of
his own cunning or maneuvering.

It is furthermore not at all true, as Holland thinks, that Mellefont "is good and does not intrigue." Intrigue he does, but designed
as he is to represent the kind of men who, to use South's words,
"are generally credulous at first," or to use Maskwell's words, "will
not hear the Serpent's hiss," and who therefore must be "bitten"
into "experience, and future caution," his credulity, along with
the failure of his intrigues, must be seen as a necessary and integral
part in the "Morality-like" infrastructure of Congreve's play. When
Lady Froth compares Mellefont to her coxcombly husband and to
Brisk, her coxcombly lover, her slighting comment that "he is too
much a Mediocrity," fatuously condescending as it is, is very much
to the point. If Mellefont is to be, in some sense, a proper Everyman
for Congreve's design, he must be more generally representative
of humanity than some so-called Hobbesian or Machiavellian "hero."
He must be designed, in Congreve's own words, as "an Open-hearted
Honest Man" posed with an adversary of such a nature that no man
(even from the first of men) could be expected to be his match—
without, of course, some outside help of a very special kind.

That Mellefont does intrigue, however ineffectually, is evident in
the opening scene of the play. Having been "surpriz'd" in his bed
that very morning by Lady Touchwood, and pressed with "all that
the most violent Love could urge," he had "with much ado" prevented his aunt, he tells Careless, from doing either of them a great
"mischief." Fearful now of further attempts by his aunt to break
off his match with Cynthia, he enlists the aid of Careless in seeing
that there is no "room for serious design" that evening: "I would
have Noise and Impertinence keep my Lady Touchwood's Head
from Working," he tells his friend, "For Hell is not more busie than
her Brain, nor contains more Devils, than that Imaginations." He
therefore wishes Careless "to engage my Lady *Plyant*" for the nonce,

so his aunt "may not work her to her Interest." He will observe Lord Touchwood himself, and has engaged Maskwell to watch his aunt and give him "notice upon any Suspicion."

In spite of such precautionary steps, however, Mellefont is immediately outwitted, for Lady Touchwood, in her "Journey-Work" under Maskwell, had already persuaded Lady Plyant, as we have seen, of his desire for her, and so when he is set upon by that lickerish loquacity that will permit no interruption, he is reduced to the impotent complaint: "So then,—spight of my care and foresight, I am caught, caught in my security." And though his frustration is most comically imposed, his language the next moment, on the entrance of Maskwell, keeps before us the tokens of the adversary he can unwittingly identify in jest, though not in fact: *"Maskwell, welcome,"* he says, "The Witch has rais'd the Storm, and her Ministers have done their work." We miss the point here if we do not see how Mellefont's words identify Lady Touchwood as one who does the devil's bidding—and most specifically in that she is identified with the ancient role of witches as "storm-raisers."* The allusions here, moreover, should cause us to hearken back to Mellefont's words when he earlier told Careless of the "Storm" Lady Touchwood had raised in his bed that morning after her advances had been repulsed. That invasion of Mellefont's sleep, taken with the repeated identification of Lady Touchwood as witch, sorceress, female demon, and raiser of storms, in bed and out, carries more than a hint that Congreve wished Mellefont's recollection of it to remind his audience of another traditional activity of infernal spirits: their visitations, as succubi or the nightmare, to the beds of sleeping men to tempt them to impious carnal intercourse.

Having been "caught" in his own "security," Mellefont falls in the more readily with Maskwell's proposal that he come, "at the critical minute," to surprise his aunt in Maskwell's embraces. He also manifests an inordinate confidence in the scheme, as well as a lamentable, and of course highly ironical, veneration for the character who

---

*See Robbins, *The Encyclopedia of Witchcraft and Demonology,* s.v. "Storm-Raising," pp. 487–89. Cf. also *Love for Love,* act 3, scene 1, lines 425–27, where Ben says: "Marry thee! Oons I'll Marry a *Lapland*-Witch as soon, and live upon selling of contrary Winds, and Wrack'd Vessels."

is serving as his bad angel: "Let me adore thee, my better *Genius!* By Heav'n I think it is not in the power of Fate to disappoint my hopes—my hopes, my certainty." So presuming is his confidence, indeed, that he seems fully deserving of Cynthia's rebuke, a bit later, when she says she would have eloped with him had he "not been so assured" of his ability "to counter-work" Lady Touchwood's "Spells, and ride the Witch in her own Bridle." But in spite of her reproofs and misgivings, Mellefont's self-assurance is such that the moment before he enters Lady Touchwood's bedchamber he is moved to exclaim, as he leaves Maskwell's presence, "Now Fortune I defie thee."

Left alone, Maskwell's next words are a contemptuous comment on Mellefont's folly; "I confess," he says to himself, "you may be allow'd to be secure in your own Opinion; the appearance is very fair, but I have an After-Game to play that shall turn the Tables." And when Maskwell's "After-Game," and Lady Touchwood's opportunistic cunning, have indeed turned the tables on Mellefont and convicted him, in his uncle's eyes, of a vile incestuous assault, the idiom of witchcraft then used by Mellefont provides the appropriate verbal connectives to tie his overthrow to Maskwell's machinations. Inexplicably overreached once more, Mellefont can only expostulate helplessly against "such Witchcraft" and the "damn'd Sorceress" who "has all the Host of Hell her Servants." He is, furthermore, given words that once again attribute the miscarriage of his efforts to a "storm-raising": "S'death," he rails, "for a Man to have the Fruit of all his Industry grown full and ripe, ready to drop into his mouth, and just when he holds out his hand to gather it, to have a sudden Whirlwind come, tear up tree and all, and bear away the very root and foundation of his hopes; What temper can contain?"

As beseemed an "Open-hearted Honest Man," Mellefont had pooh-poohed Careless's early, but undemonstrable, suspicions of Maskwell. But his misplaced trust in his own ability to "Counter-work" the "Spells" of a "Sorceress," and the repeated illustrations of his inadequacy in the face of those who have "all the Host of Hell" as their "Servants," far from being a defect in characterization on Congreve's part, is rather a necessary and constituent element in his play's design: the exemplification of an ordinarily credulous and honest man's inability to overcome, by his own sole powers and "Industry," a kind of evil whose existence he may suspect but finds difficult to apprehend or to identify.

III

In 1698, when he defended his plays against Collier's attacks on them, Congreve took particular offense at Collier's complaint that Sir Paul Plyant, who "bears the Character of a Fool," makes "mention too often of the word *Providence*":

> for says Mr. *Collier, the meaning must be* (by the way, that *must* is a little hard upon me) *that Providence is a ridiculous Superstition; and that none but Blockheads pretend to Religion.*

And then Congreve went on:

> What will it avail me in this place to signify my own meaning, when this modest Gentleman says, I *must* mean quite contrary.

In spite of so plain a declaration that the allusions to Providence in *The Double-Dealer* bore a meaning "quite contrary" to the impious or scoffing one imputed to him by Collier, critics have either denied or ignored the possibility that Congreve may have so designed the "Fable," and the outcome, of his play as to strictly reflect current belief in a Providence that intervened directly in daily life. Thus it is Birdsall's view that the final "proceedings" of the play do not "emanate from providence or from the stars," for "if justice is at last done, it is because one group of plotters has finally outwitted the other."[22] For Holland the denouement is brought about by Cynthia and Lord Touchwood—and by "chance,"[23] while Novak believes Maskwell "loses at the end only because he has a weakness—a passion for Cynthia, the one innocent woman in the play."[24] Van Voris goes so far as to say that the play's "Moral" is constructed to give the "illusion" that "divine providence has brought an enlightened order" to events, but that in reality there is, beneath the "poetic order," a "natural disorder which only the makeshift and illusory order of a class structure can hope to control."[25] There are varying degrees of contradiction in such views, but they all again raise the issue of whether the world of Congreve's art is merely a "naturalistic" one, where only the strong, the cunning, and the lucky win out in the end, or whether it is a world so theurgically controlled as to ensure, in Brisk's words, that "Love and Murder will out."

The allusions to Providence in *The Double-Dealer* which have seemed most to discredit it as a concept of any force and relevance for the play have been precisely those which Collier observed issuing so frequently from the mouth of Sir Paul, the uxorious fool who is periodically cuckholded by a wife whose "large Eye" would "centre every thing in her own Circle." Thus, when he has been led to believe that Mellefont cares nothing for his daughter but only for her portion, and would use her as a "Stalking-Horse" to get at Lady Plyant, he drags Cynthia away from Mellefont's presence, declaring that "providence has prevented all, therefore come away"—and so leaves Mellefont to the ruttish mercies of his wife. In act 3 he twice more acknowledges, much more rightfully, his obligations to a Providence which has been more than bountiful in the blessings it has accorded such a booby: "I am I thank Heaven in a fine way of living, as I may say, peacefully and happily, and I think need not envy any of my Neighbours, blessed be Providence"; and, "I have a Daughter, and a fine dutiful Child she is, though I say it, blessed be Providence I may say; for indeed, Mr. *Careless,* I am mightily beholding to Providence—a poor unworthy Sinner—."

Such words, no matter the dim and cornute head from which they come, are in themselves a most proper confession of a debt to a most benign Providence for the lot in life it has accorded him. This same Providence is scarcely to be seen as impugned when Sir Paul, in the very next act, refuses to accept from its hand the plainest possible evidence of his wife's infidelity.

The circumstances by which Lady Plyant's inconstancy are discovered to her husband have been so badly misconstrued as to lead Novak to the belief that the "only Providence that Sir Paul can thank is one which keeps fools ignorant, believing; and therefore content."[26] But let us review the evidence: Lady Plyant, having come to understand that Mellefont has no longing for her person, proves very receptive, the very next hour, to Careless's appetite for it, and their adulterous opportunities are considerably enhanced when Sir Paul enlists the aid of Careless in a campaign to persuade her ladyship to greater kindness in bed so that he may get "a Son some way or other." A notable mix-up then occurs, however, for Lady Plyant, having taken possession of a letter of accounts from Sir Paul's steward, under cover of which she may read a letter of assignation from Careless, is so "charm'd" by what will happen between them "when 'tis dark" that she *"Puts the wrong Letter hastily up"* (according to the stage direction) and so places in her husband's hands the documentary proof of her own faithlessness.

When Lady Plyant discovers her error, she rushes to Careless "in such a fright" that she is "all over in a Universal Agitation" at the "Unfortunate Mistake" and the "unlucki'st Accident" that has occurred, and they retire to think of a remedy. As for Sir Paul, when he peruses the letter, his first reaction is to exclaim, again quite justly in my opinion, "O Providence, what a Conspiracy have I discover'd." He seems to have enough sense, moreover, to see, in his own words, that he has been "conducing" to his "own Cuck-olddom" and to echo a proverb we have already touched on and which has relevance not only to his own lamentable marriage but to those of the Froths and the Touchwoods: "Henceforward, let no Man make a Friend that would not be a Cuckold: For whomsoever he receives into his bosom will find the way to his Bed, and there return his Caresses with interest to his Wife." And he goes on:

> O my Lady *Plyant,* you were Chaste as Ice, but you are melted now, and false as Water—But Providence has been constant to me in discovering this Conspiracy; still I am beholden to Provi-dence, if it were not for Providence, sure Sir *Paul* thy Heart would break.

We have seen, in *Incognita* and in *The Old Batchelour,* the ways in which "mistakes," fortunate as well as unfortunate, may serve providential ends. Here again, through an "Unfortunate Mistake" and "the unlucki'st Accident," a "Conspiracy," however low and tawdry, is "discover'd," and the reader has the choice of deciding here (as elsewhere in *The Double-Dealer,* and in plays to come) whether the discovery was due to Providence or to mere "chance" (keeping in mind, of course, the fact that most persons in the seventeenth century would have believed that "what seems accidental to us, is not Chance, but Providence"; see pp. 31ff., above). But with *"the very matter of Fact"* set fully before Sir Paul's eyes, I do not see how it can be maintained, with Novak, that Providence would keep him "ignorant": Providence rather seems, in Sir Paul's words, as "constant" to him "in discovering this Conspiracy" as it had been in bestowing those blessings of life previously mentioned. Neither can it be, in my view, a reflection on Providence when, in the next few minutes, Sir Paul proves so much a cully as to be persuaded by his wife and Careless that the letter of assignation was intended only "to make trial" of a "suspected Vertue" which, on her ladyship's part, had proved "impregnable." Having done, one presumes, all that the most solicitous Providence could be expected to do, it surely is no impeachment of Heaven's care if Sir Paul should then ignore the "Ocular Proof"* given him of his wife's infidelity and instead accept so spurious an explanation of the situation as is given him, exclaiming: "O Providence! Providence! What Discoveries are here made! Why, this is better and more Miraculous than the rest."

There are several matters of contemporary context, previously not considered, which help, I believe, to clear Congreve of any charge of irreverence of intent in Sir Paul's reiterated claims upon Providence, and which also place the "unfortunate" mix-up of the letters in a special light. In the first place, instances whereby misdirected or interrupted letters were productive of the most providential discoveries were a commonplace of both sacred and secular literature, as we can see when Jeremy Taylor lists, among the many ways God may choose to open "the cabinet of sin," such occurrences as the "Intercepting of letters, mistaking names, false inscriptions,

---

*Throughout *The Double-Dealer* Congreve, by use of phrases such as "Mathematical Demonstration" (act 2, scene 1, line 302), "demonstrative Proof" (act 4, scene 1, line 574), and "Ocular Proof" (act 4, scene 1, line 563), seems deliberately to recall, for various purposes, Rymer's sardonic comment that the "Moral" of *Othello* is instructive, in part, as "a lesson to Husbands, that before their Jealousies be Tragical, the proofs may be Mathematical" (*A Short View of Tragedy*).

errors of messengers,"[27] and as we may also see, in a most note-
worthy instance, when Hamlet, yielding to a "rashness" that "should
learn us/There's a divinity that shapes our ends," filches from
Rosencrantz and Guildenstern the letter commissioning his death,
and then, because "heaven" had been "ordinant" in providing him
with his "father's signet," is able to compose a "changeling" letter
which sends the pair to their own execution, "Not shriving time
allowed."

An even closer parallel to Lady Plyant's delivery of the wrong
letter to her husband is to be found, moreover, in Thomas Beard's
extremely popular *Theatre of God's Judgments,* that lurid and
wondrous compendium of the manifold ways by which Heaven's
justice could be administered to *"all notorious sinners, both great
and small."* There, in the chapter "Of Adulterie," Beard recounts
the story of the "wife of a certaine Duke, who"

> being a lascivious woman, wrote two letters; one to the Duke
> her husband, and another to her Lover: but it happened by
> chance, that her letter written to her lover, was delivered to
> her Husband the Duke; who thereby knowing her wickednesse,
> came no sooner home, but slew her with his owne hand.

The "chance" by which this wife's letter "was delivered to her Husband" in no way would have been considered by Beard's seventeenth-
century readers as other than "providential"—and neither, I believe,
should the "accident" by which the lascivious Lady Plyant delivers
her lover's letter to her husband be otherwise considered. What the
duke made of the evidence so placed in his hands suggests how Sir
Paul might have acted, if this were not a comedy, with the evidence
placed in his.

The fact that Sir Paul, unlike the duke, proves so much a wittol
(and consents once more to be "swath'd in Blankets" and denied
"lawful Domestick Pleasures" by a wife often "polluted by Foreign
Iniquity") should remind us once again that *The Double-Dealer*
is in great part an illustration of the way human beings may be
"punished," as Brisk says in its opening scene, for "want of apprehension," a dramatic validation of the truth, dismal though it
be, of Maskwell's aphoristic commonplace: *qui vult decipi decipiatur*

("who wishes to be deceived, will be deceived"). Providence may
do all it can to guard or enlighten the weak and foolish, but in any
realistic view of man, and particularly in the Christian view of fallen
man, there will always be those so defective of will or apprehension
as to defeat or defy Heaven's best efforts.

Far from being evidence of any impious design on Congreve's
part, furthermore, Sir Paul's expectations that Providence will
afford its blessings and safeguards, despite any neglect on his own
part, should rather be seen as the dramatic exemplification of so
orthodox a Christian premise as that stated by Archbishop Tillotson
when he wrote that "God hath promised to take care of good men,
but if they neglect themselves, or willingly cast themselves into
danger, and expect his providence and protection, they do not
trust in God, but tempt him; they try whether God's providence will
countenance their rashness, and provide for them, when they neglect
themselves; and protect them from those dangers, to which they
wilfully expose themselves."[28] As we noted in an earlier chapter,
"If you leap into a well, Providence is not bound to fetch you out."

IV

While critics have seized upon the weak-minded Sir Paul's expostulations to Providence mainly as evidence of the irrelevance of any
such divine agency to the play, very little notice has been paid to
the two remarkable allusions to Providence made by the far from
fatuous Maskwell immediately after Lady Touchwood has appointed
eight o'clock as the time to meet him in her chamber to "toy away
an hour" in dalliance. Having "lost all Appetite" for her ladyship,
Maskwell ponders to himself how he can at once deceive her and
further his own designs on Cynthia, and suddenly there comes into
his head the scheme whereby he can arrange for Lord Touchwood
to find his wife alone in her bedroom with Mellefont: "Ha! yonder
comes *Mellefont* thoughtful. Let me think: Meet her at eight—hum—
ha! By Heaven I have it—if I can speak to my Lord before—Was it
my Brain or Providence? No matter which—I will deceive 'em all,
and yet secure my self, 'twas a lucky thought!" He then immediately
discloses his rendezvous with Lady Touchwood to Mellefont, and
when the latter is puzzled as to how this can aid his own cause,

Maskwell assures him thus: "Come, come, I won't perplex you. 'Tis the only thing that Providence could have contriv'd to make me capable of serving you, either to my Inclination or your own necessity—."

One may, of course, dismiss these allusions to Providence as merely cynical on Maskwell's part, or as merely conventional on Congreve's. But in view of the way the play now begins its rush toward the "discovery" of Maskwell's "long track of dark deceit," and toward the distributive justice so emphatically announced at its conclusion, such dismissals seem, to me at least, only the rather perverse attempts of modern critics to deny to a former age the foundation and constituent elements of a mythic vision then most devoutly maintained. Maskwell's question, "Was it my Brain or Providence," should rather be considered, as I believe it would have been in 1693, as the dramatic counterpoint to the received conviction that "the instruments of Providence being free agents," nothing "can happen which may not be imputed to them," for "Divine and humane influences are so twisted and knit together, that it is hard to sever them."[29] And when he tells Mellefont that his scheme is "the only thing that Providence could have contriv'd" to serve his own "Inclination" and Mellefont's "necessity," it seems to me we have another of those many artful instances whereby Congreve has a character, often a dull or foolish one, but here most cunning, not only speak better than he knows but also remind an audience of the manifold ways they had been instructed that "what is ill done by men, and for a very ill End, may be ordered by God for Wise and Good purposes";[30] warn that God "is no idle Spectator in this vast Theatre of the World," but makes the "blackest designs" of men serve His ends: "like Watermen, they are made by Providence to row one way whilst they look another";[31] caution that man should "be not conceited and confident" of his own "wisdom and strength or ability in any kind," for

> there is a secret providence of God, which mingles itself with the actions and spirits of men, and disposeth of us unknown to ourselves; and what we think to be the effect of our own strength and resolution, of our own wisdom and contrivance,

proceeds from an higher cause, which, unseen to us, doth steer
and govern us.[32]

We should note, especially in the light of this last cautionary quotation, that Maskwell's conceit in the powers of his own brain is even
greater than that we observed in Mellefont. He is utterly confident
that "Success will attend" his "Crimes." "All's in my power," he
tells Mellefont, for he has in his "head" a "Stratagem" that "cannot
fail," and he is as certain as Lady Touchwood that he can "deceive
every body." Equally important, however, and "a strange thing, but
a true one" (to use words from a song in the play), is the fact that
his very success in contriving the ruin of Mellefont also gives rise to
the precise circumstances through which his own exposure is accomplished. That is, the master stroke by which he gives Lord Touchwood what seems to be the "Ocular Proof" of Mellefont's incestuous
guilt becomes in itself the ironical cause of the one eventuality he
knows he must prevent—a premature knowledge on Lady Touchwood's part that he has been promised the hand of Cynthia: "'tis
dangerous to delay," he muses, "let me think—shou'd my Lord
proceed to treat openly of my Marriage with *Cynthia,* all must be
discover'd and *Mellefont* can be no longer blinded.—It must not be;
nay, shou'd my Lady know it—ay, that were fine work indeed! her
fury wou'd spare nothing, tho' she involv'd her self in ruine."
As it turns out, of course, Lord Touchwood, persuaded by Maskwell himself of his "Manly Virtue," has by a bare few minutes
already told her ladyship of the blessings he intends him, driving
her into such rage at "this surprize of Treachery" that she then
indeed does "spare nothing" and so confronts Maskwell with drawn
dagger and with the clamorous recriminations which are overheard
by Cynthia and Lord Touchwood and cause them to retire behind
the "Skreen" where they learn that "this Chance" has brought
them not only the "proof of" Mellefont's innocence and Lady
Touchwood's adultery, but also the precise details of Maskwell's
"last Plot."
Maskwell's last stratagem requires a supporting cast of characters
who will don various costumes and play parts "conducing" to their
own ruin and who will be "punctual to the Minute" in following his

stage directions. Lady Touchwood must put on Cynthia's nightgown and "go privately by the back Stairs," within a bare "few Minutes," to a final confrontation with Mellefont. The latter must be "Disguis'd like a Parson" and "go by the back Stairs" to meet Cynthia in Lady Touchwood's dressing room "in half an hour," while Cynthia must be misdirected, by a "back way," to the "Chaplain's Chamber." Chaplain Saygrace must stitch up the "Gown Sleeve" of the clerical habit to be donned by Mellefont, so that he "may be puzzled, and waste time in putting it on," giving Maskwell time to take Cynthia down "a Pair of private Stairs" to the stables.

But Lord Touchwood's discovery of the "long track of dark deceit" that has been practiced in his house makes him resolve to "add" his own "Plot" to Maskwell's, altering the scenario so that he himself, in clerical vestments, will go to his wife's chamber, while Mellefont places himself in the chaplain's room, with an outcome given us in these two stage directions:

> *A great shriek from the corner of the Stage.* Lady Touchwood *runs out affrighted, my Lord after her, like a Parson.*

> *Enter* Mellefont *lugging in* Maskwell *from the other side of the Stage.* Mellefont *like a Parson.*

The clerical garb which seems so remarkably emphasized here may be regarded by some as merely the guises necessary for the successful overreach of Maskwell and Lady Touchwood. In my own view, however, the black and godly vestments which explode so suddenly and violently on stage, driving and "lugging" the wicked to public exposure and judgment, the dark flarings of cassock made the more grim and bodeful when set against the glittering sartorial foppishness of Brisk, the Froths, the Plyants, are to be seen as the visible, and deliberately electrifying, reminders of that Heavenly retribution no one, not even the devil himself, could expect, in the end, to escape. And when Lord Touchwood proceeds to declare, "We'll think of punishment at leasure" but "hasten to do Justice, in rewarding Virtue and wrong'd Innocence," the closing "judgment scene" of *The Double-Dealer* puts the play squarely in the long tradition of other English plays which also conclude, as Stroup has so well demonstrated, with the appearance of Divine Providence "in the guise of the king or duke or simply the judge who settles the conflict and metes out justice, rewards, and punishments in the last scene."

In such plays, as Stroup observes, Divine Providence does not make its appearance "in proper person," but sends its vicar, a vicarious form of itself, in its stead.[33] In *The Double-Dealer,* Lord Touchwood, who had not been in command of his own house for some time, and who in fact had withdrawn, at his wife's urging, from sight of the company, in the end emerges amidst it to reassume his rightful as well as his titular "lordship"—and to serve as the emblematic representative of quite another "Lordship." The emblematic dimension given his lordship at the end of the play should not be too surprising, moreover, if we now ponder once more Lady Touchwood's furious indictment of Maskwell at the beginning of the play:

> Have you not wrong'd my Lord, who has been a Father to you in your wants, and given you being?

And when Lord Touchwood avers that he will "add" his "Plot" to Maskwell's "last Plot," should our ears not pick up a small tintinnabulation of "that *Skilful Dramatist,* who always connecteth that of ours which went before, with what of his follows after, into good *Coherent* Sense; and will at last make it appear, that a *Thred* of exact Justice did run through all" (see p. 19 above).

We may now also lend an ear to what on the surface may have seemed the silliest of exchanges between Brisk and Lady Froth, when, in their consultation about her ladyship's "Heroick Poem," they get into a quibbling dispute over this "comparison":

> For as the Sun shines every day,
> So of our Coach-man I may say.

To Brisk's objection that "that simile wont do in wet Weather—because you say the Sun shines every day," Lady Froth responds by declaring,

> I don't say the Sun shines all the day, but, that he peeps now

and then, yet he does shine all the day too, you know, tho' we don't see him.

Brisk submits, but maintains that "the vulgar will never comprehend that." Perhaps not the vulgar, but if there were those in the audience who were not familiar with Milton's "all-ruling Sire" who oft "amidst Thick clouds and dark" resides, there would scarcely have been anyone unacquainted with the biblical texts on which such Miltonic lines are based, particularly Isaiah 45:15, "Verily thou art a God that hidest thyself, O God of Israel, the Saviour," the passage which inspired Pascal's many famous seventeenth-century pronouncements on *deus absconditus,* the hidden God. The passage may also explain the most peculiar stage direction in all of Congreve, the words *"They abscond,"* used instead of "They retire" or "They withdraw," when Cynthia and Lord Touchwood retreat behind the "Skreen" and from that vantage point, so reminiscent of the screen in the confessional stall, hear the full avowal of Maskwell's and Lady Touchwood's treacheries.

One could point to a multitude of texts in the seventeenth century in which the imagery so fatuously used by Lady Froth is made to point a moral or enhance a tale; but among all that could be chosen I quote the following for the way in which it seems so strikingly apposite to the near, and nearly tragic, success of Maskwell's machinations, and strikingly apposite also to the way in which he is brought to judgment: the "machinations of a mighty mischief," wrote Jeremy Taylor, will always be

> seen and observed by Him that stood behind the cloud, who shall also bring every work of darkness into light in the day of strange discoveries and fearful recompenses: and in the meantime certain it is, that no man can long put on a person and act a part, but his evil manners will peep through the corners of the white robe, and God will bring a hypocrite to shame even in the eyes of men.[34]

The "strangest Revolution," says Sir Paul near the end of the play, "all turn'd topsie turvey; as I hope for Providence."

The last "judgment" scene in *The Double-Dealer* establishes the pattern to be followed in the concluding scenes of Congreve's two remaining comedies; after *The Old Batchelour* he apparently acquired a deeper sense of the judgmental endings which occur in so many plays of his English dramatic forefathers, and was able to give what I consider the greatest possible imaginative turn to his own: in the last scenes of both *Love for Love* and *The Way of the World* the presiding judges or vicarious ministers of providential justice will be seen in the shape of women, one young and witty and beauteous, the other old and decayed and absurd of person— a surprising fact at first, perhaps, but not too much so if such precedents as Rosalind and Portia are brought to mind. In either case, whatever their fleshly form, they come forth in the end, as does Lord Touchwood, as reminders of a kind of justice still at work in the world.

V

The language of *The Double-Dealer,* in the speech of minor as well as principal characters, sounds and tolls with attestations of a world beyond the merely naturalistic: Heaven and Hell, Paradise and Purgatory, Grace and Damnation, Sin and Repentance, Penance and Absolution. Words often seem spoken in ways beyond the ken or intention of the characters who utter them, as when Maskwell hypocritically, but all too prophetically, responds to Lord Touchwood's promise to make him (instead of Mellefont) his heir by saying: "Now Heaven forbid—." The oath, like so many others in the play, may seem a mere convention of speech, but the events which follow so quickly thereafter suggest strongly that Congreve himself wished it to be seen as ratified in the strongest possible dramatic terms.

At times there is, on the part of certain characters, a more obviously deliberate use of religious vocabulary. When Mellefont, for example, thinks he has Lady Touchwood in his power, there occurs this exchange, reminiscent again of Hamlet's confrontation with his mother, and tensed, like it, with language of the confessional:

> *Lady Touchwood.* I'll hold my breath and die, but I'l be free.
> *Mellefont.* O Madam, have a care of dying unprepared, I doubt

you have some unrepented Sins that may hang heavy and
retard your flight.
Lady Touchwood. O. What shall I do? say? whither shall I turn?
has Hell no remedy?
Mellefont. None, Hell has served you even as Heaven has done,
left you to your self.—You're in a kind of *Erasmus* Paradice;
yet if you please you may make it a Purgatory; and with a
little Pennance and my Absolution all this may turn to good
account.

The fact that Lady Touchwood almost immediately gains the upper
hand over her "confessor" does little or nothing to erase the strongly
sacramental language of the scene, for even her most taunting
words, "I'l forgive all that's past," stem from the General Confession
of The Book of Common Prayer.

A good instance of the way a crucial issue of the play may be
phrased by one of its sillier characters is to be found in the language
of Lady Plyant when she would seem to affirm her virtue and yet
also invite Mellefont to corrupt it. "O consider," she tells him,
"what would you have to answer for, if you should provoke me to
frailty? Alas! Humanity is feeble, Heaven knows! very feeble, and
unable to support it self." And a moment later: "And no body
knows how Circumstances may happen together,—to my thinking,
now I could resist the strongest Temptation,—but yet I know, 'tis
impossible for me to know whether I could or not, there is no
certainty in the things of this life."

Such words go to the heart of a play whose main design is to
show that humanity is indeed "very feeble, and unable to support
it self" and that "no body," not even the most clever, "knows how
Circumstances may happen together." The world of *The Double-
Dealer* is one in which truth and falsehood can be so cunningly
confounded that even the shrewdest (Careless) and the most honest
(Mellefont) may be baffled and undone. It is not wit, or wisdom, or
virtue which ensures success in the end, and Mellefont is sadly wrong
to think "the Game depends entirely upon Judgment." But if
Mellefont's "care and foresight," as well as his virtue, are shown as
inadequate and unable to "support" him in his struggle against an

ancient adversary, then so too prove all the craft, the deceit, the malice, of a Maskwell when set against the "contrivances" of an almighty Providence which may work, in his own words, according to his "inclination" and yet also serve Mellefont's "Necessity."

The fact of the matter is that the ground plan of *The Double-Dealer* is that of many another seventeenth-century theodicy, and as such would have been recognized as another example of the manifold literary guises by which God's ways could be justified to man, no matter how incongrouous the idea may seem to many today, and no matter how its basic theodicean configuration has been subdued to, but not overwhelmed by, its lustrous comic substance. At bottom it is still a play about the attempts of evil to subvert and destory good, about an evil which came to understand, eons ago, that, as Maskwell says:

> One Minute give Invention to Destroy,
> What to Rebuild, will a whole Age Employ.

A "strange thing, but a true one."

8

Angelic Ministry and the "Utmost Tryal" of Virtue

> And how often the Angels help forward Mens Conversion, by working on their Imaginations, and Affections (presenting things to the Mind, and pressing them with some vehemency) we cannot tell—no doubt they do frequently.
>
> Therefore it is not unusual for God to employ good Angels in executing of his Judgments; nor is there any thing in their Nature or Office that should hinder this.
>
> Richard Saunders, *A Discourse of Angels* (1701)

Many critics have noted or explained—and sometimes tried to explain away—Congreve's unusual deployment of religious diction and imagery in *Love for Love:* as Hawkins caustically observes, the religious allusions all seem "at the whim of the individual critic who interprets them."[1] Holland, for example, observed the paradoxical theme of "real" versus "feigned" madness in the play, as well as that special sacrifice of self that brings fulfillment, and concluded that "the end of Valentine's education is to bring him to a higher kind of reality, a Providence or God's justice, that transcends the chance and show of ordinary social reality."[2] With this view, Ben Ross Schneider essentially agrees, emphasizing Congreve's use of "the central Christian paradox that loss is gain" and arguing that Valentine is saved in the end because Angelica "plays Providence to his improvidence."[3] A much more guarded treatment of such issues is that by Charles A. Lyons, who cautions that the stress he "places upon the significance of religious imagery in the determination" of the play's "structure of values does not assume that this image pattern derives from a Christian conception of the action." It is "rather the opposite," he adds, for "in Christian terms, the application of these images is profane," a charge from which he presumably

157

would save the play be declaring that it is written from within a "naturalistic perspective."[4]

No such caution, or doubt about the play's "perspective," is evinced in an outburst against it made by Collier nearly three hundred years ago. Indignant at the passage where Valentine says, "Tattle, I thank you, you wou'd have interpos'd between me and Heav'n; but Providence laid Purgatory in your way—You have but Justice," Collier exclaimed: "Thus Heav'n is debased into an Amour, and Providence brought on to direct the Paultry concerns of the Stage!"[5] He seems to view Valentine's language as unquestionably profane, and precisely because Providence, in something more than a merely metaphorical or "naturalistic" sense, does actually "direct" the events of the play.

Exploration of religious vocabulary as such has not, therefore, been decisive in determining the informing "perspective" of *Love for Love:* as Lyons, and others, have observed, the "association of spiritual and erotic love" in the play may be mere "literary convention." Such being the situation, it seems the more necessary to connect the religious vocabulary to certain configural elements of the play which have hitherto gone unremarked and which suggest that, far from being either profane or merely conventional, both language and structure in *Love for Love* are designed to show that Providence does indeed interest itself in the "concerns," even the most "Paultry," of the "stages" on which men act their "parts." As we trace these out it will help if we keep in mind the climactic scene of the play, the language and substance of which is extraordinarily judicial and judgmental.

In that scene, the roots of which are deep in the English dramatic tradition, Angelica, hitherto in the play the quintessentially young, beauteous, and very sprightly figure of a Restoration stage heiress, suddenly takes on the severe and magisterial presence proper to a judge presiding over a "trial." With the testimony of the two appellants, Valentine and his father, before her, Angelica proceeds, in these stern words to Sir Sampson, to mete out her rewards and punishments:

Learn to be a good Father, or you'll never get a second Wife.

> I always lov'd your Son, and hated your unforgiving Nature. I
> was resolv'd to try him to the utmost; I have try'd you too, and
> know you both. You have not more Faults, than he has Virtues;
> and 'tis hardly more Pleasure to me, that I can make him and my
> self happy, than that I can punish you.

Here, as so often in the long prior history of English drama, where a
persona seems partly flesh and blood, and partly emblem, Angelica
lives up to the very apparent implications of her name and takes on
the special offices traditionally assigned to angelic ministers: the
"trial" or "testing" of men, and the execution of God's justice on
earth.

I

The world of *Love for Love* is, for the most part, so enigmatic as
to defy comprehension by most of the characters, a world of secrets
and ambiguities, where people, in Ben's words, "look one way" and
yet "row another," and where a woman "is harder to be understood
than a Piece of *AEgyptian* Antiquity, or an *Irish* Manuscript." It is a
world in which people, like "a Witches Pray'r, and Dreams and
Dutch Almanacks," are "to be understood by contraries." It is a
world where things may seem, in Sir Sampson's foolish opinion, "as
plain as the Nose in one's Face," and it is also a world where a Foresight, for all his pride in reading the stars and others' physiognomies,
may be cuckolded while poring over his own face in a mirror. As
these illustrations should suggest, it is a fictive world that once again
evinces Congreve's close familiarity with the vocabularies of various
occult arts and practices: judicial astrology, witchcraft, divination by
dreams as well as by "sieve and shears," physiognomy, chiromancy,
omens and prognostications.

In this world the character of Foresight is unusually instructive,
the highly exaggerated example of a man who, in spite of his boasted
ability both to "tell and foretell," is yet totally bewildered by
goings-on that seem not only to defy all augury but also all his
"Consideration, and Discretion, and Caution." His very name, of
course, is a literal translation of "providence," a matter Congreve has
amusingly underscored in the name of his "chitty fac'd" and hoy-

denish daughter Prue (the diminutive of Prudence, from Latin *prudens,* contraction of *providens*). The family nomenclature is important, but not as a mere punning witticism or as a derogation of Providence itself. Just the reverse, for by using it Congreve promptly points to the real folly and impiety of Foresight's faith in astrology—the fact that, in the words of Henry Cornelius Agrippa, "Judicial Astrology . . . takes away the use of Faith in Religion, lessens the Reverence of Miracles, takes away Divine Providence, while it teaches, That all things happen by force and vertue of the Stars, and from the Influences of the Constellations, by a kind of fatal Necessity." Agrippa's words put us in touch with the most serious charges made against judicial astrology throughout the Renaissance: its tendency to deny not only the operations of God's Providence but also the freedom of man's will, inducing a spirit of fatalism, and thereby "excusing Vice as descending from Heaven."[6] In the words of Marcilio Ficino, those "that think all events necessitated by the stars err in three ways: they deprive God of Providence and control; they steal away the justice of angels; and they take away man's free will and tranquillity."[7]

Nothing can be more obvious than the fatalistic strain in Foresight's speech. Among his first words are these to his servant: "It is impossible that any thing should be as I would have it; for I was born, Sir, when the Crab was ascending, and all my Affairs go backward." He wishes to keep Angelica from going abroad because he remembers an old Arabian prophecy whose verses threaten cuckoldry to the "Head" of a household

> *When Housewifes all the House forsake,*
> *And leave good Man to Brew and Bake.*

It matters not that Angelica tells him she can neither make him a cuckold "by going abroad" nor "secure" his honor "by staying at home": he is concerned with the "Force" of the prophecy, not with the "force" of Angelica's "Inclinations" nor, for that matter, with the "Inclinations" of his wife. Nothing could better illustrate the deterministic character of his thought, and its impious overtones, than his resolve to be patient and resigned, not to the will of God, but to the decrees of the stars: "I will have Patience, since it is the

Will of the Stars I should be thus tormented—This is the effect of the malicious Conjunctions and Oppositions in the Third House of my Nativity; there the Curse of Kindred was foretold—."

Angelica has a good deal of impudent and bawdy fun with her uncle, goading him with intimations that he is "not Lord of the Ascendant" and that his wife is a "little Retrograde . . . in her Nature," and advising him "to erect a Scheme, and find who's in Conjunction" with her. Foresight himself is aware, to use his terminology, that his wife "was born under *Gemini,* which may incline her to Society," and that she "has a Mole upon her Lip, with a moist Palm, and an open Liberality on the Mount of *Venus.*" But even with all these "signs" from astrology, chiromancy, and physiognomy, he flounders in peevish perplexity as to his wife's chastity, consoling himself with such melancholy and fatalistic comments as this: "Well—Why, if I was born to be a Cuckold, there's no more to be said—."

Jeers directed at astrologers who pretended to know what "is done" in Heaven, but could not, while absent, "see or know what is done at home,"[8] appear to have been a Renaissance commonplace. And while certain suggestions as to Foresight's literary lineage have been advanced,* the most pertinent comment on the "seduction" (if so easy a feat can be so termed) of Mrs. Foresight by Scandal may be that provided in Agrippa's chapter "Of Judicial Astrology," where there occurs a passage remarkably suggestive of the character Congreve presents in his Dramatis Personae as "an illiterate Old Fellow, peevish and positive, superstitious." Judicial astrologers, says Agrippa, are

> a perverse and preposterous generation of men, who profess to foreknow future things, in the mean time altogether ignorant of past and present; and undertaking to tell all people most obscure and hidden secrets abroad, at the same time know not what happens in their own houses, and in their own chambers: Even such an Astrologer as *Moore* laught at in his Epigram.

*Davis, *Complete Plays,* p. 206, says that the "character of Foresight and the use of the jargon of astrology owe something to Ben Jonson's *Alchemist* and perhaps also to [Thomas] Tompkin's *Albumazar.*"

Agrippa then conflates two of Thomas More's epigrams on the cuckolding of an astrologer:

> The Stars, Etherial Bard, to thee shine clear,
> And all our future Fates thou mak'st appear.
> But that thy Wife is common all men know.
> Yet what all see, there's not a Star doth show.
> *Saturn* is blinde, or some long journey gone,
> Not able to discern an infant from a stone.
> The Moon is fair, and as she's fair she's chast,
> And won't behold thy Wife so leudly embrac't.
> *Europa Jove, Mars Venus,* she *Mars* courts,
> With *Daphne, Sol,* with *Hirce Hermes* sports.
> Thus while the Stars their wanton Love pursue,
> No wonder, Cuckhold, they'll not tell thee true.[9]

Inordinately vain of his ability to read the stars and the faces of others, Foresight's superstitious credulity is accorded a most appropriate justice when his wife acquiesces in an assignation during the very moment he studies his physiognomy in her glass. Seeking an impossible certainty from zodiac and faces, he becomes the dupe of his own astrological calculations, for we are given enough evidence to suppose that at the very time when his old nurse will bring him his urinal ("within a quarter of Twelve . . . just upon the turning of the Tide"), Scandal will have erected his own scheme within "his Wives Circle."

As the words of Ficino made clear, one of the charges against judicial astrology was that it took away not only "man's free will" but also his "tranquillity": "if a good prophecy comes true, it makes us seem worthless, for it comes (as the astrologers say) without effort on our part. If the prophecy is ill—and this is the usual case— we suffer in anticipation although the evil may never be realized."[10] Bedeviled as he is by dreams, signs, and omens, encompassed by faces he cannot read, Foresight, for all his fatalistic words, lives in querulous disquietude of mind. A fretful "Searcher into Obscurity and Futurity," he is not so much "half-crazed" (as some would say)[11] as the type or emblem of those whom the age would have seen as attempting to "bind Providence" with "forecasts and provisions" but who, "for the most part, are not only disappointed in what they hope for, but do meet with a curse instead of it."[12] While his name keeps the idea of Providence alive in the play, his life and actions are the dramatic illustrations of an anxious and therefore "impious Race of Men" who would be "attributing that to the Stars, which belongs only to God," who refuse to acknowledge that "neither the Stars are govern'd by wise men, nor wise men by the Stars; but both are govern'd by God."*

Foresight's role or function thus seems somewhat analogous to that of Sir Paul in *The Double-Dealer,* for he serves not at all to discredit Providence itself but rather to discredit wrong notions of it. In the jargon of his tribe, as well as in his perplexity of spirit despite all his "Science," he moreover contributes to Congreve's construction of a baffling and largely undecipherable world wherein both persons and events may be "kept secret" even "from the piercing Eye of Perspicuity," even indeed "from all Astrologers, and the Stars themselves," where anyone may "have a wrong Notion of Faces," where "Grey Hairs" may "cover a Green Head," where, in sum, and in his own words, *"Humanum est errare."*

II

Foresight is only the most professed physiognomist in the play, for nearly all the other characters are likewise concerned with "reading" the countenances of others while "keeping" their own. When Mrs. Foresight chides her sister for being "seen with a man in a Hackney-Coach," and further suggests she has shared, indeed, a bed with a man at the World's End, a disreputable hostel, Mrs. Frail denies all:

> *Mrs. Foresight.* You deny it positively to my Face?
> *Mrs. Frail.* Your Face, what's your Face?
> *Mrs. Foresight.* No matter for that, it's as good a Face as yours.
> *Mrs. Frail.* Not by a Dozen Years wearing.—But I do deny it positively to your Face.

*Agrippa, *The Vanity of Arts and Sciences,* pp. 95, 91. Agrippa has in mind the Ptolemaic phrase, *sapiens dominabitur astris,* which Congreve puts in the mouth of Sir Sampson in act 2 of *Love for Love.*

Mrs. Foresight. I'll allow you now to find fault with my Face;—
for I'll swear your impudence has put me out of countenance.

When Mrs. Foresight then produces a gold bodkin as evidence that
her sister had in fact been at the World's End, Mrs. Frail neatly turns
the tables by saying, "Well, if you go to that, where did you find this
Bodkin?—Oh Sister, Sister!—Sister every way," and so provokes her
"sister's" peevish aside: "O Devil on't, that I cou'd not discover her,
without betraying my self." Mrs. Foresight keeps her countenance
somewhat better in act 4 when she denies to Scandal she had shared
her bed with him the night before, leaving that astonished gentleman
to reflect: "This I have heard of before, but never believ'd. I have
been told that she had that admirable quality of forgetting to a
man's face in the morning, that she had layn with him all night, and
denying favours with more impudence, than she could grant 'em."
    The "keeping" of countenances and the "reading" of faces are the
corollary images for the play's unusual emphasis upon the "keeping"
as well as the "discovery" of "Secrets," an emphasis most amusingly,
and scathingly, illustrated in the person of Tattle, "a publick Professor of Secrets" who "will deny a Woman's name, while he gives
you the marks of her Person" and who "refuses the reputation of a
Ladie's favour" only "that it may be granted him." We see what we
need to know of his character in the first act, when he allows it to
be thought, though quite without his saying it in so many words,
that he has possessed the person of Mrs. Frail, and then agrees, when
the imminent appearance of that lady is announced, to "sacrifice
half a Dozen Women of good Reputation" to Scandal in order to
avoid the exposure of his base aspersions of her. As trivial as this
early scene may appear, it is yet the ironic preparation for that
penultimate, and highly emblematic, scene of the play when Tattle
finds to his utter dismay that somehow he has gotten himself married and in permanent possession of that lady whose favors he had so
falsely claimed.
    The marriage of Tattle to Mrs. Frail (he "hooded like a Friar" and
thinking she is Angelica, she "veil'd like a Nun" and thinking he is
Valentine) has vexed and puzzled critics for well over a hundred
years—some because it has seemed a stale and maladroit piece of

stage business, others because such a marriage was not only illegal but also invalid (at the time an illegal marriage, under some circumstances, could nevertheless be valid).* What has been overlooked by all the critics, however, is the simple fact that in this highly unrealistic yoking of two utterly rapacious characters Congreve has brought to visual life on stage an emblematic representation of a proverb commonly found in Western literature since the Middle Ages: "Cucullus non facit monachum."† So, "as we see," says Colley Cibber, "it is not the Hood that makes the Monk, nor the Veil the Vestal."[13] "Habit maketh no monk," writes Thomas Usk in his *Testament of Love* (ca. 1387), and Chaucer, in *The Romaunt of the Rose* (1:6192), sets down "Abit ne maketh neither monk ne frere." Shakespeare, in the last act of *Measure for Measure,* and just prior to the Duke's entrance in his friar's habit, has Lucio say "Cucullus non facit monachum," and so says the Clown in act 1 of *Twelfth Night* (in *King Henry the Eighth,* act 3, the Queen declares "all hoods make not monks"). Dante, Rabelais, and Erasmus use the saying, while Wycherley's "Well, the Hood does not make the Monk," issuing from the mouth of the foolish and affected Don Diego (in *The Gentleman Dancing-Master*), suggests how much a part of common parlance the proverb was.

It is, then, beside the point to object to the illegality, the invalidity, even the "unreality," of so fantastic a marriage: the impossibly unrealistic nature of the event is the very fact that should lead us to consider its various symbolic implications. Most obviously it has its place in all the "Masks," "disguises," "counterfeited Shapes," "Faces" and "Countenances," the "outsides, outsides," worn by almost everyone in the play. "You see," says Valentine to Angelica, "what disguises Love makes us put on; Gods have been in

---

*The most authoritative study of marital law at the time is *Matrimonial Law and the Materials of Restoration Comedy,* by Gilbert Spencer Alleman (Philadelphia: University of Pennsylvania Press, 1942), where the invalidity of the Tattle-Frail marriage is demonstrated. See particularly chapter 4.

†The origin of the phrase may be these lines from Saint Anselm's *Carmen de Contemptu Mundi:*

> Non tonsura facit monachum, non horrida vestis;
> Sed virtus animi, perpetuusque rigor.

counterfeited Shapes for the same Reason." It is not "Love," of course, which prompts Tattle and Mrs. Frail to agree to "be Marry'd in the dead of Night," she in the "black and white" and "long Veil" of a nun, he in the "Coul and Beads" of "a Fryar": totally mercenary and hypocritical as they are, however, they need no persuasion to put on any garb or guise by which they may swindle a fortune. And when "Suddenly" they are "trickt . . . into one another," we surely should understand that the "legality" of their marriage is not an issue: the justice done may not be statutory, but it definitely is poetical. As Ben observes, "Why there's a Match now, as tho'f a couple of Privateers were looking for a Prize, and should fall foul of one another."

But there are hints of another dimension in Congreve's emblematic staging of so old and common a proverb: this is not the first time, we should remember right off, that he has employed religious garb, in a most obtrusive fashion, in association with the discovery and punishment of treachery or lust or avarice. The terminology, furthermore, by which Tattle is made to bewail his self-inflicted torment bespeaks a kind of retribution beyond, perhaps, his mean and meager comprehension, though not beyond that of his audience: "as I hope to be sav'd," he says to Angelica of his new wife, "my Intentions were good," but "I believe I shall lead her a damn'd sort of a Life." If such hints need reenforcement, surely it is provided a few minutes later when Valentine, having been given not only Angelica's hand but also her "Blessing," turns to the man who would have so vilely usurped his love and says: "*Tattle*, I thank you, you would have interposed between me and Heav'n; but Providence laid Purgatory in your way—you have but Justice." Collier was right, however much he disapproved: Providence *is* "brought on" to "direct the Paultry concerns of the Stage."

III

Most of the characters in *Love for Love,* even the best of them, evince a degree of self-interestedness so high as scarcely to support the widespread notion that Congreve's plays represent a move toward sentimentality. Ben, for example, has totally forgotten that his brother Dick had died two years before his return from sea, while

Tattle, having taught Miss Prue the "well-bred" art of lying, leaves her to "come off" as best she can from the room where she had been striving to lose her virginity to him. Mrs. Foresight, for her part, acts the deliberate bawd to her stepdaughter, insisting that Prue and Tattle be left alone together and suggestively saying that the latter will "never miss an opportunity" for "the spoiling of a Young Thing." Mrs. Frail, having coldly decided to "wheedle" Ben into marriage, just as coldly casts him "a-drift," while Sir Sampson avows he will not "turn Pelican" (the symbol of Christian charity) to feed Valentine out of his "own Vitals." And Valentine himself is enough his father's son to wish, in the first act, that the "thoughtless two handed Whore" who had presented him with a bastard had "overlaid," or smothered, "the Child a Fortnight ago."

We have seen how exercized Collier became over what he considered the defects in Valentine's character (pp. 77–78 above), and more recent critics, too, have been distressed at what has been termed Valentine's "brutally callous" attitude toward his bastard son—and by Congreve's seeming "unawareness" of the callousness displayed.[14] We should recall, however, Congreve's defense of Valentine as "a mix'd Character" who "may pass well enough for the best Character in a Comedy, where even the best must be shown to have Faults," and at the same time remember that it is also Congreve, after all, who confronts the audience with the blatantly unsavory facts of Valentine's past.

The dramaturgical justification for so obtrusive a revelation of Valentine's past sins and present self-concern, furthermore, does not seem far to seek: the very evident peccancy of Valentine's nature, as well as the very evident peccancy of the world depicted at large in the play, is not only consistent with the received Christian view of human depravity but is also the dramatic justification for the necessity Angelica is under to "test" and "prove" the sincerity of his love for her. With a large fortune attached to her person, and beset by others who had "made Court to her," how is she to know, in view of Valentine's past debauchery and present bankruptcy, that his motives are any less sordid or self-serving than those of Tattle and Sir Sampson prove to be? The squandering of his estate in courtship of her is no evident demonstration of Valentine's love, for this could be merely the act of a gamester who ventures a stake to win a larger sum. His own father, indeed, tells Angelica at one point that Valentine "has not a Drachm of Generous Love about him: All Interest, all Interest; he's an undone Scoundrel, and covets your Estate: Body o' me, he does not care a Doit for your Person." Meeting such "faces" of love as she has, it would be the most imprudent thing in the world for Angelica to take them at face value, and the marriage of Tattle and Mrs. Frail underscores the peril of taking a lifetime partner one does not "know": as Tattle laments, it is "the most cruel thing, to marry one does not know how, nor why, nor wherefore."

Valentine, having been born, as he says, with "a huge Train of Attendants"—that is, "Reason, Thought, Passions, Inclinations, Affections, Appetites, Senses," and so on—and finding, as most of us do, that such a "Retinue" is both "craving and invincible," it is scarcely surprising that he has been as willing to resort to dissembling and trickery as have most of the other characters, and for similarly selfish reasons. But though his feigned madness is an understandably human piece of dissembling designed to gain time and "preserve the right" of his inheritance, he also "has a mind," as Jeremy tells Scandal, "to try, whether his playing the Madman, won't make [Angelica] play the Fool, and fall in love with him"— justifying the more Angelica's determination to "play Trick for Trick" and to "try" Valentine's own willingness "to throw off his Disguise of Madness," at the risk of losing his estate, "in Apprehension of losing" her.

Angelica's pleasure in trapping Valentine in his own entrapment scheme certainly suggests a vixenish streak in her character, but when he finally confesses to her that his madness has only been counterfeited, her insistence on treating him as if he were indeed a lunatic becomes also the very means by which he is instructed in the folly of all his ways—and by which we are led to the central paradox of the play. Thus when he expostulates that his pretended madness had been a mere device to preserve his estate, he is finely caught by her in this exchange:

Angelica. How! I thought your love of me had caus'd this

Transport in your Soul; which, it seems, you only counterfeited, for mercenary Ends, and sordid Interest.

Valentine. Nay, now you do me Wrong; for if any Interest was
considerable, it was yours; since I thought I wanted more than
Love, to make me worthy of you.

Angelica. Then you thought me mercenary—But how am I
deluded by this Interval of Sense, to reason with a Madman?

A few moments later she leaves him with this parting shot: "I'll
tell you two things before I leave you; I am not the Fool you take
me for; and you are Mad and don't know it."

The vocabulary of this scene leads us naturally to the play's ethical
center: its witty exploration of the traditional Christian paradox
that worldly wisdom may actually be a form of folly or madness,
and that some kinds of seeming madness or folly may be of the
highest form of wisdom. Some critics (particularly Schneider and
Holland) have taken notice of the paradox, but have not sufficiently
stressed the text to be kept in mind, Saint Paul's words in 1 Corinthians 3:18-19: "Let no man deceive himself. If any man among
you seemeth to be wise in this world, let him become a fool, that he
may be wise. For the wisdom of this world is foolishness with God.
For it is written, He taketh the wise in their own craftiness." Valentine is "taken" in his "own craftiness" by Angelica in the closing
moments of act 4. The effectiveness of the rebukes and admonish-
ments she administers at that same time may be gathered from the
fact that when we next see Valentine, in the closing scene of the
play, his first and simple words to the assembled company are these:
"here's the Fool."

IV

The traditional Christian paradox of worldy wisdom as folly is
sustained and enriched throughout *Love for Love* by an extraordinary Congrevean display of those oxymoronic expressions and
contrary (not to say dizzying) pronouncements to which the human
mind resorts when it tries to affirm or resolve the conflicting claims
of spirit and flesh, mind and matter, love and self-love—utterances,
for example, so cross and contrary, and yet so relevant to the whole

play, as this from Proverbs 13:7: "There is that maketh himself rich, yet hath nothing; there is that maketh himself poor, yet hath great riches."

The climax of *Love for Love* in its turn occurs in a conspicuously paradoxical, and seemingly perverse, human act—Valentine's decision to sign away his inheritance, an act which prompts Scandal to exclaim: "'S' death, you are not mad indeed, to ruine your self?" Yet the climax of the play is prefigured in its beginning, the opening scene where Valentine puts down the writings of Epictetus, the Greek Stoic who, "of all the antient Philosophers," according to a translator of his work only a year or so before Congreve's play,[15] "seems to have made the nearest Approaches to the true Christian Morality"—and whom Valentine, in the next moment, succinctly identifies for his servant Jeremy as "A very rich Man.—Not worth a Groat." And from moment to moment thereafter the audience is showered with reference after reference to "poor rich Rogues" or to "worthless great Men"; with advice to "feast your Mind, and mortifie your Flesh" and so have "a very fine Feast, where there is nothing to be eaten"; with comments on punks and porters who prefer "Verses" (or the carrying of them) to "Settlements" or other wages, as well as on "Young Maids" who "prefer lying in the Arms of a needy Wit, before the embraces of a wealthy Fool." Valentine tells Tattle that "to converse with *Scandal,* is to play at *Losing Loadum;* you must lose a good Name to him, before you can win it for yourself," and Scandal concludes act 1 in an even more prescient use of the same card-game image: "In my mind he is a thoughtless Adventurer,"

> Who hopes to purchase Wealth, by selling Land;
> Or win a Mistress, with a losing hand.

The nearest modern counterpart to Losing Loadum is the game of Hearts, where the idea is to give away hands rather than to take them, where the "winner" is actually the one who "loses" the most "tricks" containing hearts.* A bit more complicated than Hearts,

---

*Cf. these lines from Wycherley's "To the Duke, Written in his Absence, occasion'd from the sight of some Defamatory *Libels* on Him":

Losing Loadum seems to have derived from the French game *Reversis,* or the Spanish game *La Gana Pierde* (i.e. the winner loses). A signal feature of the game, moreover, seems to have been a progressive surrendering of the cards of value in an attempt to bring forth at the very last moment the cards "that are of most price."

Whatever melancholy, and rather self-justificatory, consolation Valentine may find in his own witty paradoxes, or in the example of Epictetus's "obstinate Contempt of Riches,"[16] the first act of *Love for Love* presents him as "mewed up" in his lodgings, unable to go "abroad" for fear of arrest by his creditors. Such "Restraint" and "forc'd Confinement" is chiefly onerous as it denies him access to Angelica, and so, "to come abroad, and be at Liberty to see her," he accepts the "hard Conditions" set him by his father. But he has no sooner bought his release from his physical "Confinement" (by accepting £4,000 cash in lieu of his full inheritance) than he enters into another, self-imposed, "confinement"—his pretended madness. Having used his liberty first to importune his father, fruitlessly, for more money, and then to importune Angelica, again fruitlessly, that she "come to a Resolution" as to her love for him, he mews up himself, voluntarily assuming the "Restraint" appropriate to his role of "Madman"—and hoping all the while to outwit both father and mistress.

The "Confinements"* and "hard Conditions" Valentine brings upon himself, whether through prodigality or his own dissembling, become emblematic of a cramped and confined understanding, and reminiscent of traditional portrayals, in both sacred and profane literature, of the unenlightened everyman or transgressor who is pent up or confined within the sinfulness of his own nature—whether he be Mankind in the "schackle" or "castel cage" of Covetousness; "every man universally prisoned" in St. Thomas More's *A Dialogue of Comfort Against Tribulation;* Robert Southwell's "prodigall

---

*Holland, *The First Modern Comedies,* pp. 161–62, notes "three confinements" of Valentine, but with an emphasis different from mine.

> Honour's a kind of losing Loadum Game,
> Whereby who loses Life, gets more of Fame,
> And never dies in his Eternal Name.

chyld" who is "cheyned in synn" and lies "in thrall, Next to the dungeon of despaire"; Milton's Sampson who, in the words of the chorus, had "become (O worst imprisonment!)" the "Dungeon" of himself, his soul "Imprison'd" in a "real darkness of the body"; or any other sinner whom God was wont to help by first "immuring him as in a castle, and shutting of him up."[17]

In terms of the play's central paradox, Valentine essentially is "confined" by his acceptance of the precepts and practices of the "wisdom of this world," two of the outward signs of which, as South had noted in a sermon on 1 Corinthians 3:19, are "a constant, continual Course of Dissimulation," and a making of a man's self "the chief, if not the sole End of all his Actions."[18] But it is not, as we have seen, by this kind of "wisdom" that Valentine can hope to win Angelica, or the "Blessing" she comes to represent, and so it is necessary for him to accept another kind of "wisdom"—the Epictetan kind, for example, that he had been able to mouth at the start of the play but was unwilling to incorporate in his own behavior. The way "out" of his "Confinement" is before him, indeed, throughout the play, implicit in all the paradoxes—Epictetan, Pauline, and otherwise—that are tossed about so frequently, so wittily, so lightly. But he cannot take the way "out" of his self-imposed "confinement" until he accepts the actual import of all such paradoxes, and so lays aside all his stratagems, all his dissimulation, all his self-interest, and thereby becomes the living proof of one who, in the earlier and scoffing but nevertheless presaging words of Scandal, would "die a Martyr to Sense in a Country where the Religion is Folly."

With his decision, out of love for Angelica, to sign away any remaining right of inheritance, Valentine may be seen as having played a last card of "most price" in the game of "hearts" so important to us all. In doing so he takes leave of the conventional "wisdom of the world": as Angelica says, "How few, like *Valentine,* would persevere even unto Martyrdom, and sacrifice their Interest to their Constancy!" In a play where the very qualities of wisdom and folly are strained to the utmost, Valentine becomes the dramatic embodiment of that paradoxical man who becomes "a fool, that he may be wise," and also that paradoxical man "that maketh himself poor, yet hath great riches."

V

One of the more artful features of all of Congreve's work is the way so many of his characters are made, in their own chat, prattle, repartee, protest, or whatever, to speak all unwittingly in ways remarkably prescient of a future event or final denouement. Thus Tattle in act 1 wonders that "the World shall think the better of any Person for his Calumniation," old Foresight inclines to the *"Turkish Opinion"* which does "reverence a man whom the vulgar think mad," and Ben, having been scorned and cast away by Mrs. Frail, puts this direct shot between her wind and water: "I'm glad you shew your self, Mistress:—Let them marry you as don't know you."

The utterances of Scandal, as we have already witnessed in several instances, seem particularly predictive of the play's climax, however unintentionally on his part, and not the least of these is his blandishing communication to Foresight of his "fear" that the "making over" of Valentine's estate, "this transferring of a rightful Inheritance," will "bring Judgments upon us." And so indeed it does, for Valentine's act of self-sacrifice notwithstanding, the final scene of *Love for Love* is essentially one of "trial" and "judgment," and is dominated by the figure of Angelica as she acts both to save his inheritance and also to preside as judge and dispenser of rewards and punishments to the claimants before her. Her very evident command over the final scene may be explained, of course, in terms of the wit, determination, and psychological acumen she has displayed throughout the play—and obviously some critics have preferred to leave it this way.[19] Yet such a reading must ignore or cavalierly dismiss the complications brought to the scene not only by its concentration of religious and judicial language but also by its figural kinship with a multitude of other scenes of final judgment in English drama. To ignore these elements in the last scene is to ignore the element of mystery in its enunciation of the justice there done.

The quasi-judicial nature of the climactic scene in *Love for Love* should itself make clear the play's firm participation in that long dramatic tradition of testing, trial, and judgment we have noted in chapter 3, as well as in discussion of *The Double-Dealer*. In the play before us the final presiding judge does not appear in the more common guise of king or duke but in the shape of a rich and clever and rather saucy young woman—and not too surprisingly, if we recall the way Rosalind makes "all even" at the end of *As You Like It,* or even Nell Gwyn's "testing" role as Angelo in *The Virgin Martyr.* Congreve's pretty young magistrate, moreover, is named Angelica, and we must not forget (though we seem to have done so) that angels, even more than such earthly vice-gerents of God as kings and dukes, had been regarded immemorially, in Saint Thomas Aquinas's words, as "the prime Instruments of God's Providence."* In the words of Archbishop James Usher's *A Body of Divinity* (reprinted many times during the Restoration period), the general function of the angels, as to the earthly creation, was to serve as "the Instruments and Ministers of God for the Administration and Government of the whole World," and in the course of their ministry to "bestow good things" upon the meritorious and to "execute Judgments upon the Wicked, and punish them for their sins committed."[20] Additionally, and most germane to Valentine's development in the course of Congreve's play, is the traditional view that if a person does suffer while under an angel's charge, "it is that he may be tried, exercised, and made better thereby."[21]

Too evidently a "Hussie" (in Foresight's view) and too much a "cunning, a wary Baggage" (in Sir Sampson's view) to be unqualifiedly "angelic," Angelica yet assumes, for a few moments at least, the stern demeanor of absolute judicial authority, and thereby, in some highly emblematic way, quite lives up to the implications of her name. We need to recall once more these extraordinary words of so young a woman to so old a man as Sir Sampson: "I always lov'd your Son, and hated your unforgiving Nature. I was resolv'd to try him to the utmost; I have try'd you too, and know you both. You have not more Faults than he has Virtues; and 'tis hardly more Pleasure to me, that I can make him and my self happy, than that I can punish you." Or we may ponder these suddenly respectful words used by so cynical a man as Scandal in this last address of the play to

---

*See *Summa Contra Gentiles,* 3:79. Cf. Archbishop Tillotson's words: "And that the Angels of God are the great ministers of his providence here in the world, hath not only been the constant tradition of all ages; but is very frequently and plainly asserted in scripture" *Works,* 3 vols. (London, 1735), 2:135.

so "angelic" a minister: "Well, Madam, you have done Exemplary Justice, in punishing an inhumane Father, and rewarding a Faithful Lover: But there is a Third Good Work, which I, in particular, must thank you for; I was an Infidel to your Sex; and you have converted me—."

Angelica declares twice that she has "tried" Valentine to the "utmost," and her words, as clear as may be, stamp *Love for Love* as a play in the "testing pattern" involving the "trial or proving of a man," and also, clear as may be, identify her role as a chary yet solicitous mistress to be, at least for certain moments, conterminous with her role as vigilant, yet also solicitous, guardian angel. If one wishes to view in strictly secular terms her manipulation of events in the play, one may say she has been prudent enough not to accept Valentine at "face value" during his prodigality, rigorous enough not to indulge him amidst his poverty and "Confinement," shrewd enough not to be duped by his counterfeit "Madness." It is my own view that a contemporary audience would have seen in her proceedings the pattern of those stratagems and ministrations by which angels were supposed to work on the "Imaginations, and Affections" of men, "presenting things to the Mind, and pressing them with some vehemency," so that the wards in their custody might "be tried, exercized, and made better thereby."[22] Womanly she is, indeed, but at the moment when Valentine takes her "Blessing" on his knees, as at other moments as well, she carries about her person an intimation of another personage, a shadowy reminder of those who "execute the divine plan for human salvation" and who also, in the words of Saint Thomas Aquinas, "free us when hindered and help to bring us home."[23]

9

The "Care of Providence" and the "Just Decrees of Heav'n"

> what can more become the Wisdom and Justice of Providence, than to make bad men the Ministers and Executioners of a Divine Vengeance upon each other, which is one great End God serves by the Sins of men.
>
> William Sherlock,
> *A Discourse Concerning the Divine Providence,* 1694

Vaguely known in our own day, by some at least, for such a line as "Musick has Charms to sooth a savage Breast," or as the source of the misquotation, "Hell hath no fury, like a woman scorned,"* *The Mourning Bride* initially "had the greatest Success, not only of all Mr. *Congreve*'s, but indeed of all the Plays" that Charles Gildon could "remember on the English Stage, excepting none of the incomparable *Otway*'s." Gildon himself could not prefer Congreve's tragedy "to the *All for Love* of Mr. *Dryden, The Orphan,* and *Venice Preserv'd* of Mr. *Otway,* or the *Lucius Junius Brutus* of Mr. *Lee,*" but he decently recorded Richard Blackmore's testimony that the play "very justly" received "universal Applause" and was "look'd on as the most perfect Tragedy that has been wrote in this Age."[1] A sour note in the chorus of praise was Collier's charge that portions of the play were a "Rant of Smut and profainness," a complaint challenged immediately by a writer who declared he had "read the *Mourning Bride* often" and that "it always inspired" him "with the noblest Ideas."[2] Matthew Prior, while expressing some sympathy with Collier's view that "our plays are too licen-

---

*Congreve's lines, "Heav'n has no Rage, like Love to Hatred turn'd,/Nor Hell a Fury, like a Woman scorn'd," may have been prompted by Dryden's "Rage has no bounds in slighted womankind" (*Cleomenes* 5.1).

176

tious," at the same time noted that "we liked the Mourning Bride thô Alphonso neither cursed like a swine or couched like a god thrô the whole piece: and there will always be found so good Sence in the Nation that some famous for having it will like what is truly good."*

Regardless of the approbation it received so immediately and claimed so long,[3] esteem for *The Mourning Bride* had so far waned by the early years of our own century that John Palmer could dismiss it in 1913 by saying, "That Congreve wrote a Tragedy will not critically concern us. . . . Distinctly it was an episode."[4] And while the play has since received, here and there, a measure of attention, the general lack of critical concern for its existence is suggested by the fact that not once is it mentioned in the latest collection of essays on Congreve's work.†

However much *The Mourning Bride* may be disdained today as an example of "tragedy," there nevertheless are compelling reasons for regarding it as something more than a merely eccentric "episode" in Congreve's career. That career, in my own view, is all of a piece throughout, and *The Mourning Bride,* because it sets forth so fully and explicitly an argument for a providentially governed universe, should help us the better to understand the theurgical vision by which Congreve's other work is shaped. There is no reason, and no evidence I can think of, to indicate that Congreve was of so bifurcated a mentality as to fashion his comedies according to one set of metaphysical assumptions and his tragedy according to another. The evidence rather points the other way, for the configurations of dramatic event in *The Mourning Bride* are in remarkable accord

---

*See H. Bunker Wright and Monroe K. Spears, *The Literary Works of Matthew Prior*, 2 vols. (Oxford: Clarendon Press, 1971), 2:877. Prior's comment (brought to my attention by Professor Richard B. Kline) rather calls into question Elmer B. Potter's contention that "no critic of standing has ever given *The Mourning Bride* unqualified praise" (see "The Paradox of Congreve's *Mourning Bride*," *PMLA*, 58 (1943):979).

† *William Congreve,* ed. Morris. Exceptions, of course, are the critiques of the play by Rothstein in *Restoration Tragedy*, by Novak in *William Congreve*, and by Van Voris in *The Cultivated Stance.* There is, in addition, David D. Mann's very helpful essay, "Congreve's Revisions of *The Mourning Bride*," *PBSA*, 69 (1975):pp. 526–46.

with those found in the rest of his work, from *Incognita* to *The Way of the World*. Here once more, whatever the differences in mood and mode, we find those whose steps are guided safely through darkness, and those who are tripped up in their own contrivances; those who are delivered from danger and affliction by "Errour" and "Mistake," and those who are trapped in their own dissembling; and, most plainly of all, those who "survive" through their "Innocence," and those on whom "the Hand of Heaven" turns "their own most bloody Purposes."

I

The Mourning Bride, one critic has recently maintained, "early sets up determinant imagery," and although "it also declares, in Osmyn's prison scene, its dependence on Providence," nevertheless "its characters at times appear 'so many ping pong balls rebounding off suddenly materializing walls of circumstances.'"[5] Such a characterization of the play's tenor and spirit seems deeply misleading to me: in the first place, it misconstrues the way the play illustrates and extolls, by the example of its virtuous characters, a deliberate "Resignation" of self to "The Care of Heaven," amidst all adversities and afflictions; in the second, it ignores, or at least depreciates, Congreve's obtrusive demonstrations, and assertions, that it is in the exercise of their own choice and craft that the wicked come to destroy both themselves and one another. In no sense can any of the characters be seen as so volitionless or helpless as to be mere "rebounding" victims of circumstance in a necessitarian universe.

The idea of such a necessitarian universe is certainly raised, in pointed fashion, in the opening moments of the play, which seem principally designed to pose the metaphysical and existential questions for which all subsequent events will provide the dramatic answer. Thus Almeria, mourning the supposed death of her husband, and the actual death of his father, bewails her plight:

> Father and Son are now no more—
> Then why am I? O when shall I have Rest?
> Why do I live to say you are no more?
> Why are all these things thus?
> Is there necessity I must be miserable?

> Is it of Moment to the Peace of Heav'n
> That I should be afflicted thus?—if not
> Why is it thus contriv'd? Why are things laid
> By some unseen Hand, so, as of consequence
> They must to me bring Curses, Grief of Heart,
> The last Distress of Life, and sure Despair.
>
> [ll. 53-63]

This series of questions, with its five emphatic *why*'s, establishes immediately the searching and interrogatory mode that is so dominant a feature of the play—the proper mode, after all, for the theodicean question of why, if there is a God of justice, the innocent are so often "afflicted" in this life. In her complaint, furthermore, Almeria clearly questions, though very inconclusively, whether her affliction is necessitated or determined, a possibility even more strongly raised in Congreve's revisions of 1710, where line 56 is completed by another question, "Is it of Force?" and where "as of consequence" in line 61 becomes "as of *sure* consequence" (my italics). So vehement, and so audacious, indeed, does her questioning of Heaven's justice appear to her lady-in-waiting that she feels called upon to chide Almeria by saying, "Alas you search too far, and think too deeply."

But however much Almeria may feel, for the moment, that Heaven has "spared" her only "for yet more Affliction," the announcement of her father's approach, and with him the man he would force her to marry, so acts upon her spirit as first to make her resolve never to be so contracted,

> No, it shall never be; for I will die first,
> Die ten thousand Deaths,

and then, kneeling, to make the following "Sacred Vow" to Heaven:

> If ever I do yield, or give consent,
> By any Action, Word, or Thought, to wed
> Another Lord; may then just Heav'n show'r down
> Unheard of Curses on me, greater far
> (If such there be in angry Heav'ns Vengeance)
> Than any I have yet endur'd.

Having manifested so "willed" a resolution, Almeria immediately finds her "Heart has some Relief" and feels herself "more at large." She is also prompted by her new feelings to think of visiting the "good *Anselmo*'s Tomb," there to repeat her vow "more solemnly."

The very opening lines of the play, where Almeria says that music not only has "Charms to sooth a savage Breast" but also the power of informing "things inanimate" as "with living Souls," had carried with them intimations of resurrection and new life, and so too does the beginning of act 2, where Heli says that his own arising "in very deed from Death" could give him no joy comparable to that of hearing that his friend Osmyn (Alphonso) was also alive. These muted notes of resurrection, however, are simply premonitory to Almeria's arrival at Anselmo's tomb, there to repeat her vows "to him, to Heav'n and . . . *Alphonso*'s Soul." The door of this tomb, like that of another and more ancient sepulcher, stands open, prompting in Almeria thoughts of her own death and reunion in Heaven with Anselmo and Alphonso, and also prompting her to stretch forth her hands and to cry out:

> O Joy too great!
> O Ecstasy of Thought! help me *Anselmo:*
> Help me *Alphonso*, take me, reach thy Hand;
> To thee, to thee I call, to thee *Alphonso*.
> O *Alphonso*.

The response to her call, of course, is designedly wondrous, and little short of sensational, for her husband, "*ascending from the Tomb*," seems instantly brought back to life before her very eyes. Alphonso, for his part, having long thought Almeria to have drowned, regards her sudden appearance as a similar return from death:

> 'tis she! 'tis she her self!
> Nor Dead, nor Shade, but breathing and alive!
> It is *Almeria*! 'tis my Wife!

The principal interrogative term of act 1 had been *why*, but in this scene of reunion, and of seeming resurrection, the leading term becomes *how*. Thus, in four different speeches Almeria asks of Alphonso: "O how hast thou return'd"; "Where hast thou been? and

how art thou alive?/How is all this?"; "How camest thou there?"
(in his father's tomb); and finally, "But still, how camest thee
hither? how thus?" Alphonso promises her, at the end of the scene,
that Heli will tell her "how" he escaped from death, "how" he is
there, and "how" he is now called Osmyn rather than Alphonso, but
the language used by all those present during the whole course of
this grave-side encounter directs us to supernatural rather than to
naturalistic explanations of both the "why" and the "how" of
events. Almeria's first exclamation, when she sees her husband
arising from his father's tomb, is clearly an echo of Hamlet's words
on first seeing the ghost of his father, "Angels and all the Host of
heaven support me," while her next words are an appeal to "Mercy
and Providence!" Her recognition of Heli causes her to exclaim,
"More Miracles," while Heli regards her reunion with her husband as
a "Miracle of Happiness!" Alphonso sums up their common bewilderment at what has befallen them, "beyond all Hope, all
Thought," by saying first that "There are no Wonders, or else all is
Wonder," and then:

> What means the Bounty of All-gracious Heav'n,
> That thus with open Hand it scatters good,
> As in a Waste of Mercy?
> Where will this end!

The extreme bewilderment, even the disorientation, of the characters in the face of the seeming "Miracles" they have experienced
is itself testimony to the inadequacy of any naturalistic or necessitarian "explanation" of their reunion. So suddenly, and so inexplicably, is each apparently "return'd" from death that both sense
and reason are staggered, and the power of their eyes to see and of
their minds to know is brought in doubt—as it is, indeed, throughout
the play. Alphonso dares not stir nor breathe lest by so doing he
"dissolve/That tender, lovely Form of painted Air/So like *Almeria.*"
Almeria is so distracted at first that she takes Alphonso to be her
own father, and later she tells him that his appearance, "with such
Suddenness," is "such Surprize, such Mystery, such Exstasy,/As
hurries all my Soul, and dozes my weak Sense." Alphonso is so
overcome, in fact, that initially at least he will seek no explanation

of the blessing accorded him:

> O I'll not ask, nor answer how, or why,
> We both have backward trod the paths of Fate,
> To meet again in Life, to know I have thee,
> Is knowing more than any Circumstance,
> Or means by which I have thee—.

The stress of the text leaves little doubt that their reunion has been brought about by an "All-powerful Heav'n" and an "All-gracious Heav'n," but the same text, by the remarkable repetition of one word on four occasions, also suggests that the Divine Will and the human will may be so conjoined as to be indistinguishable. The word is *call,* encountered first in Almeria's cry, "To thee, to thee I call, to thee *Alphonso,*" and in her husband's response while "ascending from the Tomb": "Who calls that wretched thing, that was *Alphonso*?" A bit later the still shaken Almeria exclaims, "Sure, from thy Father's Tomb, thou didst arise," and Alphonso replies, "I did, and thou didst call me," and, a moment later, "I heard thy Spirit call *Alphonso.*" In however ambiguous a way, the text endows Almeria with the mysterious power of "calling up" from the grave her supposedly dead husband.

Almeria is seemingly endowed with that power, I believe, because of the "Sacred Vow" she made to Heaven in act 1. It was on the taking of that vow that she felt relief at heart and an enlargement of her spirit, and it was then also that she was so strangely prompted to visit Anselmo's tomb to repeat her vow. We are reminded of her vow several times just before and after her voice has so dramatically, and in the most literal possible way, "called up" her husband from his father's tomb. We are left in no doubt that the "Miracle" of their "return" to each other has been contrived by an "All-powerful Heav'n," but at the same time we are also instructed, in a most teasing and certainly theatrical fashion, that Heaven may choose to work its miracles by way of a distressed but resolute human soul. Far from being the victim of "suddenly materializing walls of circumstance," Almeria is rather presented as one who has been chosen, because of her "Faithfulness and Love," as an instrument of salvation and resurrection into "new life."

II

The scenes and settings of *The Mourning Bride* are so arranged by Congreve as to present stark and powerful contrasts.[6] Opening in a brilliantly lighted "Room of State," amidst which Almeria's black garb seems an offending blot to her father, the play in act 2 moves first to an awe-inspiring "Ile of a Temple" and then to the first stirrings of life and hope, in the lovers, amidst darkness and "a Place of Tombs." Act 3 is set in the darkness of "A Prison," where Osmyn languishes in chains, and act 4 returns to the jealousies and machinations of the high and mighty amidst their "State." The last act opens amidst further rage and confusions in the "Room of State," but then "changes to the Prison," where the wicked and powerful are brought, by their own machinations, to their own destruction.

Except for the scenes in the room of state, therefore, the action of the play takes place in darkness or semidarkness, for the most part in a prison cell, and the emblematic import of such a setting should by now be readily apparent: the darkness, that is, serves here, as in Scripture, as the emblem expressive "of Straits, or Difficulties, or Adversities," while Osmyn's cell and shackles are equally expressive of the confinements and afflictions from which men may be released only by God's will and their own conversion (see pp. 29 and 171–72 above). The soliloquy with which Osmyn opens act 3 leaves no doubt as to the emblematic nature of his plight:

> But now, and I was clos'd within the Tomb
> That holds my Father's Ashes; and but now,
> Where he was Pris'ner, I am too imprison'd.
> Sure 'tis the Hand of Heav'n, that leads me thus,
> And for some Purpose points out these Remembrances.

The coincident circumstances and sufferings of father and son as pointing to the "Hand of Heav'n" would no more have been overlooked by the audience than it is by Osmyn, for it was by such strange concurrences of event that the divine administration was commonly thought to manifest itself (see pp. 27 ff. above).

Given the diction and purport of his soliloquy, what happens next in Osmyn's cell should be considered, in my opinion, as the theatrical realization of such frequently preached texts as, for example, Psalm 112:4, "Unto the upright there ariseth light in the darkness," or 2 Peter 1:19, "Ye do well that you take heed, as unto a light that shineth in a dark place, until the day dawn, and the day star arise in your hearts." Having found, "In a dark Corner" of his cell, a "Paper," Osmyn takes it to a "Light" and there finds it to be a "Petition" to Heaven, in his father's hand, imploring that his own sufferings be recompensed by doubled "Mercies" on his son. The last line of the petition, however, is incomplete (*"Not for my self, but him, hear me, all-gracious——"*), and incites in Osmyn his own questioning, analogous to that with which Almeria had opened the play, of heavenly justice:

> 'Tis wanting what should follow—Heav'n, Heav'n shou'd follow.
> But 'tis torn off—why should that Word alone
> Be torn from his Petition? 'Twas to Heav'n.
> But Heav'n was deaf, Heav'n heard him not; but thus,
> Thus as the Name of Heav'n from this is torn,
> So did it tear the Ears of Mercy, from
> His Voice; Shutting the Gates of Pray'r against him.
> If Piety be thus debarr'd Access
> On high; and of good Men, the very best
> Is singled out to bleed, and bear the Scourge;
> What is Reward, or, what is Punishment?

Here Osmyn checks himself, asking "But who shall dare to tax Eternal Justice?" Yet he also argues that man cannot help but reason and reflect upon the cause of his suffering, even though reason be but "the Power/To guess at Right and Wrong; the trembling Lamp/Of wand'ring Life."

Osmyn's soliloquy once more raises directly the theodicean question so central to the play, and does so, moreover, in a detail that recalls the crucial missing fragment of the note found by Aurelian in *Incognita*. And however remote the genre and circumstances of *Incognita* may be from *The Mourning Bride,* the complaints of the protagonists against heavenly justice in each work are countered almost immediately by events which demonstrate plainly how quickly Heaven may work, through human error or blindness or even wickedness, to bring about a happiness the complainant may have thought lost. Thus Aurelian, dejected at the loss of the fragment that would tell him the whereabouts of his beloved, wanders out into the darkness and finds his footsteps directed to her rescue, while Osmyn's questioning of "Eternal Justice" is actually interrupted by the entrance of Heli, who informs him that the tyrant Manuel's high-handed refusal to share the spoils of war with his troops has made them "ripe for Mutiny" and that others who "love *Anselmo*'s Memory" would speedily rally to Alphonso's "Cause" once thay know he is yet alive under the name of Osmyn.

Heli's words prompt Osmyn to tell him of the "Paternal Love" and "Sanctity" evinced in his father's petition, and Heli in turn offers this interpretation of the note:

> The Care of Providence, sure left it there;
> To arm your Mind with Hope. Such Piety
> Was never heard in vain: Heav'n has in Store
> For you, those Blessings it with-held from him.
> In that Assurance live; which Time, I hope,
> And our next meeting will confirm.

The "next meeting" of the two friends does of course "confirm" Heli's trust in the "Care of Providence," for they at that time prove victorious over the forces of Manuel.

More immediately, however, Heli's words cause Osmyn to regret and retract his earlier mistrustful complaint against "Eternal Justice," when, seemingly oblivious to the way his own words recall another great sufferer, he had questioned why his father, "of good Men, the very best," had been "singled out to bleed, and bear the Scourge." Now he confesses to himself, "I've been to blame, and question'd with Impiety/The Care of Heav'n," and he also attributes the "Lesson" in faith that has been given him to a kind of mystical vision granted to his father in "some Hour of Inspiration,"

> when his pure Thoughts were born,
> Like Fumes of Sacred Incense, o'er the Clouds,
> And wafted thence, on Angels Wings, thro' Ways

Of Light, to the bright Source of all. There, in
The Book of Prescience, he beheld this Day;
And waking to the World and mortal Sense,
Left this Example of his Resignation,
This his last Legacy to me, which I
Will treasure here; more worth than Diadems,
Or all extended Rule of regal Pow'r.

We do not see Osmyn, after act 3, until the closing moments of
act 5, when, having been set free by Manuel's own captain of the
guards and having defeated the tyrant's forces, he returns to the cell
where Almeria, thinking the headless body lying there is his, is ready
to drink of the poisoned cup. Convinced that her husband is "dead
at last, quite, quite, for ever dead," Almeria at first can only take his
sudden appearance before her as a "Dream," but then, in her last
words of the play, she reminds us once again of the "Miracles" that
may occur in a world where events demonstrate the "impotence of
Sight" and where "There are no Wonders, or else all is Wonder":

Giv'n me again from Death! O all ye Powers
Confirm this Miracle! can I believe
My Sight, against my Sight? and shall I trust
That Sense, which in one Instant shews him dead
And living? yes, I will; I've been abus'd
With Apparitions and affrighting Fantoms.

The world of *The Mourning Bride,* in the words of Gonsalez,
has "somewhat yet of Mystery" in it. Faced with its mystery, man
may be "amused," or blinded, by his own sight, just as he may
"exceed in thinking" and be "blinded by [his] Thoughts." It is also
a world, on the other hand, where a grief-stricken and dying father
may, "in some Hour of Inspiration," read in Heaven's "Book of
Prescience," and there find a way to leave the "Example of his
Resignation" by which his son, with all the "afflictions" heaped
upon him by an inscrutable Providence, will be strengthened and
confirmed in his faith—and thereby deserve not only his release from
a dark and underground dungeon cell (as close an analogy to a tomb
as one could find), but also deserve to be given "again from Death"
to his mourning bride.

III

For the title page of his play Congreve selected an Ovidian epigraph, *Neque enim lex aequior ulla,/Quam necis artifices arte perire sua* ("For there is no juster law than that contrivers of death should perish by their own contrivances"),[7] a pagan dictum that receives its Christian conversion in those last lines where the playwright said the "general Moral" of *The Mourning Bride* could be found when Osmyn tells Almeria that the wicked ministers, Gonsalez and Alonzo,

> both of Wounds
> Expiring, have with their last Breath, confess'd
> The just Decrees of Heav'n, in turning on
> Themselves, their own most bloody Purposes.

No doubt coincidentally, but strikingly so nevertheless, we find that in the same year *The Mourning Bride* appeared, a similar collocation of the Ovidian sentence with biblical teaching was made by William Turner, in his *Compleat History of the Most Remarkable Providences, Both of Judgment and Mercy, Which have Hapned in this Present Age,* where there appears this introductory comment to a chapter entitled "Divine Judgments by way of Retaliation":

> There is no juster Law, *saith the old Poet,* than that those who are the Authors of Contriving a Mischief for others, fall into it themselves; and the *Sacred Scripture agrees thereto; and we have many Instances of such Judgments: And Certainly, if any Evils in the World carry in them the Signature and Indication of the Cause, these do.* [See chap. 99]

Much of the stress in Turner's work, as in most other providentialist apologetics, is on the way instances of God's judgments in this world "carry in them," as he says, "the Signature and Indication of the Cause." The same emphasis can be seen in this passage from Barrow, only one of many in the age that could be chosen as remarkably congruent with both the Fable and Moral of *The Mourning Bride:*

> The proceedings of God (especially in way of Judgment, or of dispensing rewards and punishments) discover their original by

their kind and countenance, which usually do bear a near resemblance, or some significant correspondence to the actions upon which they are grounded. . . . So that the deserts of men shall often be legible in the recompenses conferred or inflicted on them;

as when

Craft incurreth disappointment, and Simplicity findeth good Success; when haughty Might is shattered, and helpless Innocence is preserved; when bloudy Oppressours have *bloud given them to drink* [Rev. 16:6], and come to welter in their own gore; (an accident which almost continually doth happen;) when Treacherous men by their own confidants, or by themselves are betrayed.

"By such occurrences," Barrow concludes, "the finger of God doth point out and indicate itself."[8]

My point here really is that a seventeenth-century audience would scarcely have needed, though they probably relished, the play's epigraph, or the "Moral" to which Congreve pointed so explicitly, in order to discern the way in which its concatenation of events, especially as they eventuate in reward and punishment, are designed to bear the "Signature and Indication" of theurgical dominion. The play, that is, carried with it an instant "legibility" for a contemporary playgoer, as it did, we may recall, for James Drake, when he observed that "*Manuel* in the prosecution and exercise of his Cruelty and Tyranny, is taken in a Trap of his own laying, and falls himself a Sacrifice in the room of him, whom he in his rage had devoted," and added that "*Alphonso* in reward of his Virtue receives the Crowns of *Valentia* and *Granada,* and is happy in his Love; all which he acknowledges to be the Gift of Providence, which protects the Innocent and rewards the Virtuous" (see p. 46 above).

The "legibility" of Providential sovereignty in the play is made the more certain by the way the wicked, with all their power and craft, are unable to enforce their own sovereignty over human nature and event. If Almeria and Osmyn are represented as baffled and amazed by the way their misfortunes are inexplicably, or "miraculously," turned into blessings, their oppressors are represented as equally perplexed by the way things turn out. They are represented, indeed, as frustrated by their own designs and actions, as being, in Zara's castigation of Selim,

> officious in contriving,
> In executing, puzzled, lame, and lost.

Selim defends himself by replying, "Avert it, Heav'n, that you should ever suffer/For my Defect; or that the Means which I/ Devis'd, should ruine your Design," but his words provide, if one is needed, the nicest possible gloss on the configuration of events in the play: the ironical way in which the very "Means" employed by connivers and self-seekers prove to be so self-destructive. Selim's very next words, moreover, intensify the existential stress of the play, for he tells her that "Prescience is Heav'ns alone, not giv'n to Man," and so we are reminded once again of the fallible nature of all human thought and forethought, sight and foresight. Whatever the glimpse in Heaven's "Book of Prescience" afforded Osmyn's father, the only predictive capacity afforded the other characters is that by which their own words or plans are fulfilled—but in a way utterly contrary to their intent or expectations. When Manuel says to Zara,

> To cast beneath your Feet the Crown you've sav'd,
> Though on the Head that wears it, were too little,

his words serve as the wholly unconscious but gruesome forecast of the moment when his head has actually been severed, and "muffled" in a corner of Osmyn's cell, just before Zara's entrance there. Again, Almeria, distracted by grief and fear over what she thinks to be the fatal discovery of Osmyn's identity, thinks she hears a voice which "cries Murder," and so resolves to "follow it" to the "Tomb" (as she calls his cell) from which "it calls"—there to find her husband not dead, but given her "again from Death."

Almeria is mistaken, at the time, in her belief that she has betrayed her husband's identity to those who would take his life, but her "mistake" nevertheless sets forward a series of choices, plots, and events whose course and outcome would unquestionably have carried, in my opinion, their own special "Signature" to audiences long habituated to the belief that God exercises "an Absolute Government over Mankind, who are Free Agents, without destroying the Liberty and Freedom of their Choice, which would destroy the nature of Vertue and Vice, of Rewards and Punishments" (see pp. 26 ff. above). In her grief, mistaken though it be, Almeria's speech is so affected that she interchanges the name of Alphonso and Osmyn and "Husband," causing Manuel, though he senses a "dire Import" in what he considers to be his daughter's ravings, to rush offstage in a fury, leaving her to make another mistake. Thinking that her father's minister, Gonsalez, alone could have had the "Policy, and Fraud, to find the fatal Secret out," she both calls a curse upon his family and plainly declares Osmyn's identity, leaving Gonsalez to soliloquize:

> *Osmyn Alphonso*! no; she over-rates
> My Policy, I ne'er suspected it:
> Nor now had known it, but from her mistake.

Almeria's disclosure, importing as it does the ·frustration of his son's own marriage to her, "concludes" Gonsalez in his decision to murder Osmyn: "To doubt," he says, "when I may be assur'd, is Folly." And so he evades Manuel's summons, causing the two of them to plot the separate courses that will have so deadly and so ironic an intersection.

From this point on, the purposes of Manuel, Zara, and Gonsalez are separately forwarded by their own counsels and choices, yet the designs and inclinations of each are manifestly the causes of their destruction. Thus Manuel, enraged at finding his daughter wedded and Zara to be false, resolves to "counterwork this Treachery," and in his fury deals a grievously offensive blow to his captain of the guards, the very man on whom he must depend to murder Alphonso and help him in his scheme to confront Zara with her perfidy. Commanding the captain to bring him Alphonso's robes, the king also orders the cell, where he will await Zara's visit to Alphonso, to "be darken'd, so as to amuze the Sight," and so he creates the very circumstances whereby Gonsalez will kill him by a "dire Mistake." Hoping to conceal the death of the king, to prevent despair among his few remaining troops, Alonzo then severs Manuel's head, causing Zara, who enters the cell a moment later, to mistake the "headless Trunk" for that of Alphonso. Thinking his murder to be the consequence of Selim's "fatal and pernicious Counsels," her own rage and despair cause her to stab him at the very moment he tries to tell her that Alphonso is still alive, and so she takes alone the poison she had brought for both.

All of the plotters—Manuel, Zara, Gonsalez, and Selim—have been drawn, by their own purposes, from their usual setting, the well-lighted "Room of State," into the cell which Gonsalez describes as being all "dark within, save what/A Lamp that feebly lifts a sickly Flame,/By fits reveals." In this so emblematic darkness, the feeble light of human reason is proven insufficient for its own purposes—but instrumental nevertheless in the accomplishment of the "just Decrees of Heav'n." The "legibility" of such events seems to me indisputable: in them "the finger of God doth point out and indicate itself."

10

Forgiving and Forgetting and the Way of the World

for nothing buth Truth can long continue; and Time is the
severest Judge of Truth.

John Dryden, Dedication of
The Spanish Friar (1681)

"Come, come, Forgive and Forget, Aunt, why you must an you
are a Christian."

Sir Wilfull Witwoud,
The Way of the World (1700)

The Way of the World was written two years after Collier first took
umbrage at the stage, a fact which may explain the more subdued
and circumspect ways in which its lineaments are designed to reflect
a Christian normative order. The play, in its basic configuration of
event, is no less illustrative than Congreve's earlier work of the
"way" things should work out in a providentially ordered world,
but its language (perhaps in response to Collier's notion that almost
any stage allusion to sacred matters would of itself be inappropriate
and even blasphemous) is throughout much less obviously religious—
except in its climactic scene of "judgment," where the richest
dimension of the situation cannot be fully appreciated apart from
Congreve's allusions to Christian liturgy and to right-minded
Christian behavior. There is a very strong flow of birth or breeding
imagery, associated closely with the passage of time and with the
idea that the truth, like "Love and Murder" in *The Double-Dealer,*
inevitably "will out": as Fainall says, "If it must all come out, why
let 'em know it, 'tis but *the way of the World.*" There is once more
the pattern wherein plotters are tripped up by their own devices, as
well as several signal instances of "opportune discovery" or seemingly happenstance event whereby villainy is exposed and rendered

impotent. Fundamental to the play also is the emphasis Congreve places on a constructive generosity of human nature, a willingness to "forgive and forget," by which family relationships (and by extension those of all society) may be made not only possible but also loving and lasting.

I

Over the past decade or so it has become the fashion among critics to perceive the principal character of *The Way of the World* as "Machiavellian Mirabell," the "Machiavellian poet as maker of society," as the "omniscient hero" who manipulates "the elements of polite society as cleverly as a Horner," as the man who has gained the greatest "mastery of conventions," as the character "who is held up for our admiration as the most accomplished manipulator," the one who "is victorious at the end of the play not because of any particular moral qualities he may have, but rather because he is a better lawyer than Fainall, and has made sure that his threats and his bargains are legally enforceable."[1]

Such perceptions of Mirabell seem badly skewed to me, and for several reasons. They ignore, in the first place, the very basic fact that all of the schemes set forward by this so-called Machiavellian master of convention and society are shown, in the play itself, as countermined and frustrated. They further ignore the equally basic fact that Mirabell gains Millamant's hand and fortune only after his very ungentlemanly schemes against Lady Wishfort have proved unsuccessful, and also only after he has agreed to appear before her ladyship and profess his "sincere remorse" for the "many Injuries" he has "offer'd to so good a Lady." They furthermore, out of some strange and aberrant esteem for an amoral Machiavellian craftiness and exploitation of others, would move *The Way of the World* off any moral center at all, as may be seen most clearly perhaps in Birdsall's view of Mirabell as the "kind of hero from whom unprincipled behavior is to be expected in such a life-and-death matter as [he] has in hand"[2]—a view which would certainly have confirmed Collier in his conviction that Congreve and other Restoration playwrights, in spite of their protests, were offering up for audience admiration a set of rake-heroes whose pursuit of a fortune justified any means, however mendacious, they might employ.

Such critical perceptions of Mirabell seem to me to originate, finally, from the widespread current assumptions that the world of Congreve's art is governed by some dubious amalgamation of Hobbesian, nihilistic, "Epicurean" premises, and that in consequence any supremacy in such a putative moral jungle could only be won, or even merited, by a "hero" in the Machiavellian mode—despite the fact that the Machiavellian Maskwell in *The Double-Dealer,* so much the honest Mellefont's superior in guile and stratagem, is exposed and expelled from the Touchwood estate at the end of the play; or that Valentine, in *Love for Love,* wins Angelica only when he renounces his impostures and his self-interest; or that Manuel and Gonsalez and Zara, in *The Mourning Bride,* are shown as finally destroyed not only by the "just Decrees of Heav'n" but also by their own inordinate cunning.

So intent, indeed, have been the critics on demonstrating that the "resolution of the play depends entirely on Mirabell's wit, charm, and knowledge of the ways of the world,"[3] or on proving that the "secular strength of his solution must not be diminished by mere luck,"[4] that they have ignored or depreciated the very large number of seemingly quite fortuitous, yet also extremely "opportune," discoveries in the play—"discoveries" which, in the end, may be seen not only as having frustrated Mirabell's own more unpalatable schemes during the course of the play but also as providing Mrs. Fainall, in the end, with the moral courage to face, and face down, a vile and mercenary husband. The chance discoveries by which Mirabell's impostures are thwarted, as well as those by which his final success is forwarded, are inconsistent with the idea of his being the consummate Machiavellian master of his milieu; they are consistent, on the other hand, with the pattern evinced in Congreve's other plays, where we find that protagonists never succeed by their own unaided devices and strength, but are rather moved, if morally disposed, through a course of defeats, mistakes, seeming coincidence, and apparently chance discovery, to ultimate reward.

Some twenty years ago Paul and Miriam Mueschke argued that Mirabell is "a developing character," of a "generous and introspective" nature, and that he "sets the moral norm" of the play,[5] a view with which I am in general agreement. At the same time, we must not overlook the ungentlemanly and even callous deceptions he practices against Lady Wishfort (offenses on his part that in my opinion are far more grievous than his one-time affair with a randy young widow Languish), and neither must we overlook the failure of his deceptions or the impediments his failures raise to his marriage with Millamant. The very beginning of the play, indeed, establishes the fact that this so-called Machiavellian Mirabell has been frustrated in his highly questionable scheme of eloping with Millamant, under cover of his "sham Addresses" to her aunt, because of the jealousy-inspired disclosure of his scheme by a lady, Mrs. Marwood, more thoroughly Machiavellian in spirit than he. With her exposure of his shamming, there of course occurs his estrangement from Lady Wishfort, and thus the creation of a most serious impediment to his hopes of wedding Millamant and also gaining that half of her fortune which depends "upon her marrying with my Lady's Approbation."

With whatever restraint Mirabell had limited his false gallantries toward Lady Wishfort (he could not undertake, he tells Fainall, "downright personally to debauch her"), his pretended passion for her is inconsistent nevertheless with the conduct expected of a "man of honor" and is demeaning of him as it is for her ladyship. Yet hard upon the miscarriage of this unbecoming behavior, he embarks on the new and even more discreditable scheme by which he hopes first to beguile Lady Wishfort into a fraudulent and unspeakably embarrassing marriage with his manservant and then to blackmail her into consenting to his own marriage with Millamant. It matters not much, it seems to me, that he has insured the illegality of such a marriage of Lady Wishfort by first having Waitwell wed to Foible, or that he has made her ladyship's daughter, Mrs. Fainall, privy to his design; for the bare outline of his scheme is enough to suggest its rather callous disregard of a lady's feelings, however ridiculous those feelings are made to appear at times.

Not only is Mirabell shown as having violated time-honored conventions of courtship and as having proceeded by way of unseemly stratagems: there is also a decided escalation in his chicanery—from relatively harmless dupery by way of flattery and innuendo to an attempted entrapment which would have culminated in demands of an extortionate nature—demands not much unlike those later actually forced upon Lady Wishfort by Fainall. Lady Wishfort's outrage at the exposure of this second scheme by Mirabell seems fully justified, no matter that her own carnal and headlong spirit may have invited such maneuverings to gain an approbation which on her part should have been more forthcoming.

The frustration of Mirabell's schemes is made the more comic, and the more instructive, I believe, when we consider the vanity and confidence of mind with which he enters upon them. When he receives word that Waitwell and Foible have been "Married and Bedded" and that all is in readiness for his plot against Lady Wishfort, his air of self-satisfaction is so evident that Fainall is moved to greet him thus: "Joy of your Success, *Mirabell;* you look pleas'd." When he discloses his scheme to Mrs. Fainall, his complacence in his own foresight is obvious when he assures her that, lest Waitwell "stand upon Terms," he has "made him sure beforehand." His certainty in the inevitable success of his scheme is also fostered by the confidence of others: Mrs. Fainall gives him her "Opinion" of his "Success," and Foible particularly assures him that he need "not doubt of Success."

In spite of all the confidence thus expressed in his success, however, Mirabell's conspiracy is utterly balked, as we know, by the seemingly fortuitous fact that Lady Wishfort requests Mrs. Marwood to retire into her closet (among that collection of books by Quarles, Prynne, Collier, and Bunyan) so that she may examine Foible "with more freedom" about her meeting with Mirabell in St. James's Park. Mrs. Marwood thus quite by chance overhears the later dialogue between Foible and Mrs. Fainall, and thereby learns of the Waitwell-Sir Rowland plot and also the fact of Mrs. Fainall's past affair with Mirabell. Armed with this information, and galled beyond endurance at hearing Foible declare that Mirabell "can't abide her," Mrs. Marwood then proceeds to enflame Fainall with the news of his wife's former frailty and also concocts the measures by which her own slighted person may be revenged and by which Fainall may seize not only his wife's fortune but the half of Millamant's as well.

Mrs. Marwood's letter of exposure, arriving as it does at the very

height of the false Sir Rowland's gasping solicitations of Lady Wishfort, effectually demolishes the last and most grandiose of schemes
by our "Machiavellian Mirabell," and renders even more remote any
likelihood of his receiving her ladyship's "Approbation." Fainall's
simultaneous threat to divorce his wife unless she make her fortune
over to him reduces Lady Wishfort, moreover, to such a despairing
helplessness that she is ready to "Compound" and to "give up all" to
Fainall, indeed "any thing, everything for Composition." Confronted with so ugly a situation as this, the direct result of his own
past guilty liaison with Lady Wishfort's daughter, and the direct
result also of his own unbecoming deportment toward her ladyship,
Mirabell at last has the good sense to lay aside thoughts of any
further stratagems and so obeys Millamant's "commands" to "come
in Person" before her aunt.

Strange as it may seem on first thought, the final scene of *The
Way of the World,* like the final scenes of *The Double-Dealer* and
Love for Love, must be regarded as another scene of "judgment,"
and in the tradition of such scenes in English dramatic history as we
have noted before. Only Holland seems to have observed the "judgmental" nature of the scene, when he remarks that in the finale
Lady Wishfort "becomes a kind of tribunal before whom the opposed forces in the play plead their causes."[6] And while my emphasis is quite different from Holland's, his comment is right in the
main, for however improbable and ridiculous a tribunal she may
seem, Lady Wishfort is nevertheless the head, however disordered
her own head may be, of the large family whose members make up
most of the characters in the play: all relationships in the play center
on her, and so there is an appropriateness, however comic, in the
fact that the main transgressors against her honor and her person,
whatever its dilapidations, are brought to judgment before her.

We must not overlook, though we seem to have done so, the remarkable fact that in this last scene Mirabell makes his first direct
appearance, and thus his first direct address, to Lady Wishfort in the
entire play, a piece of theater which tellingly points up, I believe, the
behind-the-back nature of his previous treatment of her. Now, with
the exposure of all his schemes, and faced with the savage treatment
brought on Mrs. Fainall because of her past illicit relations with

himself as well as with the extortionate demands made on her mother for the same reason, Mirabell here comes forward not only to express remorse for his behavior but also to evince clearly the fundamental generosity of spirit which the play, in spite of his disposition to "shamming," affirms to be so much a part of his character. One need not, if one chooses, take Mirabell's expressions of remorse here totally at face value, but then I see no reason to take his words and behavior as totally insincere, especially if we consider the religious terminology that is made so basic a part of this scene of "judgment"—and consider also what seems to be that terminology's direct source and proper context: the General Confession in the Anglican order of Holy Communion.

In the Anglican service, a communicant is required specifically to "acknowledge" his "manifold sins," and to "earnestly repent" and be "heartily sorry" for his "misdoings," before he can ask for mercy and be forgiven for "all that is past." Mirabell's first words to Lady Wishfort express his "deep sense of the many Injuries" he has offered her, and are followed by a declaration of "a sincere remorse, and a hearty Contrition," as well as a "confession" that he has "deservedly forfeited the high Place" he once held of "sighing" at her feet. There are no stage directions to require his kneeling, but his words suggest he does in fact kneel before her (as would communicants during the General Confession), for he goes on to appeal that she not "turn" from him "in disdain," adding that he is "a Suppliant only for Pity." And when he asks to be "pitied first; and afterwards forgotten," honest Sir Wilfull is so moved that he exclaims: "By'r Lady a very reasonable request; and will cost you nothing, Aunt—Come, come, Forgive and Forget, Aunt, why you must an you are a Christian."

Mirabell proceeds to "confess" that though his "device" had a "Face of guiltiness," it was "at most an Artifice which Love Contriv'd," and then he pleads that "errours which Love produces have ever been accounted *Venial.*" He asks that Lady Wishfort "think it is Punishment enough" for him to have lost what he holds most dear, his love, and with that love his "Peace and Quiet"—nay, all his "hopes of future Comfort." Again Sir Wilfull intercedes, and with his second behest that she "forgive quickly" her ladyship agrees to stifle her

"just resentment" and to endeavor what she can "to forget." A bare
fifty lines later, after Mirabell has offered his "Remedy" against
Fainall's unconscionable demands, she declares to him, in those
words Congreve had also put in quite a different lady's mouth (see
p. 155 above), that she will "forgive all that's past"—an almost
word-for-word reminder once more of the petition of the Anglican
priest during the General Confession: "Forgive us all that is past"
(I quote from a 1691 edition of The Book of Common Prayer).

Some critics of late have argued that Congreve "deliberately"
excluded any kind of religious imagery or "any cluster of religious
allusions" from *The Way of the World.*[7] Yet such a cluster of allusions is unmistakably present in this final scene, and there is no hint,
as far as I can see, that the language of confession and penitence and
forgiveness is being used in any way that could be considered blasphemous or sardonic—a mocking of the Anglican service or a jeer at
a ridiculous old woman. Of course I am not trying to turn the scene
into a ponderous enactment of a liturgical event, or Lady Wishfort
into a grotesque caricature of the Deity. I am arguing that the
visually emblematic nature of the scene, and the language which
accompanies it, both serve to evoke the substance and the form, the
spirit and the letter, of a Christian ceremony of penitence and forgiveness, and that an awareness of these elements serves to heighten
and complicate, rather than overturn, the comic mood of the play's
climactic scene.

II

The title of *The Way of the World* does not admit of an easy
glossing, in part because of the unsettling fact that the titular phrase
is employed three times in the play, and with different implications
on each occasion. There is Fainall's association of it with a "rank"
state of marriage, wherein spouses become "Rank-Husband" and
"Rank-Wife"—"all in the Way of the World," an association mag-
nified by those closing lines of the play which declare that "marriage
frauds too oft are paid in kind." Not too removed from such an
association, perhaps, is Mirabell's use of the phrase in describing
Mrs. Fainall's precautionary conveyance of her estate to himself
as "*the way of the World,*" more particularly the way "of the

Widdows of the World." Quite apart from these uses of the titular
phrase, each in its own way reflective of certain unsavory facts of
life in the play, there is, however, Fainall's statement in the last
scene, when so many events of the past have come to light, that "If
it must all come out, why let 'em know it, 'tis but *the way of the
World*," an observation that seems especially applicable to the way
the play moves from revelation to revelation, a movement enforced
by a pattern of diction constructed out of such terms as "Discovery," "Exposure," "Detection," and supported also by a strain
of birth imagery which insists that all events in the womb of time
will inevitably be born, that truth, like murder, will out.

The importance of the birth imagery is suggested by the fact that
nearly all the characters employ it, beginning in the first scene when
Mirabell tells Fainall that Lady Wishfort, in "her Detestation of Mankind," will "let Posterity shift for it self," for "she'll breed no
more," and then, a moment later, confides that in pursuance of his
blandishments of her ladyship, and to "compliment her with the Im-
putation of an Affair with a young Fellow," he had "told her the
malicious town took notice that she was grown fat of a suddain; and
when she lay in of a Dropsie, persuaded her she was reported to be
in Labour." Witwoud, alluding to a treaty proposed between Millamant and Mirabell's counterfeit uncle, describes it as "being in
Embrio" and adds that "if it shou'd come to Life; poor *Mirabell*
wou'd be in some sort unfortunately fobb'd," while Petulant, equally
gullible about the rumored treaty, advises Mirabell that he could be
"disinherited" if the supposed uncle "shou'd marry and have a
Child." Mrs. Marwood cattily urges Millamant to own publicly her
love for Mirabell: "indeed," she says, "'tis time," "for the Town has
found it: The secret is grown too big for the Pretense: 'Tis like Mrs.
Primly's great Belly; she may lace it down before, but it burnishes on
her Hips." Fainall, upon learning of his wife's premarital amour with
Mirabell, somehow, in the rankness of his own imagination, updates
that long dead affair into a here-and-now act of infidelity and
cuckolding of himself: "'S death," he exclaims, "to be an Anticipated Cuckold, a Cuckold in Embrio. Sure I was born with budding
Antlers like a young Satyre, or a Citizens Child."

Lady Wishfort at one point feels "as pale and as faint" as "Mrs.

Qualmsick the Curate's Wife, that's always breeding," and in her indignation at Foible's part in the Sir Rowland plot denounces her as a "frontless Impudence, more than a big-Belly'd Actress." She is, moreover, rendered utterly despondent when Mrs. Marwood, in the rankness of *her* imagination, conjures up a nasty vision of the court scene which may ensue if Fainall is driven to "prove" her daughter's "Caprices" and "Cuckoldomes":

> Prove it *Madam*? What, and have your name prostituted in a pub-lick Court; Yours and your Daughter's reputation worry'd at the Barr by a pack of Bawling Lawyers? To be ushered in with an *O Yez* of Scandal; and have your Case* open'd by an old fum-bling Leacher in a Quoif like a Man Midwife to bring your Daughter's Infamy to Light. . . .

Sir Wilfull, in a drunken allusion to the match proposed between Millamant and himself, exclaims, "If she has her Maidenhead let her look to 't,—if she has not, let her keep her own Counsel in the mean time, and cry out at the nine Months end." Mirabell, in his exchange of "Conditions" during the "contract scene" with Millamant, fails not to bring up the "Item" of her "Breeding" the son which "may be presum'd" as a "blessing" on their "endeavours." And hovering in our thoughts, and behind so much of the play's action, there is, of course, that suspected pregnancy which led the young Widow Languish to marry Fainall—and which, by the end of the play, has produced some very unpleasant consequences.

We have seen such imagery of breeding and birth before this in Congreve, particularly in the closing "Moral" of *The Double-Dealer,* which assured us that "Howe're in private, Mischiefs are con-ceiv'd,/Torture and shame attend their open Birth." And in a non-dramatic context, his poem called *The Birth of the Muse,* published about three years before *The Way of the World,* Congreve gives us an explicit statement of what I take to be the import of the imagery of conception and birth that was later to be used so profusely in his

---

*An obvious pun on *case* as the female genitalia. Cf. *Romeo and Juliet,* act 3, scene 3, lines 84–85: "*Nurse.* O he is even in my mistress' case. Just in her case!"

play. Writing of the moment "When first the frame of this vast
Ball was made," Congreve goes on:

> Then *Time* had first a Name; by firm Decree
> Appointed Lord of all Futurity.
> Within whose ample Bosom Fates repose
> Causes of Things, and secret Seeds enclose,
> Which ripening there, shall one Day gain a Birth,
> And force a Passage thro' the teeming Earth.

The Way of the World is a play simply teeming with private plots,
secret infamy, sham addresses, past and present liaisons, all ripe and
pressing for delivery and disclosure, and it is to foster our sense that
the course of time will inevitably expose all such matters that Congreve crowds his play with all its talk about "bellies," "breeding,"
"embryos," "laboring," "midwifery," "nine-Months end," "discovery," "exposure," "bringing to light."

The idea of time as the great revealer of truth is an old and commonplace idea, of course, reflected in contemporary quotations of
Cicero to the effect that "Time wipeth out groundless conceits, but
confirms that which is found in nature and real,"[8] as well as in
Dryden's comment that "nothing but Truth can long continue; and
time is the severest Judge of Truth."[9] Congreve's own use of imagery
of parturition to convey a sense of time's inevitable exposures is
itself probably to be regarded as quite traditional, however wittily,
and even at times crudely, he has adjusted such imagery to the
vigorous, and the often coarse and savage, personalities of his play.
There is, for example, the old Latin tag, noted before in chapter 6,
Veritas filia temporis, with its implicit suggestions of time's par-
turitive process, and there are of course the opening verses of *Eccle-
siastes*, chapter 3, beginning with "To every thing there is a season,
and a time to every purpose under heaven," a contemporary gloss on
which by Bishop Wilkins associates time not only with imagery of
birth but also with the designs of an overruling Providence:

> The Wise man says there [in Proverbs, 27: 1], that the day brings
> forth events, *Partura est dies;* alluding to a teeming-Mother,
> to whom there is a set date for her delivery. So doth Time

travel with the decrees of Providence, and for each several action there is a pregnancy, a fulness of time.[10]

In *The Way of the World* one does not find, as in Congreve's earlier work, explicit reference to Heaven's justice or Providence's decrees. Nevertheless, the play's configuration of events—its progress, along a course of chance concurrences, fortunate mishaps, opportune discoveries, self-defeating triumphs, to a final scene of justice—is utterly in keeping with the configurations to be found in all the Congreve canon. Such a configuration, I believe, would have been as "legible," as "scrutable," to a contemporary audience, as that to be found in *The Double-Dealer* or in *The Mourning Bride.*

III

References to time—time past, time future, and the "mean time"—in *The Way of the World* are as copious as those to breeding and birth. In the play's opening scenes, Mirabell tells Fainall he is "engag'd in a Matter" (the sham marriage) which "is not yet ripe for discovery," while his question to Betty of "what says your Clock?" gets the pert reply, "Turn'd of the last Canonical Hour, Sir." Lady Wishfort's "Female Frailty" and "deprav'd" appetite are the "Green Sickness of a second Childhood; and like the faint Offer of a latter Spring, serves but to usher in the Fall; and withers in an affected Bloom." Her ladyship's further variance with time is suggested as much when she is put "out of all patience" as it is by her desire to "make haste," even "all imaginable haste," or by her desire that the false Sir Rowland be so importunate in his courtship that she "may unbend the severity of *Decorum*—and dispense with a little Ceremony," and so enter the sooner upon lawful carnal delights without being put "to the necessity of breaking her Forms." To a spiteful remark by Mrs. Marwood, Millamant replies that she is amazed to think what Mirabell can see in herself, for, she goes on, "I'll take my Death, I think you are handsomer—And within a Year or two as young—If you cou'd but stay for me, I shou'd overtake you—But that cannot be."

The insistent allusions to time throughout the play make the more noticeable the attempts, inevitably unsuccessful, of the principal intriguers to manipulate or exploit time to their own sole advantage. Mirabell's scheme to hasten his marriage by an elopement with Millamant is a violation of a proper pace in the betrothal process: in violating the decorum of courtship he violates time's decent measures. Similarly, in his plot to get Lady Wishfort in his power by means of a precipitous and fraudulant marriage, he displays as unbecoming a desire as she does for the breaking of time and form and ceremony. But he does seem to learn. At the end of the "contract scene," when he is told by Millamant to hold his tongue, and by Mrs. Fainall that there is a "Necessity" for his "Obedience," for he has "neither time to talk nor stay," he finally exhibits an acquiescence to the moment: "I am all Obedience," he says.

Mirabell's next appearance on stage is preceded by Millamant's statement that he has accepted her "Commands" to "come in Person" before Lady Wishfort and there "make a Resignation" of their "Contract," and that furthermore he "waits" her ladyship's "leave" to appear before her for the "last time." His unbecoming stratagems behind him, and having "resign'd" his "pretensions" to Millamant, Mirabell seems more the partner of time as he becomes less the manipulator of it. Thus, when Fainall appears to tell Lady Wishfort that her "date of deliberation" is "expir'd," Mirabell not only is able to offer her a "Remedy" for all her wrongs but gains from her ladyship an "approbation" which, when we consider that the word *generous* is one that "epitomizes the ethical substratum of Restoration comedy in general,"[11] is surely not to be taken lightly: "How!" she exclaims, "dear Mr. *Mirabell,* can you be so generous at last!"

And so "at last," and with the "leave" of Lady Wishfort twice granted him, Mirabell summons the various other "Offenders" and "Penitents" who, he tells her, will "in good time" relieve her from Fainall's savage treatment. Telling Witwoud and Petulant they "now" shall know the contents of the parchment they once had witnessed, he informs Fainall "it is now time" he should know that his wife had set her hand to a deed bearing "an Elder Date" than the one Fainall had wheedled from her. Having submitted to Lady Wishfort (as he should have from the very beginning) his "pretensions" to Millamant and to a place in her family, Mirabell seems "at last" to move in keeping with time's own measures and to find, in the end, that he has both time, and her ladyship, on his side.

If Mirabell, by ill-timed stratagems, seeks to manipulate time, his intriguing adversaries, Mrs. Marwood and Fainall, seem unfailingly primed to exploit moments and occasions as they arise: like all such fortune-hunters, they are thoroughly opportunistic in their grasp of time's occasions. They exploit the immediate moment, moreover, because they seem to know, better than Mirabell, the inevitable exposures time itself will bring, as may be seen when Mrs. Marwood reminds her lover that Foible "knows some passages," and then goes on: "Nay I expect all will come out—But let the Mine be sprung first, and then I care not if I'm discover'd." As early as their quarrel in act 2, Mrs. Marwood had warned Fainall of an inescapable future: "It shall all be discover'd," she says, "You too shall be discover'd; be sure you shall. I can but be expos'd—If I do it myself I shall prevent your Baseness." And when he then begs of her, "Will you yet be reconcil'd to Truth and me?", her retort provides the best possible rationale for their own inevitable unmasking: "Impossible. Truth and you are inconsistent."

Lady Wishfort, in a remark expressive of at least some worldly wisdom and even, perhaps, of a certain sad self-knowledge, at one point asks, "Ah dear *Marwood,* what's Integrity to an Opportunity?" and the trenchancy of her insight could hardly be better illustrated than in Mrs. Marwood's own advice to Fainall, a few pages later, that he shake off his condition of "Scurvy Wedlock": "You have often wish'd for an opportunity to part;—and now you have it." Hardly a moment passes, moreover, before she again would have him grasp time's forelock and "take the opportunity of breaking" the news of his wife's past misconduct to Lady Wishfort "just upon the discovery" of Mirabell's conspiracy—a "discovery" she will ensure by contriving "a Letter which shall be deliver'd to my Lady at the time when that Rascal who is to act Sir *Rowland* is with her." Subsequently, after they have overwhelmed Lady Wishfort with revelations of the deceptions and disloyalties within her immediate family, they coldly beset her with their threats and insinuations, pressing time and their advantage to the utmost, granting her ladyship only such "time" as will be necessary for the "drawing" of the "Instrument" they would force her to sign.

But there are, of course, those two other matters in time's ample wallet which now come to light and utterly frustrate their efforts to usurp the time. One is that "most opportune thing" by which their own opportunism is taken aback: Foible's disclosure that the two of them had been found abed "in the Blew garret." The other, of course, is the emergence of that deed of "an Elder Date" by which Mrs. Fainall had conveyed her estate, "in trust," to Mirabell, a disclosure that, to my mind at least, is not so much a stroke of Machiavellian genius on Mirabell's part as it is a sharp example of the way falsehood and fraud may be cast down by an outbreak of truth and actual fact: the "deed of Conveyance" here brought forth is not, after all, part of any prescient master plan by which Mirabell had hoped to win Millamant's hand. It is instead a precautionary document that was drawn up, as Mirabell himself says, on the "wholesome advice of Friends and Sages learned in the Laws of this Land," to forestall any possibility that Mrs. Fainall would be unduly the victim of her husband's "Inconstancy and Tyranny of temper." Its appearance is demanded by the actual occurrence of such a possibility and by the real exigencies of the moment; the timing of its appearance, or its importance in his winning of Millamant, could scarcely, in my opinion, have been foreseen by Mirabell.

The critical view that Mirabell wins out in the end by means of some uncanny Machiavellian cast of mind has been encouraged, I believe, by the attribution of certain vague symbolic, even magical, qualities to the "Black box" produced in the final scene: in Novak's words, "the black box is a magical key for a worldly victory."[12] But attributions of deep symbolic value or high talismanic powers to the black box seem to be made without any cognizance of the simple fact that such a box would have been instantly perceived by a contemporary audience as the standard and, indeed, only appropriate receptacle, on stage or off, for either a deed or a will: that is, it would have been an instantly identifiable seventeenth-century "deed box," made of tin-plate that had been japanned to a durable glossy finish by means of a black enamel or lacquer. Such boxes were as proverbial a badge or token of the legal profession as were the "green bags" in which lawyers also carried their papers and documents. As a matter of fact, in *A New Dictionary of the Terms Ancient and Modern of the Canting Crew,** a work which appeared in 1699, the year before *The Way of the World,* one finds that a "green bag" and a "black box" both appear as cant terms for lawyers in general.

When Waitwell, at the end of act 4, makes his escape from Lady Wishfort's presence with the promise that, as proof of his "Truth and Innocence," he will "go for a black box, which contains the Writings" of his "whole Estate," his words are born of the dire straits in which he has been placed by Mrs. Marwood's totally unexpected and unforeseen letter identifying him as a "disguis'd and suborn'd" rascal, and can scarcely be taken as a prearranged item in Mirabell's grand imposture: his allusion to a "black box," moreover, suggests again how commonly such boxes were understood to be the usual containers of deeds and wills. And when, in the last moments of the play, he reappears to hand over to Mirabell the "Black box at last," a contemporary audience would simply have recognized the only kind of box they could expect to see: a black box of the kind in which they would have kept their own deeds, and which they would ordinarily have seen stacked about a lawyer's chambers—much as they are, in certain parts of England, to this day.

By seeing the black box as some kind of symbol for Mirabell's "omniscience," critics have tended to depreciate the import of the box's contents: that deed which Mrs. Fainall, "by the wholesome Advice of Friends and of Sages learned in the Laws," had delivered "in trust," as the play twice reminds us, to Edward Mirabell. The play in no way suggests her decision as taken solely on the advice of Mirabell, though he certainly may have been among the friends alluded to, nor does the play suggest in any way that the contents of the black box are part of some grand strategy. The contents

---

*See the entry, "Black-box." There is, of course, a specific "Black Box" of great political interest, the one in that "idle story," as Macaulay terms it, which was supposed to have contained the contract of a marriage between Charles II and Lucy Walter, mother of the Duke of Monmouth. That "story," however idle, again suggests the ordinariness of a black box as a container for family papers.

rather suggest that not only Mrs. Fainall but also her best advisers considered Mirabell to be a person in whom a lady could place her trust, both in "Act" and in "Deed." Mirabell's triumph in the end is far from being the consequence of "unprincipled behavior" or "Machiavellian manipulations." He wins, rather, because he was a man held "in trust"—and so proves himself, in the end, to be.

IV

As many readers have noticed, family relationships in *The Way of the World* are so unduly complicated as to be downright baffling, prompting at least one critic to a diagram of the Wishfort family tree in order to clarify the play's "welter of consanguinity."[13] The affiliations of kith and kin, moreover, seem to have been made purposely obtrusive, as when Mirabell observes to Fainall that he has "the Honour to be related" by marriage to Sir Wilfull Witwoud, and gets this reply: "Yes; he is half Brother to this [Anthony] *Witwoud* by a former Wife, who was Sister to my Lady *Wishfort,* my Wife's Mother. If you marry *Millamant* you must call Cousins too." Fainall's words are gratuitously explicative, for surely there is no need to inform Mirabell that Lady Wishfort is mother to the former mistress whose marriage to Fainall had been prompted by Mirabell himself.

Such intrusive comments, along with a daisy-chain of other relationships (Lady Wishfort wooed by the false Sir Rowland, Waitwell, who is married to Foible, her ladyship's maid; Mrs. Marwood, mistress to Fainall, who longs for a liaison with Mirabell, the one-time "Friend" of the Arabella Languish who is now Mrs. Fainall, and so on) seem, as others have noted, to make the family itself—and by extension perhaps the larger family of society itself—into a central image and preoccupation of the play. And not merely the family itself, but also the very conditions by which the family may be sustained, for there are a multitude of suggestions that family "Composition" can be achieved and maintained only through an indispensable "forgiving and forgetting" of the frailties and follies to be found in even the best of its members. On one side there are to be found those who, like Foible (a name not without its own pertinence to my theme), had concealed her knowledge of Fainall's adultery because, in her words, she loves "to keep Peace and Quietness" by "good will" and "had rather bring friends together, than set 'em at distance"; and on the other side those who, like Mrs. Marwood, would "play the Incendiary," and would not fail to keep Lady Wishfort "warm" if "she should Flag" in her readiness to "Sacrifice Niece, and Fortune, and all."

One of the more important revelatory moments in *The Way of the World* occurs early in the first act when Fainall, commenting on a nonchalant appraisal of Millamant made by Mirabell, says to him: "For a passionate Lover, methinks you are a Man somewhat too discerning in the Failings of your Mistress." Mirabell, in a neat chiastic rejoinder, replies: "And for a discerning Man, somewhat too passionate a Lover." And then he goes on to evince both his passion and his discernment in a declaration that seems to me expressive of the play's ethical groundwork: "for I like her with all her Faults; nay, like her for her Faults." "I'll tell thee, *Fainall*," he continues,

> she once us'd me with that Insolence, that in Revenge I took her to pieces; sifted her and separated her Failings; I study'd 'em, and got 'em by rote. The Catalogue was so large, that I was not without hopes, one day or other to hate her heartily: To which end I so us'd my self to think of 'em, that at length, contrary to my Design and Expectation, they gave me every Hour less and less disturbance; 'till in a few Days it became habitual to me, to remember 'em without being displeas'd. They are now grown so familiar to me as my own frailties; and in all probability in a little time longer I shall like 'em as well.

The language of love and courtship was never more wittily adjusted to that great commandment, "Thou shalt love thy neighbour as thy self"—even so near a neighbor as a mistress or wife.

The play's emphasis on the need for mutual forbearance in human relationships, no matter how amorous and no matter one's own "discernment," is most brilliantly and appealingly displayed, no doubt, in the so-much admired "contract scene," when Mirabell and Millamant negotiate the terms of give-and-take whereby she may only "by degrees dwindle into a Wife" and he "may not be beyond Measure enlarg'd into a Husband." But even the more vain or silly or

surly characters are made to exemplify the reciprocal sufferance
recommended in the play not merely to fellows but also to bed-
fellows. When Mirabell, for example, rallies Witwoud by saying that
Petulant thinks himself his superior in wit, he replies:

> Come, come, you are malicious now, and wou'd breed Debates.—
> *Petulant*'s my Friend, and a very honest Fellow, and a very
> pretty Fellow, and has a smattering—Faith and Troth a pretty
> deal of an odd sort of a small Wit: Nay, I'll do him Justice. I'm
> his Friend, I won't wrong him neither—And if he had but any
> Judgment in the World,—he wou'd not be altogether contempt-
> ible. Come, come, don't detract from the Merits of my Friend.

In spite of the fact that Witwoud's "defence" of his friend is as snide
as snide may be, the lengthy scene of which this is only a small part
establishes firmly the forbearing accommodation—even, one may
say, the kind of "marriage"—they have made to one another, a
metaphor I would justify by the fact that when Millamant asks Witwoud if he and Petulant have "compos'd" their "Animosity,"
he replies that they "have no Animosity," for the "falling out of
Wits is like the falling out of Lovers—We agree in the main, like
Treble and Base." And if man and wife should ideally be made
"one" by virtue of matrimony, let us remember that Witwoud and
Petulant "were enroll'd Members" of the female cabal so that there
"might be one Man of the Community." Let us remember also
that when Mirabell observes to Witwoud that Petulant "wants
Words" as well as learning, Witwoud's rejoinder is this: "Ay; but I
like him for that now; for his want of Words gives me the pleasure
very often to explain his meaning." Witwoud, the play makes clear,
likes Petulant not only with his faults, but for his faults, and I do
not hesitate to see in his liking a splendidly comic, yet broadly
humane, parallel to Mirabell's liking of Millamant "with all her
Faults" and, indeed, "for her Faults."

"We have all our Failings," says Witwoud excusing Petulant's way
of speaking before he thinks, and whatever the coxcombly mouth
from which the words come, they remind us of our brotherhood in
frailty and of the sufferance of one another required by it. We are
reminded of it in other ways too: when Witwoud, for example,

describes Sir Wilfull as "the Fool, my Brother," and would console himself with the thought that the knight is but a "half Brother," and "no nearer," Mirabell suggests to him that "Then 'tis possible he may be but half a Fool." And then there is that signal alliance near the end of the play when the oddest couple of all—the countri-fied Sir Wilfull and the urbane Edward Mirabell—have become "sworn Brothers and fellow Travellers": "We are to be *Pylades* and *Orestes,* he and I," says Sir Wilfull, an allusion that, apart from its legendary import, is most appropriate for their future kinship—Mirabell as the "son" of Lady Wishfort, Sir Wilfull as her nephew.*

Set apart from those who are able to bear the failings of others as easily as they live with their own are Mrs. Marwood and Fainall, especially the former, who at moments seems as full of self-loathing as she is of hate for her paramour and the world in general: during their quarrel in act 2 she declares to him that it is not "too late" for her to "loath, detest, abhor Mankind, my self, and the whole treach-erous World." She tells him further that he has urged her infidelity with such "deliberate Malice" that she "never will forgive it," and when he pleads for reconciliation, she exclaims, "I hate you, and shall for ever." The hatefulness that is so much a part of their nature, and by which they estrange themselves from everyone else, becomes in fact the very means by which Fainall attempts to patch up their rift: "Come," he says, "I'll hate my Wife yet more, Dam her, I'll part with her, rob her of all she's worth." Later on, having browbeaten Lady Wishfort into despair, his full hatefulness of nature is nakedly exposed when he tells her ladyship, in words of the utmost malice, that if his wife's fortune is not made over to his own sole use, then her "Darling Daughter's turn'd a drift, like a Leaky hulk† to Sink or Swim, as she and the Current of this Lewd Town can agree." As for the malice of Mrs. Marwood, it is surely *malice prepense,* and nowhere more clearly so than after she has heard

---

*Orestes was the son, and Pylades the nephew, of Agamemnon, and united in the execution of justice against him (as Mirabell and Sir Wilfull are against Fainall). They became legendary for their travels as well as for their friendship.

†A traditional image of unchastity. Cf. Dryden's translation of Lucretius, 3. 1008–12.

Foible describe Mrs. Fainall as "the Pattern of Generosity." "I," she vows, "shall not prove another Pattern of Generosity."

The bitter exchanges between Mrs. Marwood and Fainall during their quarrel not only reveal their essential malevolence of nature, but also betray the disquietudes and cross-purposes all too likely to beset any alliance between two such basically selfish individuals. And while their altercation is patched up, Mrs. Marwood clearly emerges from it as the dominant personality, reducing Fainall, in spite of his all-too-justified suspicions of her infidelity, to the most abject, extravagant, and, I believe, ludicrous apologies and expostulations. "Come," he says, "I ask your Pardon—No Tears—I was to blame," and then, "I believe you; I'm convinc'd I've done you wrong; and any way, every way will make amends": "we'll retire somewhere, anywhere to another World. I'll marry thee—Be pacify'd." One is tempted to say, in spite of everything, "Alas, poor Fainall!"

On several occasions in the play Mrs. Marwood is specifically alluded to as "That Devil," seen as a conceiver of "Ingenious Mischief," charged to her face, in the end, with being "as False as Hell." By no means as heavily invested with satanic traits as was Maskwell in *The Double-Dealer,* the terms applied to her are nevertheless unusually obtrusive in a play whose language is otherwise remarkably free, for Congreve, of reference to any kind of preternatural order of existence. Such terms, as well as her actions in the play, give her the lineaments and the role, however vestigial, of the malevolent prompter of Christian story. Inclined to viciousness though Fainall himself may be, Mrs. Marwood clearly emerges less as his mistress than as his mentor, prompting and instructing and "playing the Incendiary." A malevolent tutelary spirit, a fomenter of discord among everyone, an "officious" spoiler of even her own lover's designs, a "Mischievous Devil" who "loaths" both herself and all "Mankind," she so works upon Lady Wishfort that her ladyship comes to consider her (much as Maskwell was considered by Mellefont in *The Double-Dealer*) as her "good Genius," an appellation by which Congreve both establishes her ancestry and suggests at the same time how insidiously her bad tutelary spirit has usurped the appearance of a good tutelary spirit.

One critic, we may remember, has recently argued that Congreve's plays "cannot embody any transcendental moral doctrine"
because "the evil of characters like Marwood is matched by no
saintly goodness on the other side" (see p. 76 above). Such a view
has little to do, as we have seen, with either Christian conceptions of
human nature or Restoration theories of dramatic characterization.
As should be readily apparent, moreover, I would no more view
Mirabell as a character of "saintly goodness" than I would view him
as that most successful and "unprincipled" Machiavel he is considered to be by some. Nevertheless, he has enough "goodness" to
merit his reward in the end, and to affirm the ethical "ground" of
the play, because his transgressions, as opposed to the deliberate
evil of Mrs. Marwood and Fainall, are such as may be considered, in
those words of Dryden, as "the sallies of youth, and the frailties of
human nature," such "to which all men are obnoxious," or "sus-
ceptible," and consequently such "as may be forgiven, not such as
must of necessity be punish'd" (see p. 74 above). As Mirabell himself says to Lady Wishfort, the "errours which Love produces have
ever been accounted *Venial*"—and we must not fail to note that,
quite apart from its traditional associations with the language of the
confessional, the word *Venial* also has its own distinct place in the
play's vocabulary of forgiving and forgetting, for literally it means
"easily excused or forgiven," and comes from the Latin *venia,*
meaning forgiveness.

Mirabell's reward also comes, furthermore, from the defeat rather
than the success of his major conspiracy—a defeat that one may, if
one wishes, view as deriving solely from the happenstance over-
hearing of his plans by Mrs. Marwood, but one which I would view
as having its place in the prevailing providentialist pattern so dis-
cernible in all of Congreve's work. It comes finally after a public
"act" of contrition for his past misdeeds and after a public and
proper submission to Lady Wishfort's dispensing powers within the
family she heads. Mirabell is no saint, nor does he need to be, to gain
full admission to the Wishfort family: there have been, all along,
certain bounds and limits to his intrigues, and with even these laid
aside, he seems worthy, in the end, of a "Blessing" on his endeavors.
Mrs. Marwood and Fainall, on the other hand, do not hesitate to

break all bounds and bonds, and as they storm off the stage in the very last scene, they seem to have banished themselves from all those blessings that come only with the acceptance of family bounds and bonds.

I would stress, in conclusion, the way the failings and transgressions of most characters in *The Way of the World* are placed within a framing diction which accentuates the very human fact, even the human weakness, of "forgetfulness"—and also accentuates the value and even the necessity of such "forgetting." One may, as Witwoud does, forget what one "was going to say," or even, as he also does, forget the half-brother he has not seen "since the Revolution." One may forget one's gloves or the "Motto" on one's "Crest," as Sir Wilfull does, or forget, as does Lady Wishfort, that her nephew will be coming for dinner. One may even forget one's own self, as Waitwell fears he may do in his transformation into Sir Rowland, as Foible is said to do in her new "Preferment" as Waitwell's wife, or as Lady Wishfort apologizes for doing: "As I'm a Person I am in a very Chaos to think I shou'd so forget my self."

So human a failing, however, may also be put to the most virtuous and saving of purposes, and most especially when one endeavors "to forget" past injuries, or to "stifle" a "just resentment," as Lady Wishfort does after Mirabell has begged that the past "be forgotten" and that he "be pitied first; and afterwards forgotten." And indeed, as Sir Wilfull maintains, you must "Forgive and Forget," most especially "you must, an you are a Christian." By the end of *The Way of the World* a goodly number of characters have shown that our acts of "forgetfulness" may be something more than mere foibles or signs of infirmity—they may be the best evidence we can give of a most estimable human trait.

Notes

CHAPTER 1

1 See Gladys Scott Thomson, *Life in a Noble Household, 1640–1700* (Ann Arbor: University of Michigan Press, 1959), pp. 73–74.

2 See Foster Watson, *The English Grammar Schools to 1660: Their Curriculum and Practice* (Cambridge: Cambridge University Press, 1908), p. 534, and also W. H. L. Vincent, *The Grammar Schools: Their Continuing Tradition, 1660–1714* (London: John Murray, 1969), pp. 86–87.

3 See Gilbert Burnet, *Some Passages in the Life and Death of John Earl of Rochester, With a Sermon, Preached at the Funeral of the said Earl by the Rev. Robert Parsons* (London, 1819), p. 24.

4 "Theory of Comedy in the Restoration," *MP* 70 (1973): 302.

5 *A Defense of Dramatick Poetry: Being a Review of Mr. Collier's View of the Immorality and Profaneness of the Stage* (London, 1698), p. 67. Once attributed to Edward Filmer, this work has recently been ascribed to Elkanah Settle.

6 Hume, "Theory of Comedy in the Restoration," p. 302.

7 See, e.g., Charles O. McDonald, "Restoration Comedy as Drama of Satire: An Investigation into Seventeenth Century Aesthetics," *SP* 61 (1964): 527. In spite of my complaint, I find McDonald's essay a very stimulating piece.

8 Preface to *De arte graphica: The Art of Painting, by C. A. du Fresnoy* (1695), in *Of Dramatic Poesy and Other Critical Essays*, ed. George Watson, 2 vols. (London: J. M. Dent & Sons, 1962), 2: 184.

9 Virginia Ogden Birdsall, *Wild Civility: The English Comic Spirit on the Restoration Stage* (Bloomington: Indiana University Press, 1970), p. 8.

10 W. H. Van Voris, *The Cultivated Stance* (Dublin: The Dolmen Press, 1965), p. 22.

11 *Works*, 12 vols. (London, 1748), 8: 118.

12 *Of the Principles and Duties of Natural Religion: Two Books* (London, 1675), p. 85.

13 *The Role of Providence in the Social Order*, The Jayne Lectures for 1966 (Philadelphia: American Philosophical Society, 1972), p. 19.

14 *The Mourning Bride,* act 5, scene 2. All quotations from Con-
    greve's plays are taken from *The Complete Plays of William
    Congreve,* ed. Herbert Davis (Chicago: University of Chicago
    Press, 1967).
15 See *The First Modern Comedies* (Bloomington: Indiana Uni-
    versity Press, 1967), p. 14.
16 Preface to *de Arte Graphica* (Watson, 2: 184).
17 *The Correspondence of Samuel Richardson,* ed. Anna Laetitia
    Barbauld, 6 vols. (London, 1804), 2: 128–29. This passage was
    called to my attention by James L. Fortuna.
18 Burnet, *Some Passages,* pp. 51, 77, 79, 81, 83–84, 87, 93, 99,
    112, 118–19, 126–27.
19 Ibid., p. 111.
20 Ibid., pp. 79, 84.
21 Ibid., p. 127.
22 See *A Life of Gilbert Burnet, Bishop of Salisbury,* ed. T. E. S.
    Clarke and H. C. Foxcroft, 2 vols. (Cambridge, 1907), 1: 160.
23 *The First Modern Comedies,* pp. 116–20.
24 For a healthy correction of Holland's view, see the essay by
    Henry Knight Miller, "Some Useful Lies about the Eighteenth
    Century: History of Ideas and Literature," in *Lex et Scientia*
    2 (1975): 128–51.
25 See *Sermons Preached Upon Several Occasions* (London, 1678),
    p. 413.
26 See *A Letter in Answer to a Book Entituled, Christianity Not
    Mysterious. As also to All those who set up for Reason and
    Evidence in Opposition to Revelation and Mysteries,* 3d ed.
    (London, 1703; 1st published 1697), pp. 120–21.
27 Bruce King has suggested that portions of Saint Catharine's
    argument reflect sermons by Archbiship Tillotson. See "Dryden,
    Tillotson, and *Tyrannick Love,*" *RES,* n.s. 16 (1965): 364–77.
28 *The Works of John Dryden,* vol. 10, ed. Maximillian E. Novak
    and Robert George Guffey (Berkeley and Los Angeles: Uni-
    versity of California Press, 1970), p. 383.
29 See entry for 27 February 1668.
30 *The Works of John Dryden,* 10: 385.
31 See Ehrenpreis, *Literary Meaning and Augustan Values* (Char-
    lottesville: University Press of Virginia, 1974), p. 22.
32 John Arrowsmith, *Armilla Catechetica: A Chain of Principle;
    Or, An orderly concatenation of Theological Aphorism and
    Exercitations; Wherein, the Chief Heads of Christian Religion
    are asserted and improved* (Cambridge, 1659), p. 400.
33 See, among other passages, the one in which Prospero tells
    Miranda of their deliverance, "By Providence Divine" (act 1,
    scene 2, lines 92 ff.).

34 William Sherlock, *A Discourse Concerning the Divine Providence* (London, 1694), p. 42.
35 November 19, 1668.
36 See the introduction to *The Diary of Samuel Pepys,* ed. Robert Latham and William Mathews (Berkeley and Los Angeles: University of California Press, 1970), I, xxxix, cxix.
37 See Harriet Hawkins, *Likenesses of Truth in Elizabethan and Restoration Drama* (Oxford: The Clarendon Press, 1972), pp. 112, 97.

CHAPTER 2

1 Holland, *The First Modern Comedies,* pp. 118-20.
2 See Viner, *The Role of Providence in the Social Order,* pp. 16-17, and also Francis C. Haber, "The Darwinian Revolution in the Concept of Time," in *Studium Generale* 24 (1971): esp. 291-300.
3 *Armilla Catechetica,* p. 402.
4 *Select Discourses* (Cambridge, 1673), p. 139.
5 *Reason and Religion* (London, 1689), p. 163.
6 *A Discourse on Divine Providence,* pp. 133, 136.
7 *The Reasonableness of Scripture Belief* (London, 1672), pp. 18, 22.
8 *Forty Eight Sermons and Discourses on Several Subjects, and Occasions,* 4 vols. (London, 1715), 1:301.
9 *A Discourse Concerning the Divine Providence,* p. 69.
10 For Battenhouse, see "The Doctrine of Man in Calvin and in Renaissance Platonism," *JHI* 9 (1948):447-71, and *Marlowe's Tamburlaine: A Study in Renaissance Moral Philosophy* (Nashville: Vanderbilt University Press, 1941), esp. pp. 124-26. For Stroup, see *Microcosmos: The Shape of the Elizabethan Play* (Lexington: University of Kentucky Press, 1965), esp. pp. 7-36.
11 *A Collection of Sermons,* 2 vols. (London, 1713), 2:39.
12 *The Spectator,* no. 219 (Nov. 10, 1711).
13 *Marlowe's Tamburlaine,* pp. 124-25.
14 *True Intellectual System of the Universe* (London, 1678), pp. 879-80.
15 See chap. 8 of *An Explanation of the Grand Mystery of Godliness,* in *The Theological Works of Henry More* (London, 1708), p. 31.
16 *Fifteen Sermons Preached on Several Occasions,* 2d ed. (London, 1701), p. 436.
17 *Sermons Preach'd Upon Several Occasions Before the King at White Hall . . . To which is added, A Discourse Concerning the Beauty of Providence* (London, 1680). See p. 148 of *A Discourse.*

18   *Works,* 9: 311–12.
19   Ibid., 8: 149.
20   *A Discourse Concerning the Divine Providence,* pp. 223–24.
21   *Works,* 1: 172, 178.
22   *A Collection of Sermons,* 2: 34.
23   *Works,* 8: 118.
24   *A Collection of Sermons upon Several Occasions* (Oxford, 1701), p. 106.
25   *A Discourse Concerning the Divine Providence,* pp. 35, 48.
26   *A Discourse,* p. 125.
27   Ibid., p. 137.
28   South, *Twelve Sermons Preached Upon Several Occasions,* 1: 361–62.
29   *Select Discourses,* pp. 427–28.
30   Hickes, *A Collection of Sermons,* 2: 21–22.
31   For Barrow, see *Sermons Preached Upon Several Occasions,* pp. 419–39. For Hickes, see *A Collection of Sermons,* 2: 22–40.
32   *Resolves* (London, 1634), pp. 244–45.
33   *Works,* 3: 111.
34   *Forty Sermons* (London, 1676), p. 125.
35   *Fifteen Sermons Preached on Several Occasions,* p. 179.
36   *A Discourse Concerning the Divine Providence,* p. 341.
37   *Armilla Catechetica,* pp. 434–35.
38   *A Discourse Concerning the Divine Providence,* p. 341.
39   *The Wonders of the Little World: Or, A General History of Man, In Six Books* (London, 1678), p. 620.
40   *A Discourse,* p. 125.
41   *A Discourse Concerning the Divine Providence,* p. 42.
42   *Forty Eight Sermons and Discourses on Several Subjects, and Occasions,* 1: 294, 299.
43   *The Works of the Right Reverend Father in God, Dr. William Beveridge,* 2 vols. (London, 1720), 2: 577.
44   *Works,* 8: 119–20.
45   *A Collection of Sermons,* 2: 32.
46   *An Elegant, and Learned Discourse on the Light of Nature,* p. 16.
47   The Dedication of the *AEneis* (1697).
48   *Origines Sacrae,* p. 474.
49   Tillotson, *Works,* 3: 24, 127.
50   Arrowsmith, *Armilla Catechetica,* p. 410.
51   *A Discourse Concerning the Divine Providence,* p. 41.
52   "Some Useful Lies about the Eighteenth Century," p. 147.
53   *Works,* 8: 213–14.
54   Ibid., 12: 236.

55 George Stanhope, *A Paraphrase and Comment upon the Epistles and Gospels,* 4 vols. (London, 1706–09), 4: 277.
56 Étienne François de Vernage, *The Happy Life: Or, The Contented Man* (London, 1708), p. 282.
57 Arrowsmith, *Armilla Catechetica,* p. 399.
58 Sherlock, *A Discourse Concerning the Divine Providence,* pp. 251–52.
59 Tillotson, *Works,* 8: 248–49.
60 Arrowsmith, *Armilla Catechetica,* p. 474.
61 Samuel Clarke, *An Exposition of the Church-Catechism,* 2d ed. (London, 1730), p. 266.
62 *Works,* 1: 172.
63 *A Paraphrase and Comment upon the Epistles and Gospels,* 2: 141.
64 *Works,* 2d ed., 3 vols. (London, 1687–92), 3: 144, 153–54.

CHAPTER 3

1 James Drake, *The Antient and Modern Stages survey'd. Or, Mr. Collier's View of the Immorality and Profaneness of the English Stage Set in a True Light* (London, 1699), p. 226.
2 See Curt A. Zimansky, *The Critical Works of Thomas Rymer* (New Haven: Yale University Press, 1956), pp. xxviii–xxix, 201–02. Cf. also Hooker, *The Critical Works of John Dennis,* 2: 439.
3 *The Advancement of Learning,* bk. 2, chap. 4, para. 2. For a useful, but limited, study of the concept, see M. A. Quinlan, *Poetic Justice in the Drama: The History of an Ethical Principle in Literary Criticism* (Notre Dame, Ind.: Notre Dame University Press, 1912).
4 *The Critical Works of Thomas Rymer,* pp. 22, 75, 161.
5 See "Heads of An Answer to Rymer" (1677), Watson, 1: 218, 213.
6 Preface to *Phæton* (London, 1698).
7 *The Critical Works of John Dennis,* 2: 437; 1: 183.
8 Ibid., 2: 436.
9 In the preface to *Fables Ancient and Modern.* See Watson, 2: 283.
10 Pp. 204–06.
11 *The Critical Works of Thomas Rymer,* p. 27.
12 *The Grounds of Criticism in Tragedy,* prefixed to *Troilus and Cressida* (1679). See Watson, 1: 248.
13 Pp. 215–17.
14 See John Barnard, "Passion, 'Poetical Justice,' and Dramatic Law in *The Double-Dealer* and *The Way of the World,*" p. 109,

in *William Congreve,* ed. Brian Morris (London: Ernest Benn, 1972).

15 See *Microcosmos,* pp. 22–23, and *Marlowe's Tamburlaine,* p. 126.

16 *Microcosmos,* esp. chap. 6.

17 Clarke, *Expositions of the Church Catechism,* p. 266.

18 J. Harold Wilson, "Nell Gwyn as an Angel," in *N&Q* 193 (February 1948): 71.

19 See the words of Dryden, chap. 2, p. 54.

20 Robert L. Root has maintained that there is little evidence of a "testing pattern" in plays of the Restoration before 1688. See *PMLA* 90 (October 1975), letter to Forum, pp. 925–27.

21 Pp. 155–56.

22 Ibid., p. 155.

23 *A Farther Defence of Dramatick Poetry: Being the Second Part of the Review of Mr. Collier's View of the Immorality and Profaneness of the Stage* (London, 1698), pp. 64–65. Once attributed to Edward Filmer, this work has recently been ascribed to Elkanah Settle (see Zimansky, *The Critical Works of Thomas Rymer,* p. 287).

24 See *Five Restoration Adaptations of Shakespeare* (Urbana: University of Illinois Press, 1965), pp. 11–12.

25 *A Discourse Concerning the Divine Providence,* p. 113.

26 Dedication to *The Rival Ladies* (Watson, 1: 2, 4).

27 *Sermons Preached Upon Several Occasions,* pp. 438–39.

28 *The Advancement and Reformation of Modern Poetry* (1701), in Hooker, 1: 230.

29 Ibid., pp. 202–03.

CHAPTER 4

1 *A Short View of the Immorality, and Profaneness of the English Stage* (London, 1698), pp. 54–55, 287.

2 *Amendments of Mr. Collier's False and Imperfect Citations, &c.* (London, 1698), pp. 7–9.

3 See *The Antient and Modern Stages Survey'd,* p. 97, and *A Defence of Dramatic Poetry,* p. 34.

4 *A Second Defence of the Short View of the Prophaneness and Immorality of the English Stage* (London, 1700), pp. 103–04.

5 *A Defence of the Short View of the Prophaneness and Immorality of the English Stage* (London, 1699), p. 10.

6 *The Stage Condemn'd* (London, 1698), p. 80. Horneck's "Scheme" appeared in *Delight and Judgment: Or, a Prospect of the Great Day of Judgment, And its Power to Damp, and em-*

bitter Sensual Delights, Sports, and Recreation (London, 1684), p. 210.

7   Cf. *A Short View*, p. 220.
8   *A Second Defence*, pp. 100–01.
9   See *A Short View*, pp. 124, 139, 175.
10 *A Defence of Dramatick Poetry*, pp. 1–2.
11 *A Short View*, p. 3.
12 *Maxims and Reflections Upon Plays* (London, 1699), pp. 55–56.
13 *A Short View*, p. 3.
14 *The Antient and Modern Stages Survey'd*, p. 238.
15 Anon., *The Stage Acquitted* (London, 1699), pp. 81–82.
16 *A Short Vindication of the Relapse and the Provok'd Wife* (London, 1698), pp. 45–46.
17 *The Stage Acquitted*, p. 81.
18 *The Antient and Modern Stages Survey'd*, pp. 118–19.
19 *A Short Vindication*, p. 46.
20 Anon., *A Letter to A. H., Esq.; Concerning the Stage* (London, 1698), p. 15.
21 *The Antient and Modern Stages Survey'd*, p. 272.
22 Epilogue to *The Pilgrim* (1700).
23 See pp. 115, 71, 128–30, 36, 33.
24 *A Letter to A. H., Esq.*, p. 11.
25 *A Defence of Dramatick Poetry*, p. 84.
26 *Amendments*, pp. 14–15.
27 *The Stage Acquitted*, p. 76.
28 *A Defence of Dramatick Poetry*, p. 81.
29 *The Stage Acquitted*, p. 77.
30 *A Vindication of the Stage* (London, 1698), pp. 26–27.
31 *A Defence of the Short View*, p. 16.
32 *A Defence of Plays* (London, 1707), pp. 69–70.
33 *The Antient and Modern Stages Survey'd*, pp. 120–21.
34 See *Reflections on the Stage, and Mr. Collier's Defence of the Short View. In Four Dialogues* (London, 1699), pp. 116–17.
35 *The Antient and Modern Stages Survey'd*, p. 122.
36 *The Stage Defended* (1726), in Hooker, 2:308.
37 *A Letter to A. H., Esq.*, p. 16.
38 *The Stage Acquitted*, pp. 44–45.
39 *A Defence of Dramatick Poetry*, pp. 72, 86–89.
40 *A Defence of Plays*, p. 57.
41 *A Farther Defence of Dramatick Poetry: Being the Second Part of the Review of the Immorality and Profaneness of the Stage* (London, 1698), p. 64.
42 *A Short View*, p. 234.

43 *The Usefulness of the Stage* (Hooker, 1: 169). See also Drake, *The Antient and Modern Stages Survey'd*, pp. 114–15.
44 *A Letter to A. H., Esq.*, pp. 16–17.
45 *A Defence of Dramatick Poetry*, p. 71.
46 *A Vindication of the Stage*, pp. 25–26.
47 *The Usefulness of the Stage* (Hooker, 1: 182).
48 *A Defence of Dramatick Poetry*, pp. 89–90.
49 *A Short View*, p. 11.
50 *A Defence of Plays*, p. 16.
51 *The Antient and Modern Stages Survey'd*, p. 291.
52 *Amendments*, pp. 59, 63.
53 *The Antient and Modern Stages Survey'd*, pp. 271–72.
54 *A Defence of Plays*, p. 76.
55 Birdsall, *Wild Civility*, p. 4.
56 *The Antient and Modern Stages Survey'd*, pp. 235–37.
57 *A Short View*, pp. 140ff.
58 Ehrenpreis, *Literary Meaning and Augustan Values*, p. 21.
59 *The Antient and Modern Stages Survey'd*, pp. 233–34.
60 *A Farther Defence of Dramatick Poetry*, pp. 10–11.
61 *A Short View*, pp. 142–44.
62 *Amendments*, pp. 89–90.
63 Ibid., p. 9.
64 *A Defence of the Short View*, pp. 108, 10–11.
65 *The Antient and Modern Stages Survey'd*, pp. 222, 327–28.
66 *A Second Defence*, p. 120.
67 *A Defence of Plays*, p. 30.
68 *Reflections on the Stage*, pp. 11–12.
69 *The Antient and Modern Stages Survey'd*, pp. 220–22.
70 *Reflections on the Stage*, p. 129.
71 *Amendments*, pp. 12–15, 35–36.
72 *A Defence of the Short View*, pp. 20–21.
73 *The Antient and Modern Stages Survey'd*, pp. 220–21.
74 *Amendments*, pp. 9–10.
75 *A Defence of the Short View*, pp. 14–15, 18.
76 Preface to *Fables Ancient and Modern* (1700).
77 Pp. 55–56. Cf. also Oldmixon, *Reflections on the Stage*, p. 43.
78 *Amendments*, p. 23.
79 *A Defence of the Short View*, pp. 30–31.
80 See Sister Rose Anthony, *The Jeremy Collier Stage Controversy, 1698–1726* (Milwaukee: Marquette University Press, 1937), p. 160.
81 *Amendments*, p. 23.
82 *A Defence of the Short View*, p. 33.
83 Anon., *Some Remarks Upon Mr. Collier's Defence of his Short View of the English Stage* (London, 1698), pp. 6–7.

84 *Amendments,* p. 25.
85 *A Defence of the Short View,* pp. 13–14.
86 *A Short View,* p. 62.
87 *Amendments,* pp. 37–38.
88 *Reflections on the Stage,* p. 53.
89 *A Defence of the Short View,* p. 41.
90 *A Short View,* p. 83.
91 *Amendments,* pp. 55–56.
92 *A Defence of the Short View,* pp. 63–64.
93 *A Vindication of the Stage,* p. 14.
94 See Emmett L. Avery, *Congreve's Plays on the Eighteenth-Century Stage* (New York: Modern Language Association, 1951), and also the three volumes comprising part 2 of *The London Stage,* ed. Emmett L. Avery and Arthur H. Scouten (Carbondale: Southern Illinois University Press, 1960, 1961).
95 See *The Evil and Danger of Stage Plays* (London, 1706) and *A Serious Remonstrance In Behalf of the Christian Religion* (London, 1719).

CHAPTER 5

1 Samuel Johnson, *Lives of the English Poets,* 3 vols., ed. G. B. Hill (Clarendon Press: Oxford, 1905), 2:214. Macaulay's review ("Comic Dramatists of the Restoration") of Leigh Hunt's edition of *The Dramatic Works of Wycherley, Congreve, Vanbrugh, and Farquhar.* See *Dictionary of National Biography,* 4:931. Sir Edmund Gosse, *Life of William Congreve* (London, 1888), p. 20. H. F. B. Brett-Smith, *Incognita: or Love and Duty Reconcil'd* (New York and Boston: Houghton Mifflin Co., 1922), p. xii. Bonamy Dobrée, *The Mourning Bride, Poems, & Miscellanies* (Oxford: University Press, 1928), p. vii. F. W. Bateson, *The Works of Congreve* (London: Peter Davies, 1930), p. xxv. D. Crane Taylor, *William Congreve* (Oxford: University Press, 1931), p. 21. H. Norman Jeffares, *Congreve: Incognita and the Way of the World* (London: Edward Arnold, 1966), p. 16. Irène Simon, "Early Theories of Prose Fiction: Congreve and Fielding," in *Imagined Worlds: Essays on Some English Novels and Novelists in Honour of John Butt,* ed. Maynard Mack and Ian Gregor (London: Methuen & Co., 1968), pp. 20, 23. Maximillian Novak, *William Congreve,* chap. 3, esp. pp. 69, 73.
2 These comments come from Brett-Smith, pp. vi, xii, and Jeffares, p. 16.
3 Sherlock, *A Discourse Concerning the Divine Providence,* p. 340.

4   See, e.g., Isaac Barrow's sermon, "Of Patience," in *The Works of Isaac Barrow,* 3 vols. (New York, 1845), 1:461ff.
5   For a more extensive account of Providential interventions in Fielding, see my essay "Interpositions of Providence and the Design of Fielding's Novels," *SAQ* 70 (Spring 1971):265–86.
6   Novak, *William Congreve,* pp. 68–69.
7   Anthony Tuckney, *Forty Sermons* (London, 1676), p. 125.
8   Étienne François de Vernage, *The Happy Life: or, The Contented Man, Showing the Art, How to Live Well; With Reflections Upon Divers Subjects of Morality* (London, 1708), p. 74.
9   Barrow, *Sermons Preached Upon Several Occasions,* p. 425.
10 See the preface to Wilkins's *A Discourse Concerning the Beauty of Providence.* ¹

CHAPTER 6

1   See *William Congreve: Letters & Documents,* ed. John C. Hodges (Macmillan & Co.: London, 1964), p. 151.
2   *The Lives and Characters of the English Dramatick Poets* (London, 1699), p. 25.
3   *Lives of the English Poets,* 2:219.
4   *Amendments,* p. 39.
5   *The Cultivated Stance,* p. 49.
6   *Lives of the English Poets,* 2:217.
7   See Holland, *The First Modern Comedies,* chap. 12; Novak, *William Congreve,* chap. 4; Van Voris, *The Cultivated Stance,* chap. 2; Birdsall, *Wild Civility,* chap. 8.
8   Anon., *An Essay in Defence of the Female Sex,* 2d ed. (London, 1696), pp. 111–12.
9   Anon., *The Art of Complaisance or the Means to oblige in Conversation,* 2d ed. (London, 1677), pp. 8–9.
10 *An Essay in Defence of the Female Sex,* pp. 110–11.
11 *The First Modern Comedies,* p. 135.
12 *Wild Civility,* pp. 185–90.
13 Ibid., p. 182.
14 Holland, *The First Modern Comedies,* p. 137.
15 Van Voris, *The Cultivated Stance,* p. 43.
16 *William Congreve,* p. 88.
17 See Davis, p. 7.

CHAPTER 7

1   See Hartley Coleridge, *Lives of Northern Worthies,* 3 vols. (London, 1852), 3:318–19n.
2   See "Comic Dramatists of the Restoration."
3   *The Complete Plays,* p. 10.

4 See *William Congreve: Letters & Documents*, pp. 95–96.
5 Robert Sanderson, *XXXVI Sermons* (London, 1689), pp. 371–72. Cf. a comparable passage from Barrow, p. 28 above.
6 *The Cultivated Stance*, p. 64.
7 See *The London Stage*, pt. 1, p. lxix.
8 See act 3, scene 1, lines 169, 187, 233, 260; act 4, scene 1, lines 52, 514, ii, 8; act 5, scene 1, line 493.
9 *Restoration Comedy: 1660–1720* (London: Oxford University Press, 1962), p. 128.
10 *The Cultivated Stance*, p. 65.
11 *Restoration Comedy*, p. 128.
12 *Wild Civility*, pp. 198–203.
13 See Rossell Hope Robbins, *The Encyclopedia of Witchcraft and Demonology* (New York: Crown Publishers, 1959), pp. 66–67.
14 See *The Oxford Dictionary of English Proberbs*, ed. F. P. Wilson, 3d ed. (Oxford: Clarendon Press, 1970), p. 183.
15 For a good account of this particular form of necromancy and its currency in the seventeenth century, see George Lyman Kittridge, *Witchcraft in Old and New England* (New York: Russell & Russell, 1956), chap. 11, passim. See also Keith Thomas, *Religion and the Decline of Magic* (New York: Charles Scribner's Sons, 1971), pp. 117, 186, 215, 221, 250, 254, for additional illustration of contemporary practice of such divination.
16 *Purchas his Pilgrimage, Or Relations of The World and The Religions Observed in All Ages And places discovered, from the Creation unto this Present* (London, 1613), p. 310. The curious reader may wish to read Sir James George Frazer's account of superstitions concerning mirrors in *Taboo and the Perils of the Soul*, part 2 of *The Golden Bough*, 3d ed. (London: Macmillan & Co., 1963), pp. 92ff.
17 See the First Partition, sect. 3, no. 3.
18 See Peter S. French, *John Dee: The World of an Elizabethan Magus* (London: Routledge & Kegan Paul, 1972), pp. 12–13.
19 Part 1, vol. 1, p. 428.
20 *Twelve Sermons Preached Upon Several Occasions*, 2 vols. (London, 1715), 1: 369–70.
21 *The First Modern Comedies*, p. 157; *Wild Civility*, pp. 195–96.
22 *Wild Civility*, p. 207.
23 *The First Modern Comedies*, p. 158.
24 *William Congreve*, p. 101.
25 *The Cultivated Stance*, p. 60.
26 *William Congreve*, p. 99.
27 *Works*, 10 vols. (London, 1855), 4: 265.

28 *Works,* 7: 92.
29 Barrow, *Sermons Preached upon Several Occasions,* p. 413.
30 Sherlock, *A Discourse Concerning the Divine Providence,* pp. 54–55.
31 John March, *Sermons Preach'd on Several Occasions,* 2d ed. (London, 1699), pp. 243, 254. First edition of this collection was 1693.
32 Tillotson, *Works,* 6: 224–25.
33 *Microcosmos,* pp. 280, 184, 187, 202–04.
34 *Works,* 4: 265–66.

CHAPTER 8

1 *Likenesses of Truth in Elizabethan and Restoration Drama,* p. 107.
2 *The First Modern Comedies,* p. 164.
3 *The Ethos of Restoration Comedy* (Urbana: University of Illinois Press, 1971), pp. 69, 71, 95.
4 "Congreve's Miracle of Love," in *Criticism* 6 (Fall 1964): 346.
5 *A Short View,* p. 76.
6 I use the 1676 English translation of Agrippa's *The Vanity of Arts and Sciences,* p. 97.
7 Quoted by Don Cameron Allen in *The Star-Crossed Renaissance* (Durham, N.C.: Duke University Press, 1941), p. 15 n.
8 See John Melton, *Astrologaster, Or, The Figure-Caster* (1620), ed. Hugh G. Dick, no. 174x in The Augustan Reprint Society Series (Los Angeles: William Andrews Clark Memorial Library, 1975), p. 24.
9 *The Vanity of Arts and Sciences,* pp. 93–94.
10 Allen, *The Star-Crossed Renaissance,* p. 15 n.
11 See the editors' prefatory note to the Augustan Reprint Society publication no. 174x.
12 Wilkins, *A Discourse Concerning the Beauty of Providence,* p. 167.
13 *An Apology for the Life of Colley Cibber,* ed. B. R. S. Fone (Ann Arbor: University of Michigan Press, 1968), p. 80.
14 See George Parfitt, "The Case Against Congreve," in *William Congreve,* ed. Morris, pp. 23–24.
15 See *Epicteti Enchiridion: The Morals of Epictetus Made English, in a Poetical Paraphrase,* by Ellis Walker (London, 1716), B 2 v. Walker's translation was first issued in 1692.
16 *Epicteti Enchiridion,* B 1 v.
17 See G. A. Starr, *Defoe and Spiritual Autobiography* (Princeton: Princeton University Press, 1965), p. 101.
18 *Twelve Sermons Preached Upon Several Occasions,* 1: 335–73.

19 See Hawkins, *Likenesses of Truth in Elizabethan and Restoration Drama*, p. 112.
20 I cite the 8th edition of *A Body of Divinity: Or, the Sum and Substance of Christian Religion* (London, 1702), pp. 104-05.
21 See Richard Saunders, Ἀγγελογραφία Sive Πνεύματα λειτυργικά, ΠΝΕΥΜΑΤΟΛΟΓΙΑ: *Or A Discourse of Angels: Their Nature and Office, or Ministry* (London, 1701), p. 168.
22 Ibid., pp. 266-67.
23 *Commentary on the Four Books of the Sentences*, vol. 2, sentence xi, trans. Thomas Gilby, in *St. Thomas Aquinas: Theological Texts* (London: Oxford University Press, 1955), p. 91.

CHAPTER 9

1 *The Lives and Characters of the English Dramatick Poets* (London, 1699), p. 23.
2 Anon., *Some Remarks Upon Mr. Collier's Defence of his Short View*, p. 7.
3 See the essay by Potter, and also Emmet L. Avery, *Congreve's Plays on the Eighteenth-Century Stage* (New York: Modern Language Association, 1951), esp. pp. 19-24.
4 *The Comedy of Manners* (London, 1913), p. 170.
5 Rothstein, *Restoration Tragedy*, p. 159.
6 Taylor, pp. 101-02 of *William Congreve*, noted such "skilful use of contrast."
7 See *Artis Amatoriae*, ed. J. H. Mozley (Harvard Univ. Press: Cambridge; William Heinemann: London, 1947), I, 655-56.
8 *Sermons Preached Upon Several Occasions*, pp. 435-37.

CHAPTER 10

1 See Van Voris, *The Cultivated Stance*, pp. 151, 132; Philip Roberts, "Mirabell and Restoration Comedy," and R. A. Foakes, "Wit and Convention in Congreve's Comedies," in *William Congreve*, ed. Morris, pp. 52, 44, 68; Harold Love, *Congreve* (Totowa, N.J.: Rowan and Littlefield, 1974), p. 91; Ian Donaldson, *The World Upside-Down* (Oxford: Clarendon Press, 1970), pp. 146-47.
2 *Wild Civility*, p. 230.
3 Novak, *William Congreve*, p. 153.
4 Bernard, in *William Congreve*, ed. Morris, pp. 107-08.
5 *A New View of Congreve's Way of the World* (Ann Arbor: University of Michigan Press, 1958), pp. 38, 77.
6 *The First Modern Comedies*, p. 186.

7 See, e.g., Hawkins, *Likenesses of Truth in Elizabethan and Restoration Drama*, p. 113.
8 From Isaac Barrow, *Works*, 3 vols. (London, 1687), 2:133.
9 Dedication of *The Spanish Friar*.
10 *A Discourse Concerning the Beauty of Providence*, p. 105.
11 See Schneider, *The Ethos of Restoration Comedy*, p. 21.
12 *William Congreve*, p. 153.
13 Holland, *The First Modern Comedies*, p. 177.

Index

Addison, Joseph: quoted, 23, 37n, 41–42

Afranius, 78

Agrippa, Henry Cornelius: quoted, 160–63

Angels: guardian, 33, 50, 157; as ministers of justice, 49–50, 157, 158–59, 174–75

Anselm, Saint, 165n

Anthony, Sister Rose: cited, 48n

Aquinas, Saint Thomas: quoted, 174, 175

Aristotle: definition of comedy, cited, 59–60; cited, 70; cited against Collier, 71

Arrowsmith, John, D.D.: quoted, 15, 21, 30, 33, 35

Art of Complaisance, The: quoted, 110

Augustine, Saint, 30, 105

Bacon, Sir Francis: quoted, 39, 40

Baker, Sir Richard: quoted, 65–67

Barnard, John: quoted, 47, 194

Barrow, Isaac, Rev.: quoted, 8, 27–29, 36, 55–56, 101, 103, 106, 149, 187–88, 191, 202

Bateson, F. W.: quoted, 91

Battenhouse, Roy W., 22–23; cited, 47

Beard, Thomas, D.D.: quoted, 24, 147

Bedford, Arthur, Rev.: quoted on stage impiety, 89

B. E., Gent., *A New Dictionary of the Terms Ancient and Modern of the Canting Crew:* quoted, 116, 207

Beveridge, William, Rev.: quoted, 31–32

Biblical citations: Rom. *8:28,* 16, 26; Prov. *16:1,* 26; *11:5,* 30; *28:10,* 30; *16:33,* 31; *16:9,* 103n; *13:7,* 170; *27:1,* 202; Psal. *34:21,* 30; *91:6,* 134; *112:4,* 184; Mat. *10:29-31,* 31; Book of Esther, 31–32; Luke *10:31,* 33; *1* Pet. *1:6-7,* 34; Isa. *45:15,* 153; *1* Cor. *3:18-19,* 169; *2* Pet. *1:19,* 184; Rev. *16:6,* 188; Eccl. *3,* 202

Birdsall, Virginia: quoted, 4, 74, 115, 130–31, 139, 143, 193

Blackmore, Richard: quoted, 176

Bossuet, Jacques Benigne (bishop): quoted on Plato, 62–63; quoted on marriage, 83–84

Boyle, Robert, 19

Boyle, Roger (earl of Orrery), 55, 79

Brett-Smith, H. F. B., 91, 92

Browne, Peter, Rev.: quoted, 8

Bunyan, John, 196

Burnet, Gilbert (bishop): quoted, 7; rebuke to Charles II, 8

Burton, Robert: quoted, 136

Cartwright, William, 48n

Casaubon, Meric: cited, 136

Chance: equated with Providence, 16, 31–34, 56–57, 146

Charles II, 8, 207n

Chaucer, Geoffrey, 81; quoted, 165

Christianity: education, 1, 2–3; Book of Common Prayer, 1, 158, 198–99; Thirty-nine Articles, 3; Providential interposition on stage of world, 3–4, 8, 14–16, 18; relation of

229